PRACTICING CATHOLIC

D1246193

Essays Historical, Literary, Sporting, and Elegiac

George Weigel

A Crossroad Book
The Crossroad Publishing Company
New York

The Crossroad Publishing Company
831 Chestnut Ridge Road
Chestnut Ridge, NY 10977
www.crossroadpublishing.com

Printed in the United States of America.

The text of this book is set in Adobe Garamond Pro.
The display face is Adobe Garamond Pro.

Library of Congress Cataloging-in-Publication Data

Weigel, George, 1951-
  Practicing Catholic : essays literary, historical, sporting and elegiac / George Weigel.
    p. cm.
  ISBN 978-0-8245-0022-1
  1. Catholic Church--History--20th century. I. Title.

BX1389.W34 2013
282.09182'10904--dc23

2012029077

Books published by The Crossroad Publishing Company may be purchased at special quantity discount rates for classes and institutional use. For information, please email sales@crossroadpublishing.com

ISBN 978-0-8245-0022-1

Contents

Part IV: The Sporting Life

Part V: Remembrance

For
David and Joyce Brewster

Preface

Practicing Catholic: Essaying on Almost Everything

M ichel de Montaigne, the sixteenth-century French writer who invented it, didn't know what to call the thing at first. Then he hit on the idea of dubbing this new form of literary reflection an *essai*, an "attempt." It was an inspired choice because, as one commentator on his work neatly put it, Montaigne "wrote mostly to find out what he was writing about, to discover what he thought, or, on second thought, didn't think." The essays collected here touch two-thirds of Montaigne's trifecta; for in each case they were written to puzzle out something or someone, and in the course of writing them I not infrequently found that I had to think (and write, and edit) again.

I have been writing essays on various matters—political, historical, theological, sporting, literary, philosophical, humdrum—for over thirty years. And while the products of all that trying have doubtless been trying to some readers, I have always found the essay form uniquely congenial. The op-ed column, of which I have committed something well north of a thousand, is a limited medium in which one idea can be proposed (at most) and very cursorily explored (at best). Books are a different beast altogether: books, like children, tend to take on lives of their own, often unanticipated. In the development of a book, the narrative sometimes fights back, pushes the author in unanticipated directions, demands that attention be paid *here* and not *there*. There's a lot of thinking-by-writing in crafting a book; some of it is surprisingly pleasant, but more often than not, there is also heavy lifting involved.

In my experience, the essay is a different, and very friendly, form of thinking-by-writing. Unlike the column, where pith is of the essence, an essay allows a writer to stretch a bit, flap the wings, try a new maneuver or two, yet all within reasonable spatial and temporal boundaries. Unlike books, in which the length of production and publishing schedules dictates that the fruits of one's wrestling with the subject matter are only visible a year or so after the writer has downed tools, an essay offers a more immediate, or at least less languorous, form of authorial gratification: for better or worse, it's out there in print, sooner rather than later; and if the essayist has done the job, an interesting discussion, perhaps even an argument, rather quickly ensues. In the Internet age, columns provide almost instant gratification (and controversy), but both the satisfactions and tempests tend to be fleeting. Good essays, by contrast, have staying power—as the pleasures of reading Montaigne's literary rambles, or the more tightly worked gems of America's premier contemporary essayist, Joseph Epstein, demonstrate, whether centuries or decades after their first publication.

My serious writing life, and thus my first steps in essaying (or trying, in Montaigne's sense) began in late high school, when Father W. Vincent Bechtel, a fearsome English teacher who makes a cameo appearance in one of the essays gathered here, insisted that his charges learn to write lengthy term papers; the first I produced, if memory serves, was on the poet e. e. cummings and is happily lost to posterity. Term papers and academic essays remained a staple of my college and graduate school life, but if the truth be told, by the time I had finished at the University of St. Michael's College in Toronto in 1975, my prose style was likely at its nadir. It hadn't helped that I had spent a lot of time, in college and graduate school, reading German theology and biblical criticism: disciplines in which literary grace may have been valued but was rarely achieved. Whatever the reasons, however, I left St. Michael's wanting to write but not really knowing how to do so in a compelling, literate manner. I knew how to lay out an argument, but, like most graduate students, I was addicted to the passive voice, convoluted sentences, and other banes of crisp writing. So I needed further tutelage. My wife provided some very useful criticism of my earliest efforts at columns, but my life as a writer (and public intellectual, a term I've never really liked but have had to accept) was launched in earnest from an entirely unexpected literary shipyard.

After losing the academic job that had drawn me to Seattle in 1975, I had cast my lot with America's only pro-democracy, anti-communist peace organization, the World Without War Council. This unique combination of think tank and activist agency brought me into contact with a lot of interesting people, far beyond the boundaries of the rather small Puget Sound Catholic community I had come to know while teaching at the St. Thomas Seminary School of Theology and conducting adult education programs for the Archdiocese of Seattle. In the course of the Council's work with some of the Seattle area's most accomplished political people, media personalities, and academics, I ran into David Brewster, who changed my life by taking a chance on a theologian-without-portfolio and making me into a writer.

David, another refugee from the groves of academe, had founded an alternative newspaper/newsmagazine, the *Weekly*, in 1976, thinking (correctly) that there was room for serious reporting and commentary, done with flair, in a major city burdened by two unreadable newspapers. It was the golden age of such enterprises in American journalism, and while the *Village Voice* was undoubtedly better known nationally, the *Weekly* quite probably produced, pound for pound, a larger number of writers who went on to find national audiences and build national (and international) reputations than any of its journalistic cousins.

This had something to do with the available talent pool, of course. But lots of cities have lots of talented people, eager to be writers. What *the Weekly* uniquely had going for it was David Brewster, his remarkable capacity for energizing others, his own considerable skills as a writer and editor, and his refreshingly quirky disdain for what the world presumed to be expertise. Thus the *Weekly* thrived on writers writing, or "trying," outside the box of their normal occupations.

David himself, who had done his doctoral work in English at Yale, produced a lot of the local and regional political commentary, became something of an expert in urban planning and design, and with no training (but a refined palate) turned himself into the Pacific Northwest's most respected (and feared) restaurant critic. Alan Furst, the *Weekly*'s football writer, went on to an enormously successful career as the author of upscale espionage fiction set in the cauldron of interwar and World War II Europe. Roger Sale, a truly great basketball writer who was a professor of English at the University of Washington and the author of a well regarded history of Seattle, covered the Seattle Supersonics of the NBA in the *Weekly*. The baseball writers, one year, were yours truly and John Miller, who went on to become a four-term Member of Congress and the U.S. Special Ambassador to Combat Human Trafficking. One of our staff members, Tim Appelo, became a book critic for Amazon.com, while Laura Schapiro, who did all sorts of cultural writing for the magazine, became the dance critic of *Newsweek*. Terry Tang, a recovering lawyer, took a massive salary cut to work (and fight) with David Brewster at the *Weekly* and ended up serving a sentence as op-ed editor of the *New York Times*.

No one, including me, imagined that the *Weekly* was also incubating a future papal biographer. David, however, was interested in getting the Seattle religious scene covered in a bracing way, and thus, in our first conversation, he asked me if I would be interested in doing "sermon reviews" for the magazine. Seattle was, in those days, a self-consciously secular town, and has become even more so since. But David, whose interests were catholic, thought that something of the cultural temper of the place could be measured by the quality of the preaching going on there, as well as by the quality of the local musical and dramatic offerings, the sports scene, the culinary possibilities, the intellectual life at the area's universities, and so forth.

I have to say that I thought the suggestion of "sermon reviews" a little crazy—not least because I had professional and personal contacts in the local clergy that I could easily imagine getting frayed if the brethren were subjected to extensive critique of their exegetical, theological, and rhetorical accomplishments. So while I welcomed the suggestion that I write for the *Weekly*, I counterproposed that, while doing the occasional article on a religious topic (John Paul II was just coming into view, and I relished the thought of explaining this unexpected figure to an audience that generally regarded Catholicism as troglodytic, at best), I would concentrate on writing about foreign policy and international affairs, thus connecting my work with the *Weekly* to my day job.

Generous soul that he is, David accepted the proposal and I began writing for him: which is to say, I began getting edited by him. Over the ensuing three decades, I would work with many brilliant and demanding editors, including Norman Podhoretz and Neal Kozodoy at *Commentary* and Richard John Neuhaus at *This World* and *First Things*, but in retrospect no one did more for me as a writer than David Brewster. And he did it, not only by becoming my personal Strunk & White, a style guide and mentor, but by giving me my head and letting me write on just about any topic, and without any ideological preconditions. This caused more than a few raised eyebrows over time, since the *Weekly* reflected, if often in a critical way, the general liberal sensibility of Seattle, and I had begun the intellectual journey that would eventually get me tagged a neoconservative. But David's catholicity extended to my political heresies, which he believed ought to be part of any civilized mix of argument, and he regularly defended me against the wannabe censors of the authoritarian Left, of whom I had my first experience in Seattle, the city that imagines it invented "tolerance."

It was also through the *Weekly* that I discovered a vocation of explaining Catholicism both to pagans and to ill-catechized Catholics. The latter were also at my mercy when I began writing a column for the *Catholic Northwest Progress*, the weekly newspaper of the Archdiocese of Seattle. But it was in the *Weekly* that I was first compelled to unpack, analyze, and, not infrequently, defend the teachings and practices of the Catholic Church in ways that made sense to readers who were quite intelligent, but who had no formal training in theology; who regarded religious conviction and practice as (at best) one among many optional lifestyle choices; and who, insofar as they had been exposed to any serious religious thinking and writing, had gotten a horse-doctor's dose of liberal Protestantism. It was, in other words, a challenging environment in which to explain the Catholic Church and its leader, a mediagenic Pole of obvious compassion and integrity who nonetheless insisted that there were truths to be known and followed in leading a truly human and humane life, and that those truths were, on the moral side of the ledger, to be found in classic biblical religion and its teaching.

This was not, to put it gently, the generally received cultural wisdom among the great and good of the Puget Sound region. Thus I found myself the center of controversy through this form of trying-by-writing, which I suppose amounted to a distinct form of apologetics. As things worked out, of course, all of this was exceptionally helpful training in preparing me to take on the task of describing John Paul II's life, thought, and work for a global audience, most of which was, if not overtly hostile, then at least unpersuaded by what the pope was teaching. It also helped armor me against the slings and arrows of criticism, even as I was being introduced to some of the woollier forms of anti-Catholicism.

I wrote regularly for the *Weekly* during the Reagan years, a period in which I also learned a lot about the limits of liberal tolerance. In the second decade of the twenty-first century, it is almost impossible to convey something of the passions that were roiling the American Left in the 1980s, passions centered on nuclear weapons and U.S. policy in Central America. I first broke with the Left on the latter; the occasion was the murder of two American representatives of the AFL-CIO's American Institute for Free Labor Development in El Salvador. One of the two, Mike Hammer, had discussed that tortured country's chaos with me two weeks before his assassination in January 1981; the other, Mark Pearlman, was a Seattle native. So I suggested to David Brewster that a memorial column to two heroes of democracy was in order; David agreed; and, having written the piece, I was quickly under assault from those who could not acknowledge that these two brave men represented an alternative to "oligarchs struggling to maintain their privilege [and] Marxists fighting to establish a new order of privilege," as I put it in my essay.

Then there was the nuclear question. Here, the beau ideal of the Seattle liberal community was the Catholic archbishop, Raymond G. Hunthausen, who described the Trident submarine base in his archdiocese as the "Auschwitz of Puget Sound," who withheld those portions of his federal income taxes that he deemed were being spent on nuclear weapons, and who encouraged his congregants to do the same. I found all of this wanting, both morally and politically; it seemed to me that unilateral American nuclear disarmament would have no impact on the Soviet Union except to strengthen its hand at a time when I could begin to see cracks in the totalitarian system being opened by the human rights activists of Poland, Czechoslovakia, the USSR, and elsewhere behind the Iron Curtain. However willing they were to have the archbishop of Seattle publicly commend committing felonies, though, the Seattle Left was not willing to let my dissent from its fierce, anti-Reagan consensus go unremarked. So my efforts to articulate a human rights-based solution to the Cold War in the pages of the *Weekly* became another source of controversy with the party of "tolerance."

Yet this experience, too, was useful in my evolution as a writer: once I learned that the Left held no monopoly on intelligent or compassionate or principled politics, I was liberated to do some serious trying-by-writing in pondering the innumerable dilemmas of foreign and domestic policy. In that sense, I wrote my way into neoconservativism, as I consistently found that the usual liberal "answers" to those dilemmas were no answers at all, once I tried to analyze or defend them on paper. My break with the Seattle peace fundamentalists—who were in fact anti-American-power fundamentalists (and worse, as the release of the Mitrokhin KGB archive demonstrated)—had one further, happy side effect: it brought me into contact, in the last years of his life, with a true statesman, Senator Henry M. Jackson. "The World According to Scoop," the lengthy memorial essay that David Brewster commissioned for the *Weekly* immediately after Jackson's unexpected death on September 1, 1983, was probably the best piece of writing I ever did for the magazine.

B y the time that my family and I left Seattle in 1984 so that I could take up a year's fellowship at the Woodrow Wilson International Center for Scholars, then lodged in the old Smithsonian castle, I had, with David Brewster's encouragement and under his editorial guidance, found a way to deploy my philosophical and theological training in essays that addressed topics rarely thought susceptible to theological or philosophical analysis: human rights, world history, international relations, foreign policy, literature, business, and sports. I had also found myself as an apologist. Trying-by-writing had made me more thoroughly convinced of the truth of what Catholicism taught, and I discovered that it was a lot of fun, if also occasionally exasperating, to try to explain that truth to others (including Catholics). And in this, I think, the essay form was crucial, for the medium fit the message particularly well.

After my relocation to the East Coast, my life as an essayist took on a national, and even international, cast, as I began writing for such journals as *Commentary*, *Crisis*, *This World*, and *First Things*, which was planned on the deck of Richard Neuhaus's Ottawa Valley cottage as the two of us talked through the possibilities over bourbon and adult tobacco products. *Commentary* was, of course, the intellectual and literary epicenter of neoconservatism, and I had, over the years, heard numerous tales of Norman Podhoretz's editorial ferocity. I must confess, however, that I found Norman (and his worthy successor, Neal Kozodoy) a joy to work with. Perhaps David Brewster's tutelage was so effective that Norman and Neal laid aside their editorial hacksaws and worked on my material with scalpels; in any event, I recall no fierce arguments, no writhings in the pain reported by other *Commentary* writers. And, as at the *Weekly*, I found in Norman and Neal editors who let me range widely, over everything from contemporary Catholicism to foreign policy to the future of Europe to sports. The same ecumenism has always prevailed during my twenty years' association with *First Things*, where I have done everything from travel diaries of papal pilgrimages to literary criticism to political theology to U.S. Catholic history. Jim Nuechterlein, longtime deputy to Richard Neuhaus at *First Things*, is not only a lucid writer in his own right; he was a fine editor with a keen eye for fustian and a sharp pencil in exterminating it. Richard himself was, of course, one of the Anglosphere's finest essayists, and his example was one I was happy to try to follow.

My books opened up other avenues for essays, a goodly chunk of which were rendered in other languages—a sometimes tricky business, given how fragile nuance proves in translation, but one that can pay unexpected dividends. My lengthy review essay in *Crisis* on Tad Szulc's unfortunate biography of John Paul II, translated into Polish and published in the distinguished Polish monthly *Więz* [Link], played a small role, for example, in my taking on the task of papal biographer myself in 1995. The Internet, of course, has vastly increased the quantity (at least) of those who are trying-by-writing, and a few years into the new century I found myself "essaying" for audiences in cyberspace. Thus I spent several years as a regular contributor to the print and online editions of *Newsweek*, where Jon Meacham was kind enough to let me explain John Paul II and Benedict XVI to readers who were, I expect, not altogether thrilled by my defense of these two great men. Since 2008, I have found a regular outlet for essays that address immediate, breaking news in the cyberpages of *National Review Online*; Kathryn Jean Lopez invited me to write for *NRO* and has been my guardian angel there, with occasional editorial assistance from the sharp-eyed Linda Bridges.

The essays collected here reflect both facets of my authorial vocation: my theological, or perhaps better, theotropic, interpretation of literature, history, public policy, culture, sports, and large-scale personalities; and my efforts to explain what the Catholic Church teaches, why, and how that teaching might cast needed light up some otherwise dark alleys of the human condition. There was perhaps more of the latter in the first collection of my essays published by Crossroad, *Against the Grain: Christianity and Democracy, War and Peace.* Here, I am "practicing Catholic" across a wider canvas—thus demonstrating, I hope, that Catholic means catholic, and that theological insight opens up new pathways of understanding in a variety of fields.

For if I have made any contribution to the art of the essay over the past three decades, it is likely here: in demonstrating how a theologically-driven optic on the human condition lets us see the human person, and the human condition, in full. The secularist cast of mind flattens the horizon of both our perception and our aspiration: we see less, and we aim lower, when we give a resigned (or stoic) "Yes" to Peggy Lee's question, "Is that all there is?" At a historical moment in which the temptation to reduce human beings to manipulable matter, and to do so in the name of compassion, is widespread, the theological optic lets us see that we are not congealed stardust, but something more, something greater, in both origin and destiny. In a culture fascinated by technology and technique, politics can quickly get reduced to process and "narrative"; reading history and politics through lenses ground with the tools of theology shows us the deeper dimensions involved in the ordering of public life. Wrestling with what Peter Berger once called "rumors of angels" has long been a dynamic within Anglo-American literature; thus a theological reading of fiction often unveils layers of a story or novel that cannot be approached or grasped any other way. Even our games comes into sharper, clearer focus when we see them through the intuition that *homo ludens*, the human person at play, is, in the pursuit of athletic excellence, reaching for transcendence and not just for victory (or salary).

Thirty-plus years of practicing Catholic have taught me that no one really knows what they think about a subject unless and until they write about it. And if "lifetime learning" is a good thing, as I think it is, I know of no better way to retain a love of learning that by practicing the art of the essay. The results can be, sometimes, surprising, even discomforting. But they can also be satisfying, invigorating, and exciting: both in terms of what an author receives and, just as importantly, in terms of what an author gives to readers.

Part I

In Our Times

The Sixties, Again and Again and Again

C ampaigning for the French presidency in 2007, Nicolas Sarkozy ran hard against "1968," describing the post-1968 New Left as "immoral" and "cynical" and defining the choice before the French electorate in stark terms: "In this election, the question is whether the heritage of May '68 should be perpetuated, or if it should be liquidated." Evidently, French politics has yet to discover the warm fuzzies of the focus group.

"1968" was a bad year throughout the Western world, a moment in which history seemed to career out of control. It was worse in Europe, and the impact of "1968" there was more profound. In western Europe, the agitations of "1968" aimed to effect a deep rupture with the past, and if those who took to the Paris barricades failed politically, they succeeded culturally; the dis-spirited western Europe that languishes in a crisis of civilizational morale today is in no small part a product of "1968"—as Nicolas Sarkozy, Marcello Pera, Giuliano Ferrara, Joseph Ratzinger, and others have recognized. "1968" is remembered differently in the United States. It was, to be sure, a terrible year, replete with political violence. But it is the Sixties as a whole, not some apocalyptic moment called "1968," that has had an enduring impact on our culture and our politics.

I don't propose to revisit here the question of whether what we call "the Sixties" was in fact hatched in the Fifties, or whether it unfolded its full plumage in that low decade, the Seventies. Rather, I want to revisit six crucial moments in the Sixties with an eye to how they reshaped American political culture, with effects still being felt more than a half-century later. What a large segment of American political culture learned from those moments constitutes the issues beneath "the issues" in the United States in the early twenty-first century—and in that important sense, America is still fighting battles begin in the Sixties, like it or not.

We had better learn to like it, because those fights involve the first principles of politics, rightly understood.

The First Moment: The Assassination of President John F. Kennedy (1963)

John Fitzgerald Kennedy would have been ninety-five years old in 2012—a circumstance virtually impossible to imagine. When Lee Harvey Oswald's bullets struck home on November 22, 1963, the national memory of the thirty-fifth president of the United States was frozen in a kind of memorial amber. It's hard enough to picture a sixty-year old JFK as the proprietor of a great newspaper (a postpresidential career he was considering). It is simply impossible to conjure up images of him at seventy-five, much less ninety-five. He remains forever young in the national consciousness.

Do we understand why he died, though? And does the regnant interpretation of the Kennedy assassination mask the truth about his presidency, about his place in the spectrum of American political opinion, and about the effects of his assassination on the decade that, at its outset, he seemed to embody?

In a marvelous piece of revisionist history, *Camelot and the Cultural Revolution*, James Piereson argues that the answers to those questions are "No" and "Yes." By re-examining the early Sixties absent the befogging romanticism of the Kennedy hagiographers, Piereson makes us think again, not only about events and personalities, but about the political culture of an entire era. And he compels us to reckon with how the interpretation (or, as he insists, misinterpretation) of the most dramatic event in that era continues to shape the politics of our own time.

Why did John F. Kennedy die? According to the interpretation advanced by admiring biographers (and former Kennedy aides) Arthur M. Schlesinger, Jr., and Theodore Sorensen—both influenced by Richard Hofstadter's essay, "The Paranoid Style in American Politics"—JFK's assassination was the by-product of a culture of violence that had infected the American far-Right. Right-wing paranoia about communism and civil rights activism was abroad in the land; this paranoia turned the city of Dallas into a seething political madhouse. Something awful was very likely to happen; it happened to John F. Kennedy, who had gone to Dallas to defend the politics of reason against the politics of irrational fear. Kennedy was martyred by unreason.

Thus the account from the court historians—which, interestingly enough, is the story told to visitors of the museum on the sixth floor of the Texas School Book Depository in Dallas, from which Oswald fired the lethal shots. Schlesinger and Sorensen were not operating in a hermeneutic vacuum, of course. As Piereson usefully reminds us, Schlesinger and Sorensen followed the lead of the mainstream media of their day in proposing that Kennedy's death was the tragic result of right-wing irrationality. For both print and electronic coverage of Kennedy's assassination and Oswald's subsequent murder had bathed these events in a torrent of introspection about an America allegedly fearful of the world, fearful of social change, and addicted to violence.

The Schlesinger/Sorensen interpretation was congenial to Jacqueline Kennedy, and may well have owed something to her understanding of what had happened and why. After Lee Harvey Oswald was arrested and identified, Mrs. Kennedy lamented that her husband hadn't even had the satisfaction of being killed for civil rights; his murderer had been a "silly little communist," a fact Mrs. Kennedy thought had robbed JFK's death of "any meaning."

So meaning would be created. And thus was born the familiar imagery of the Kennedy White House as an American Camelot, a "brief shining moment" that must "never be forgot" (as Alan Jay Lerner's lyrics, from the contemporary Broadway musical, put it).

Yet certain stubborn facts remain, as Pierson rightly insists: Lee Harvey Oswald was a convinced communist, a former defector to the Soviet Union, and a passionate supporter of Fidel Castro; the Kennedy administration was a sworn foe of Castro's communist regime, had authorized the Bay of Pigs operation, and had negotiated the removal of Soviet IRBMs from Cuba, much to Castro's chagrin. Hatred of Kennedy's Cold War policies was Oswald's motivation for assassinating President Kennedy. John F. Kennedy was not a victim of the irrational American right wing; he was a casualty of the Cold War—a Cold War, Pierson reminds us, that he prosecuted vigorously, if not always wisely or successfully.

The failure to acknowledge this in a country still jittery over the 1962 Cuban Missile Crisis was perhaps understandable. But too long an indulgence of historical fantasy, and the enduring effects of the Camelot myth, had long-term and serious effects on our political culture. By turning John F. Kennedy—the embodiment of pragmatic, rationalist, results-oriented anticommunist liberalism—into a mythical figure whose idealism could never be recaptured, Mrs. Kennedy, the court biographers, popular historians like Theodore H. White, Jr., and the mainstream media helped undermine the confidence in progress that had once characterized the liberalism of FDR, Truman—and John F. Kennedy. When that confidence dissolved, conspiracy theorizing migrated from the Bircher fever swamps of the extreme Right and began to infect American liberalism. And since the glorious Camelot past could never be recaptured, American liberalism became less a matter of substantive change than of style—and eventually of lifestyle. The net result was the liberalism we know today, a liberalism for which the legal recognition (indeed, promotion) of lifestyle libertinism is the paramount concern.

The Kennedy assassination was the event that ignited the firestorm in American political culture that we call "the Sixties." Of course some of the tinder was already there, waiting to be lit. A year before the president's death, Students for a Democratic Society issued what would become a key text for the New Left of the Sixties, the Port Huron Statement. The Kennedy assassination seemed to confirm Port Huron's lament for a generation's lost political innocence: as Tom Hayden and his SDS colleagues put it, "what we had originally seen as the American Golden Age [i.e., post-World War II America, come to its Periclean apogee in the Age of the Kennedy Camelot] was actually the decline of an era." With JFK dead, there were no answers left in the old pragmatic liberalism—hence the New Left's loathing of two of the last standing pragmatic liberals, Hubert H. Humphrey and Henry M. Jackson, and of the most legislatively successful liberal president in history, Lyndon Johnson. Take two measures of lost innocence, one large jigger of demonology, infuse it with the Marxist moonshine of Herbert Marcuse and his ilk, and what do you get? Within a few years, you got the lethal political cocktail that spelled "America" with a "k"—"Amerika," a Nazi-like authoritarian polity built on injustice at home and posing a grave danger to the world.

This rapid declension of the political imagination and discourse of the American Left in the wake of JFK's assassination led, in time, to another surprise: a reversal in the gravitational field of American political ideas. In 1949, Lionel Trilling, the literary embodiment of the old liberalism, deplored those American conservatives who do not "express themselves in ideas but only in actions or in irritable gestures which seek to resemble ideas." Less than twenty years later, it was the New Left that embodied Professor Trilling's grim description, while a revitalized conservative movement was taking its first steps in developing the economic, cultural, social welfare, and foreign policy ideas that would dominate American public life from 1980 through 9/11. During that period and down to the first decades of the twenty-first century, it would be conservatives and neoconservatives who would challenge Americans to bear great burdens to "assure the survival and the success of liberty," as JFK had put it in his Inaugural Address, while those who imagined themselves the heirs of Kennedy promoted a kind of American withdrawal from the world that was far more reminiscent of Joseph P. Kennedy than of his second son.

All of which, one suspects, was not quite what Jacqueline Kennedy, Arthur Schlesinger, Jr., Ted Sorensen, and Teddy White had in mind in creating the mythology of Camelot. Irrespective of what the widow and the courtiers had in mind, though, we can be quite sure that John F. Kennedy did not think of himself or his politics as Tom Hayden and SDS did: as a kind of American analogue to Weimar Germany.

The Second Moment: *Griswold v. Connecticut* (1965)

In 1961, the executive director of the Planned Parenthood League of Connecticut, Estelle Griswold, opened a birth control clinic in New Haven in collaboration with Dr. C. Lee Buxton, a professor at the Yale School of Medicine. Their purpose was to test the constitutionality of Connecticut's 1879 law banning the sale of contraceptives, a law that had never been enforced and which the U.S. Supreme Court had recently declined to review. What appears to have been a carefully-crafted strategy then unfolded: the state authorities acted; Griswold and Buxton were charged, tried, convicted, and fined $100 each; and the lower court decision was upheld by the relevant Connecticut appellate courts (including the splendidly named "Connecticut Supreme Court of Errors").

Griswold and Buxton then appealed to the U.S. Supreme Court, which accepted the case and, in the 1965 decision *Griswold v. Connecticut*, struck down both the convictions and the Connecticut statute on the ground that the law violated what Justice William O. Douglas's majority opinion called "the right to marital privacy." Justice Douglas conceded that the Constitution did not mention a "right to privacy," marital or otherwise, but famously opined that such a right was to be discerned in "penumbras formed by emanations" from the Constitution's enumerated rights. (To compound the jurisprudential confusion, Justice John Marshall Harlan argued in a concurring opinion that "privacy" is protected by the due process clause of the Fourteenth Amendment, while Justice Arthur Goldberg's concurrence argued that "privacy" was among the unenumerated rights "retained by the people" according to the Ninth Amendment.)

In dissent, Justice Potter Stewart described the Connecticut law he believed constitutional as "uncommonly silly"—which, in retrospect, was a phrase he could have used to describe *Griswold v. Connecticut*, adding "pernicious" to "silly." Why? Because, in terms of our legal culture, *Griswold* was the Pearl Harbor of the American culture war, that fierce debate over the moral and cultural foundations of our democracy that has shaped our politics for two generations.

As Edward Whelan neatly put it, who knew that contraception could have such generative power? For *Griswold* begat *Eisenstadt v. Baird*, the 1972 decision in which the Court extended the protections of the "right of privacy" to nonmarried couples. Then *Eisenstadt* begat *Roe v. Wade*, in which the "right to privacy" was cited to strike down the abortion law of all fifty states, in what Justice Byron White would describe as an exercise in "raw judicial power." *Roe*, in turn, begat *Casey v. Planned Parenthood of Southeastern Pennsylvania*, which described the "right to abortion" as a liberty right under the Fourteenth Amendment. *Roe* and *Casey* then begat the 2003

Supreme Court decision in *Lawrence v. Texas*, which struck down a state antisodomy statute, with Justice Anthony Kennedy making an explicit reference to *Griswold*'s "right to privacy" as "the most pertinent beginning point" for the line of reasoning that led the Court to *Lawrence*. And if *Eisenstadt, Roe, Casey,* and *Lawrence* were the direct descendants of *Griswold*, it is not difficult to see how *Goodridge v. Department of Public Health*, the 2003 Massachusetts Supreme Judicial Court decision mandating so-called "gay marriage," was a collateral descendant of Justice Douglas's discovery of a constitutional "right to privacy."

*G*riswold, this paradigmatic judicial artifact of the Sixties has had, and continues to have, a tremendous impact on our public culture. *Griswold* helped set the constitutional conditions for the possibility of the sexual revolution, as the oral contraceptive pill was the technological condition for its possibility. Governmental indifference to contraception was soon construed to imply governmental indifference to abortion, via the misconstrual of abortion as a matter of sexual "privacy" rather than as a matter of public justice; and the "right to abortion" soon became a defining issue in our politics. For as Hadley Arkes has put it, "the 'right to abortion,' with its theme of sexual liberation, has become the central peg on which the interests of the Democratic Party have been arranged," just as "since the days of Ronald Reagan, the Republican Party has become . . . the pro-life party in our politics."

Careful observers will note here a profound inversion. If the abortion issue and related life issues are in fact the great civil rights issues of our time—in that they test whether the state may arbitrarily deny the protection of the law to certain members of the human community—then *Griswold* eventually led to a situation in which the Democratic and Republican positions on civil rights flipped, with today's Democratic Party playing, as a whole, the role that its southern intransigents played during the glory days of the American civil rights movement.

The Supreme Court was not the only actor in these momentous changes, of course. The development of the oral contraceptive pill must rank with the splitting of the atom and the unraveling of the DNA double helix as one of the three scientific achievements of the twentieth century with world-historical impact. The sexual revolution was also influenced by trends in philosophy, particularly existentialism's emphasis on "authenticity." The inability of many modern moral philosophers to get beyond Hume's fact/value distinction in order to think their way through to a contemporary form of natural law moral reasoning (which would in turn have helped discipline legal thinking) also played its role. The supine surrender of most religious authorities removed one cultural obstacle to the sexual revolution's triumphant progress, which was sped by developments (that is, deteriorations) in popular culture.

Still, in measuring the impact of the Sixties on the politics of the twenty-first century, it is the legal consequences of *Griswold* that must be underscored. Here, the Supreme Court began to set in legal concrete the notion that sexual morals and patterns of family life are matters of private choice or taste, not matters of public concern in which the state has a legitimate interest. That this trend should have eventually led to claims that "marriage" is whatever any configuration of adults-sharing-body-parts declares it to be ought not have been a surprise. Nor should it have been a surprise that the Court, having successfully claimed for itself the authority to write a "living Constitution" based on penumbras and emanations, should go on to assume the roles of National Metaphysician and National Nanny (as it did in *Casey*, with its famous "sweet mystery of life" passage and its hectoring injunction to a fractious populace to fall into line behind the Court's abortion jurisprudence). The royal road to the imperial judiciary may not have begun with *Griswold*, but *Griswold* certainly accelerated the pace of the coronation procession.

The Third Moment: *The Secular City* (1965)

At the beginning of the 1960s, the National Council of Churches, ecumenical embodiment of mainline Protestantism's large role in American culture, was as secure in the pantheon of influential American institutions as the American Medical Association and the American Bar Association. Thirty years later, to cite Richard John Neuhaus's formula, the mainline had become the oldline and was on its way to being the sideline: which unenviable position it has now achieved, the National Council of Churches having been reduced to renting a few offices at 475 Riverside Drive, the famous "God-Box" it had once occupied to capacity. As mainline/oldline/sideline Protestantism ceased to be a culture-forming force in American public life, the void was filled by a new Catholic presence in the public square and, perhaps most influentially in electoral terms, by the emergent activism of evangelical, fundamentalist, and pentecostalist Protestantism in what would become known as the Religious New Right—a movement that formed a crucial part of the Republican governing coalition for more than a quarter-century. The pivotal moment in this tectonic shift in American religion's interface with American public life came in the Sixties, when the mainline imploded, theologically and politically.

The political side of the tale is a familiar one: what had begun as mainline Protestant support for the classic civil rights movement quickly morphed into liberal Protestant support for black militancy, the most strident forms of anti-Vietnam protest, the most extreme elements of the women's movement and the environmental movement, the nuclear freeze and similar agitations, and, latterly, the gay liberation movement (which, among other things, now bids fair to destroy the most mainline of mainline American churches, the Episcopal Church USA). All of this must be considered a sadness, for it was the mainline/oldline/sideline that provided moral-cultural ballast to the American democratic experiment from the colonial period through World War II. (The decline and fall of the mainline also occasioned one of the funniest pieces of religio-political commentary in the last quarter of the twentieth century. At the height of the nuclear freeze enthusiasm, New York Episcopal Bishop Paul Moore and the dean of his Cathedral Church of St. John the Divine, Dr. James Morton—two men who incarnated the radicalization of liberal Protestantism in the Sixties—declared the cathedral a "nuclear-free zone." To which then-Pastor Neuhaus replied with the quip that this was good news, since their behavior over the past twenty years had made it quite clear that neither Bishop Moore nor Dean Morton could be trusted with nuclear weapons.)

Harvey Cox's 1965 bestseller, *The Secular City*, with its argument for a radically secularized Christianity in which the world sets the agenda for the Church, has not worn well; virtually no one reads it today, save perhaps as a period piece. In its time, however, *The Secular City* put into play virtually all the major themes that, while they led mainline Protestantism into a wilderness of religious marginality, nonetheless had a decided influence on the politics of the Sixties—and of the American twenty-first century today. The cult of the new; the fondness for revolutionary rhetoric; evil understood in therapeutic categories; worship conceived as self-realization; the celebration of action detached from either contemplation or serious intellectual reflection; insouciance toward tradition; moralism in place of moral reasoning; the identification of human striving with the in-breaking of the Kingdom of God—whatever Harvey Cox's intentions (and he is one of the nicest men you'll ever meet), these are the things that people learned from *The Secular City* and its many offspring in the world of liberal American religious thought. By the time the Hartford Appeal for Theological Affirmation tried to redress the balance in 1975, the damage had been done. *The Secular City* helped accelerate the secularization of American elite culture, which created both new openings in the public square for more traditional religious bodies and new fault lines in our politics—fault lines which are as visible as twenty-first- century headlines and op-ed pages.

The Fourth Moment: Tet and the Canonical Narrative of Vietnam (1968)

The American war *in* Vietnam spanned the entire decade of the Sixties. The American war *over* Vietnam continues, as President George W. Bush discovered in 2007 when he used the Vietnam analogy to warn against the likely consequences of a precipitous withdrawal of U.S. forces from Iraq. "A risky gambit," *Time* called it. "Nonsense," said historian Robert Dallek. "Irresponsible and ignorant," harrumphed our leading senatorial expert on the riverine vagaries of the Vietnam-Cambodia border, John Kerry. "Ludicrous," sneered the *Nation's* Robert Scheer. "Surreal," opined the editors of the *New York Times* (whose familiarity with the surreal is, it must be conceded, extensive). Why, asked Senator Majority Leader Harry Reid, was Bush tying his "flawed strategies" to "one of the worst foreign policy blunders in our nation's history"?

To judge by the bludgeoning Bush took from his Democratic, academic, and media critics, you'd have thought that he'd committed blasphemy. Which, in a sense, he had: for if there is any set of convictions on the post-Sixties American Left that resembles the most stringent interpretation of biblical inerrancy among certain Protestant fundamentalists, it's the commitment to the canonical narrative of Vietnam. That narrative, according to historian Arthur Herman, rests on four theses.

T he first of these holds that an America obsessed with communism blundered mindlessly into an internal Vietnamese struggle in which no vital American interest was at stake. That obsession, in turn, led the United States to fight a war against an indigenously supported native guerrilla movement for which the U.S. military was unprepared; so American forces resorted to barbaric tactics and then lied to the American people about them. According to the third thesis in the canonical narrative, a losing struggle in the fetid jungles of Vietnam destroyed American troop morale and discipline; this disintegration led to rampant drug abuse, the murder of unpopular officers, atrocities like the My Lai murders, and a generation of physically and psychologically scarred veterans. Finally, the canonical narrative insists that the entire enterprise was doomed from the start; and in any event, America's failure led to desirable effects, such as the reunification of Vietnam. If atrocities happened after the communist takeover of South Vietnam and Cambodia, well, those atrocities were triggered by our "meddling" in affairs that were none of our business.

The Vietnam fundamentalists of the academic, media, and cultural Left believe the canonical narrative they created (the origins of which may be traced to the reporting of David Halberstam and Neil Sheehan from Vietnam) with a fervor as great as the Rev. Bob Jones's belief in the world's creation in seven twenty-four hour periods. Yet the Vietnam fundamentalists of the Left have a serious problem: for a decade's worth of work by historians using primary source materials from former Vietcong and North Vietnamese figures suggests that each of the four theses in the canonical account is wrong.

The details of this new historical-critical account of the history of America's war in Vietnam are interesting, for they point toward the sad conclusion that American seized defeat from the jaws of a modest victory in Southwest Asia. But however one assesses that judgment, the enduring effect of the canonical account of Vietnam on contemporary politics is unmistakable.

T he antiwar domestic American politics of Vietnam were a volatile expression of what might be called, following the existentialist fashions of the time, the "politics of authenticity." In the politics of authenticity, what counts is the nobility of my feelings; what does not count is evidence, and what is not required is an examination (or re-examination) of conscience in light of the evidence. The politics of authenticity lead us by a short route to a public morality of feelings, impervious to data and dismissive of a moral calculus of possible consequences. Or to put it in Max Weber's terms, the morality of *intentions* trumped the morality of *responsibility*. The irresponsibility that characterized the Carter and Clinton administrations' responses to the threat of global jihadism—a fecklessness deeply influenced by the canonical Vietnam narrative—followed.

This irresponsibility in the name of putatively superior moral intentions and sensibilities has gotten worse in the first decades of the twenty-first century, having been goaded to hitherto unimaginable extremes by the distorting psychological impact of what the American Left considered an illegitimate presidency since December 12, 2000, when the U.S. Supreme Court effectively awarded the 2000 president election to George W. Bush. Senator Majority Leader Harry Reid's premature 2007 proclamations of defeat in Iraq—a defeat the impact of which the majority leader seemed to relish—is difficult to explain unless you understand that. For Reid and those of his persuasion, George Bush's suggestion that a precipitous American withdrawal from Iraq would lead to bloodbaths similar to those in postwar Vietnam and Cambodia is blasphemy by a political heretic and usurper.

The Tet Offensive of January 1968 was the point at which the liberal canonical account of America's Vietnam, which was deeply influencing American journalism, began to have a marked impact on policy, and thus on events. Lyndon Johnson, taking Walter Cronkite's misreporting of Tet seriously, lost heart; the Democratic party largely abandoned the war that John F. Kennedy had begun (and would certainly have continued, the mythmakers notwithstanding); public opinion, shaped by what now appears to have been some of the worst reporting of the television age, turned decisively against the war. Today, no responsible historian considers Tet anything other than a colossal military defeat for North Vietnam and the end of the Vietcong as a major force in the struggle for Vietnam's future. Why? Because North Vietnamese and Vietcong sources frankly admit that that was the case. But when David Halberstam died in an auto accident in 2007, not a single obituary notice I read suggested that he (and Neil Sheehan, Walter Cronkite, and all the rest) had been terribly wrong about Tet, or that this wrongheadedness in propagating the canonical account had helped create a political situation that had had lethal consequences for millions.

The point here is not media-bashing. The point is that the canonical narrative continues to distort the worldview of many of those charged with responsibility for our national security. Barack Obama and others may well wish to "get beyond" the Sixties. But here is a question for those who take that line: With whom do you stand on the question of Vietnam and its relationship to our global responsibilities today? Do you stand with the fundamentalists of the Left, impervious to evidence? Or does the new, evidence-based historical-critical approach to understanding America's war in Vietnam shape your way of thinking about American responsibilities in the twenty-first-century world?

The Fifth Moment: The Kerner Commission and the Politics of Victimhood (1968)

The Sixties began with the American civil rights movement at the height of its classic phase; the Sixties ended with the leaders of classic civil rights activism dead or marginalized. At the end of the decade, the leadership of what had once been a movement for national reconciliation in a color-blind society had been seized by race-baiters who preached a gospel of victimization and identified the struggles of black America with the revolutionary theories of such Third World ideologues as Frantz Fanon.

This happened in an astonishingly short period of time. When Lyndon Johnson signed the Civil Rights Act of 1964, he shared presidential pens with men like Martin Luther King, Jr., Roy Wilkins, and Thurgood Marshall; within half a decade, King was dead, men like Wilkins were charged with being "Oreos" by the new black militants, and a culture of victimization had settled like a thick, choking fog over America's inner cities. Dr. King's dream of a nation come to the mountaintop of justice had been displaced by chants of "Burn, baby, burn!" Equality of opportunity was passé; racial quotas masquerading under the euphemism of "affirmative action" were the new cause; King's righteous demand that his children be judged by the content of their characters rather than the color of their skins was inverted by race-hustlers and shakedown artists— an inversion subsequently validated by activist judges. The net result? The alienation of the majority population and the descent of American inner cities into a miasma of broken families, illegitimacy, crime, substance abuse, and poverty.

Why and how one part of the American drama of race played out this way can be debated. But that it happened, and that the terms in which it happened continue to shape the American politics of the early twenty-first century, seems reasonably clear. Perhaps the pivotal moment was the Kerner Commission Report of 1968, formally known as the Report of the National Advisory Commission on Civil Disorders, created by President Johnson to determine the cause of the racial riots that had burned across America in the summer of 1967.

By that year, the United States, a country whose original sin was black slavery, had made immense strides in building what is today the most racially egalitarian major nation on the planet. Segregation of public institutions had been declared unconstitutional and segregation of public facilities outlawed. The poll tax in federal elections had been banned by the Twenty-fourth Amendment, Americans of African descent had been rapidly enfranchised, and as the 1964 Democratic National Convention demonstrated, black America had begun to play a significant role in national politics. That all of this had been accomplished by a religiously-grounded movement of national moral and legal reform, in which blacks and whites organized, worked, marched, and bled together, held out the prospect of further progress in sustaining racial equality before the law, creating equality of economic opportunity, and strengthening the culture of responsibility throughout American society.

The Kerner Commission, however, seemed blind to many of these positive dynamics, proposing an analysis in which black "frustration" and white "racism" were the two forces shaping American urban life. Black America was a victim, and a victim could not be held morally responsible for lashing out against his victimization. According to the Kerner Commission's analysis, racist white America was similarly bereft of moral resources, such that government, rather than the institutions of civil society that had been so central to the classic civil rights movement, had to become the principal agent of enforced social change in order to deal with the crisis of an America "moving toward two societies . . . separate and unequal."

W hile the Kerner Commission was rewriting the national narrative on civil rights in favor of a story line of racial victimization and irresistible irresponsibility—precisely what King, Wilkins, and others of their generation had fought against— what all this might mean on the ground was being played out in the furious 1968 controversy over local control of public school faculty appointments in the Ocean Hill-Brownsville neighborhood of Brooklyn. By the time things simmered down, Brooklyn's inner-city schools were in considerably worse shape, white liberals had become accustomed to making excuses for black violence, and the old alliances between the civil rights movement, on the one hand, and the American labor movement and organized American Jewry, on the other, had been put under severe strain. Albert Shanker and the American Federation of Teachers may have won some of the battles in Brooklyn, but they lost the larger war, as American liberalism, forced to choose between maintaining its classic emphasis on a race-blind society and keeping pace with the new black militancy, eventually chose the latter. As for the black-Jewish alliance, that, too, shattered over time, to the point where Jesse Jackson could refer to New York as "Hymietown" and not pay any serious price for it.

The emergence of what presidential historian Steven Hayward has called a "therapeutic victim culture" that would have a profound impact on American politics began with the collapse of the classic civil rights movement in the mid-Sixties: which is to say, at its greatest moment of triumph. The classic civil rights movement, once determined to reshape America through moral reason, was distorted through the victim culture into a twisted parody of itself, and infused with a moralism self-consciously detached from reason that would prove incapable of calling anyone, black or white, to the great cause of equal justice for all.

As usual, those who paid the heaviest price were those with the least resources to withstand the breakdown of moral reason and the culture of responsibility in entire neighborhoods: the underclass. But among those with the resources to indulge irresponsibility, the new, late-Sixties' culture of victimization would eventually set in motion two trends in American public life that are very much with us in the twenty-first century: the gay movement (which successfully, if quite implausibly, identified itself and its grievances with the grievances of pre-civil-rights-era black America), and leftist celebrity activism (which would end up providing political cover for the likes of Saddam Hussein and Hugo Chavez).

The Sixth Moment: Earth Day and the Rise of Environmentalism (1970)

That human beings cannot live without transcendent points of spiritual and moral reference is nicely illustrated by the fact that, as liberal mainline Protestantism was collapsing, those who might have been expected, in previous generations, to have been among its staunch adherents found a new god: the Earth. The transformation of the quite sensible and admirable American conservation movement into an "ism"—environmentalism—is best understood, I suggest, as a matter of displaced religious yearning. Having found the God of liberal Protestantism implausible or boring, American liberal elites discovered a new deity, the worship of which involved a drastic transformation of virtually every sector of American life by the new liberalism's favorite instrument of salvation, the state.

Inspired in part by bestsellers like Rachel Carson's 1962 *Silent Spring*, conservation-become-environmentalism evolved in the Sixties into a movement highly critical of technology and its impact on global ecology and deeply skeptical about markets; it also cross-pollinated politically with the antiwar movement. Which is at least a bit strange, in that it was an artifact produced by the much-deplored military-industrial complex—the photographs of Planet Earth taken by the astronauts of Apollo VIII on their Christmas 1968 circumnavigation of the moon—that gave the new environmentalism its icon and something of its emotional power. That irony notwithstanding, antiwar activist John McConnell, having seen the pictures taken by Frank Borman, Jim Lovell, and Bill Anders from the command module windows of Apollo VIII, created the "Earth Day flag" from one of those photos and in 1969 proposed a global holiday in celebration of the Earth to a UNESCO conference being held in San Francisco (of course). The Earth Day Proclamation signed by U Thant, Margaret Mead, and others followed, as did the now-annual celebration of Earth Day.

The new environmentalism was not only peopled by many of the same activists who had been instrumental in the anti-America's-war-in-Vietnam movement; in subsequent decades, the new environmentalism has displayed similar characteristics to the fundamentalism or fideism of those who cling to the wreckage of the canonical narrative of America-in-Vietnam. Among those characteristics (in addition to a certain apocalypticism) is an imperviousness to contrary data and scientific evidence. As the Danish statistician Bjørn Lomborg (a veteran of the European Green movement) has shown in study after empirical study, life expectancy is increasing on a global basis, including the Third World; water and air in the developed world are cleaner than in five hundred years; fears of chemicals poisoning the earth are wildly exaggerated; both energy and food are cheaper and more plentiful throughout the world than ever before; "overpopulation" is a myth; and the global picture is, historically speaking, one of unprecedented human thriving.

Acknowledging this, however, would call into question the revelation vouchsafed to another of the new environmentalism's ideological allies, the population-control movement: namely, that people are a pollutant—a pernicious idea, born of the earlier progressivist eugenics movement and brought to a popular boil in the Sixties by evidence-light propagandists like Paul Ehrlich, that continues to affect U.S. foreign aid policy to this day. Now as always, the worship of false gods tends toward bad politics.

From the Sixties to the Twenty-first Century

Taken together, these six moments suggest that something of grave and enduring consequence happened to liberal politics, and thus to American political culture, during the Sixties. A politics of reason gave way to a politics of emotion, and even flirted with the politics of irrationality. The claims of moral reason were displaced by moralism. The notion that all men and women were called to live lives of responsibility was displaced by the notion that some people were, by reason of birth, victims. Patriotism became suspect, to be replaced by a vague internationalism. Democratic persuasion was displaced by judicial activism. Each of these consequences is much with us today; what one thinks about them defines the substratum of the politics of the early twenty-first century, the issues-beneath-the-issues.

That this trajectory was virtually unaffected by the victory of democracy and the free economy in the Revolution of 1989 tells us something important about the post-Sixties phase of the story. Beginning in the late Sixties, American liberalism followed the path of the global Left, substituting social issues and lifestyle libertinism for its previous concerns with economics and participatory politics. Which is to say that American liberalism, like its European counterpart, adopted the strategy of the Italian Marxist theorist Antonio Gramsci and began a long march through the institutions—first, the universities, the media, the philanthropies, the religious communities; now, the institutions of marriage and the family. That this has had the most profound impact on our politics is obvious: the American culture war, which is one of the preeminent issues-beneath-the-issues, shapes the public discourse on both domestic and foreign policy questions every day.

The transformation of the pragmatic, results-oriented, rationalist liberalism of John F. Kennedy, first into the New Left and subsequently into postmodern American liberalism, has put the imperial autonomous Self at the center of one pole of American public life, where it has displaced the notion of the free and virtuous society as the goal of American democracy. This raises the most profound and urgent questions about the future. Can a common culture capable of sustaining institutions of self-governance be built out of a congeries of autonomous selves? Can a politics detached from moral reason give reasons why toleration, civility, and persuasion are superior to coercion in doing the public business? What can the politics of autonomy—which is the distillation of the politics of the Sixties—say in the face of the existential threats that confront the United States: the threat of jihadism (which has a very clear, and very different, idea of the good society), and the threat of a slow descent, via biotechnology, into the stunted humanity of the brave new world? Is freedom understood as autonomy and willfulness a freedom worth sacrificing for? Or will only a renewal of the idea of freedom for excellence—freedom tethered to moral truth and ordered to goodness—see us through the political and cultural whitewater of the early twenty-first century?

The Sixties are indeed much with us—including, it is important to add, that part of the Sixties that called the American people to live nobly in the defense and promotion of liberty, rightly understood, and of equality for all before the law. Whether *that* legacy of the Sixties wins out over the less happy residues of that turbulent decade is a very large question facing twenty-first-century Americans.

Scoundrel Time

The Beltway conventional wisdom on the 2008 presidential election was summed up, unsurprising, by a *Washington Post* column published on November 2, 2008, forty-eight hours before the vote. Barack Obama, David Broder wrote, had demonstrated an "impressive" capacity to "convert strangers into friends" and had had the good sense to hire a staff who "knew what they were doing" in the cauldron of presidential politics. Moreover, Broder contended, Obama had dealt with "the classic American dilemma of race" by demonstrating "repeatedly how to bridge the racial divides that still remain," thus symbolically conveying a "powerful, positive message to the world" of a new "national maturity."

It would be churlish to deny that there were grains of truth here. In its result, the 2008 campaign was a historic one, which we may hope has at least partially vindicated the moral goal of the classic civil rights movement: the building of an America in which character, not pigmentation, is the standard by which we measure our neighbors and fellow citizens. From the point of view of salesmanship, the Obama campaign was virtually flawless, having turned a relatively unknown backbencher with the Senate's most liberal voting record into a vessel of hope into which people across a good part of the political spectrum poured their aspirations.

Yet it is also true that the 2008 campaign was a disturbing one—not because it coincided with an economic crisis of historic proportions, but because it revealed some serious flaws in our political culture. Prominent among those flaws is our seeming inability to discuss, publicly, the transformation of American liberalism into an amalgam of lifestyle libertinism, moral relativism, and soft multilateralism, all flavored by the identity politics of race and gender. Why can't we talk sensibly about these things? From 2000 through 2008, no small part of the reason why had to do with the phenomenon that Charles Krauthammer, in a nod to his former incarnation as a psychiatrist, dubbed "Bush Derangement Syndrome."

Raising this point was not, for Krauthammer at the time or for any serious analyst later, a matter of electoral sour grapes. Given an unpopular war that had been misreported from the beginning, plus George W. Bush's unwillingness to use the presidential bully pulpit to help the American people comprehend the stakes in Iraq, plus conservative frustration over a spendthrift Republican Congress and Administration, plus the Administration's failure to enforce discipline on its putative Congressional allies, plus public exhaustion with a familiar cast of characters after seven years in office, plus an economic meltdown—well, given all that, it seems unlikely that any Republican candidate could have beaten any Democrat in 2008. Indeed, the surprise at the presidential level may have been that President Obama didn't enjoy a success on the magnitude of Eisenhower's in 1952, Johnson's in 1964, Nixon's in 1972, or Reagan's in 1984.

Still, I would argue that the basic dynamics of the 2008 campaign, evident in the passions that led Obama supporters to seize control of the Democratic Party and then of the presidency, were not set in motion by the failures and missed opportunities of the previous seven years of Republican presidential governance, but by Bush Derangement Syndrome. Bush Derangement Syndrome emerged as a powerful force in American public life on December 12, 2000: the day American liberalism's preferred instrument of social and political change, the U.S. Supreme Court, determined that the candidate with fewer popular votes nationally, George W. Bush, had in fact won Florida, and with it a narrow majority in the Electoral College. Here was the cup dashed from the lips—and by a Court assumed to be primed to deliver the expected and desired liberal result yet again. Here was the beginning of a new, millennial politics of emotivism (displayed in an astonishing degree of publicly manifested loathing for a sitting president) and hysteria (fed by the new demands of a 24/7 news cycle).

O ne might even drive the analysis back two years further. For the seeds of Bush Derangement Syndrome were sown during the 1998–1999 impeachment crisis. William Jefferson Clinton was acquitted by the U.S. Senate on February 12, 1999—but more to the point, he had been absolved by liberal political culture months earlier.

In the summer of 1998, it seemed not unlikely that President Clinton would be successfully impeached and removed from office, or compelled to resign on the Nixon model—not least, because of the self-preservation instincts of the Democratic Party and its Congressional leadership. Then, around Labor Day 1998, Maureen Dowd and others in the media commentariat successfully re-framed the issue in the debate over Clinton's continued fitness for office. As defined by the late, great Henry Hyde in the Judiciary Committee of the U.S. House of Representatives, the question throughout 1998 had been, "Can a felon who has perjured himself before a federal grand jury and obstructed justice continue to serve as president, that is, the country's chief law enforcement officer?" Or, as Henry was wont to put it, "Can a man live in the White House when several hundred people who have committed precisely the same crime are living in federal prisons?" The issue, in other words, was the rule of law.

That changed, in the virtual twinkling of an eye, when the commentariat decided that this was really all about sex, and that if Clinton (whom many ideologically hardened liberals despised) crashed and burned, so would the sexual revolution. Even worse, if Clinton fell, the zealots of the great unwashed Moral Majority would be vindicated—and who knew who would be sent to the stake next? Liberal America decided that, if the price to be paid for saving the sexual revolution was to permit a felon to serve as president of the United States, then it was worth it. So the issue was redefined in the political culture; tremulous Republican leadership in the U.S. Senate acquiesced, at least tacitly, to the redefinition; and the president was acquitted.

But anger remained on a high boil in Democratic breasts. How could the natural party of governance (as Democrats continued to imagine themselves even after the 1994 Gingrich revolution), indeed the righteous party (as liberal Democrats had imagined themselves since the Sixties), have been brought to such a pass? Not, certainly, by its own sins, offenses, and negligences, but by an unholy conspiracy of yahoos, philistines, scolds, and censors, to whom the runt of the Bush litter, the arch-moron, "Dubya," had blatantly appealed by declaring Jesus Christ his favorite political philosopher during the 2000 presidential primaries. Thus vengeance was the order of the day in 2000. The natural party of governance would be vindicated. Imagine, then, the rage when a combination of hanging chads and a controversial Supreme Court decision determined otherwise.

From the beginning of the Bush Administration, then, a passionately held conviction that dared not speak its name smoldered in many Democratic and liberal hearts: *George W. Bush is an illegitimate president*—morally, if not quite constitutionally. That conviction hardened over time, not least because of President Bush's disdain for Washington tastemakers, his indifference to what others said or wrote about him, his inability or unwillingness to strike back wittily, and his loyalty to subordinates who were incompetent or who had run out of gas. To make matters worse, Bush was a serious Christian who made no bones about the fact that conversion to Christ had changed his life and that prayer played a large role in his daily routine; who knew what bizarre transmissions from the Great Beyond this pious idiot might be receiving? This secularist plank in the anti-Bush platform received regular reinforcement from western European opinion merchants, who feared that their Kantian utopia

of perpetual peace was on the verge of being destroyed by an ignorant Yankee cowboy evangelical apocalyptic—and who regularly
instructed their American liberal colleagues to *Do something about
this fool before he gets us all killed.*

Thus, despite a brief post-9/11 rallying of emotional and political support for the president, Bush Derangement Syndrome
was well entrenched by the 2004 election cycle, which resulted in
yet another severe disappointment for the natural party of governance: this time, not because of the Supreme Court, but because
several hundred thousand Ohio evangelicals decided to register in
order to vote against so-called "gay marriage"—and punched in
for George W. Bush at the same time. All of which only confirmed
to both American and European elite opinion that the barbarians
were not outside the gate, but at the control panels of the U.S.
government.

The boiling rage of Bush Derangement Syndrome thus set the
emotional context for the 2008 electoral cycle, even as Republican idiocies and corruptions in Congress set the political context
for the return of the House and Senate to Democratic control in
2006—which seemed to guarantee, in the mind of the natural party
of governance, a return to the White House on January 20, 2009.
The cowboy would be sent packing, back to his ranch in loathsome
Texas; his supporters would retreat into the enclaves from which
they had first sallied forth during the Carter years; the right order of
the universe would be restored.

To be sure, other cultural factors played into the distinct
dynamics of the politics of 2008. Perhaps the most over-
used word in twenty-first-century political commentary has been
"narrative," which seems to have succeeded "story line" as the go-to
term for describing the ebb and flow of politics: "He's created a
compelling narrative." Or, "Can he change the narrative?" And so
forth and so on.

Yet this verbal tic is not, well, just a verbal tic. It reflects, usually unreflectively, the rhetoric of postmodernism, which has migrated from the campuses into the mainstream media and into everyday life. Post-modern assertions to the contrary, however, post-modern rhetoric is not just rhetoric. It reflects a cast of mind in which human beings have no secure grasp on the truth of things, be that historical truth or moral truth. There is only "your truth" and "my truth," which is to say, you've got your story and I've got my story. "Narrative" is all, and "narrative" has no tether to an objective truth-of-things that we can know by the exercise of our reason.

In Europe, this epistemological skepticism has brought several European countries and the European Union itself perilously close to what a distinguished European intellectual once described as the "dictatorship of relativism:" the imposition of relativism by state power. Perhaps the most notable example is contemporary Spain, where, thanks to the now-defunct Zapatero government, Juan can walk into his local civil registry office, declare himself "Juanita," and have his national identity card changed accordingly, without any surgical folderol. Human nature is what my "narrative" declares it to be. As I quipped to a Spanish colleague, "The dame in Spain is mainly in the name."

Things have not quite come to that pass in the United States. But the same trajectory is evident in a culture in which the creation and marketing of a compelling personal "narrative" has replaced the contest of issues and ideas as the driving force of electoral politics. Everyone knows that this is what's going on; a senior producer at a major mainstream media network told me, early in the 2008 presidential primary season, that she was appalled by the callousness, indeed cynical craftiness, with which "narrative" was manipulated for minute electoral advantage by focus-group besotted campaign managers. Alas—but not surprisingly—her concerns didn't drive that network's coverage of the politics of 2008. One has to wonder whether it would have made any difference if they had. In a country in which *American Idol* has become a major cultural reference point, is it any wonder that we have elections that resemble *American Idol* in their dominance by "narrative"—which is to say, elections that are substantively vacuous?

F or there were surely things for Americans to debate in 2008. We could have argued about the nature of terrorism and the appropriate response to it. We could have discussed why the State Department, the Defense Department, and the CIA remain stubbornly obtuse about the religious dynamics of jihadism. We could have had a morally serious debate about the borderline between aggressive interrogation and torture, about rendition, about what is to be done with the murderously dangerous men incarcerated at Guantanamo. Americans could have debated how housing policies intended to empower the poor ended up creating the subprime mortgage crisis—an example of unintended consequences if there ever was one. We could have had an interesting debate about China, and whether assertive human rights pressures on a regime that throws a hissy fit when the Dalai Lama meets with Lech Wałęsa in Gdańsk can move that global giant into a less threatening international posture. We could have debated the status of *Roe v. Wade*, the moral limits of biotechnology, the resurgence of Russian nationalism, the collapse of Pakistan, the crime of human trafficking, the future of the Bush Administration's AIDS and malaria initiatives in Africa, the fate of Darfur and Zimbabwe, and the economic, social, and political consequences of the European birth dearth. We might even have debated a national grand bargain that would reinvent the American automobile industry while defunding jihadism.

Some of that happened; but not nearly enough of it. The American people elected a young president with less governmental experience than any major party nominee since Wendell Willkie because—well, because he was the winner on *American Idol: The 2008 Election Edition.* Thus on Inauguration Day 2009, one crucial point ought to have been clear: Narrative, not substance, is what put the forty-forth president into the White House.

Narrative shaped the 2008 election in another way. In *Dreams from My Father* (a far more interesting book than his campaign manifesto, *The Audacity of Hope*), Barack Obama unveiled a compelling personal narrative, which became the chief focus of the Democratic primaries and the general election. Framing the election cycle that way was undoubtedly an impressive technical accomplishment on the part of Obama and his campaign team. Yet that very accomplishment tended to crowd out everything else, such that it precluded any serious conjuring with Obama's political pedigree and his relationships with some of the more unsavory creatures from the violent fever swamps of the Sixties. Had any Republican candidate refused to acknowledge or explain a longstanding and mutually profitable relationship with a domestic terrorist like Timothy McVeigh, he would have been regarded, and rightly, as too radioactive to touch. Yet the trail of destruction and death left by longtime Obama colleagues Bill Ayers and Bernadine Doehrn was less than McVeigh's only by reason of capacity and circumstance, not intent—and that by Ayers's own account.

The problem here is more serious than it may first appear on the surface. American liberalism has never engaged in the kind of cleansing of the Augean stables that William F. Buckley, Jr., conducted among American conservatives in the 1950s. Buckley drove the right-wing full-mooners out of the conservative big tent; the left-wing full mooners remain firmly inside the liberal big tent. Indeed, they help define the liberal big tent, not least by conducting ongoing moral blackmail against their less pervfervid (or more prudent) liberal colleagues. A Left that cannot come to grips with its own scoundrel time during the Sixties is a Left that will continue repeating the lies that marked Lillian Hellman's memoir (I use the term loosely) of that title.

A Left that cannot confront its failures of analysis, nerve, and moral seriousness during the last half of the Cold War is also a Left that is unlikely to understand, much less cope with, and still less defeat, the multiple threats to freedom that define the post-Cold War, post-9/11 world. A Left that refuses to see that its embrace of abortion on demand is a self-indulgent exercise and a betrayal of the legacy of the classic civil rights movement is a Left that is unlikely to chart a path away from a brave new world of manufactured humanity, in which misguided ideas of compassion are married to technological marvels to produce dehumanizing consequences. An American Left that cannot look at Europe and see the human, social, economic, financial, and cultural failures of debonair nihilism is not a Left that can grasp, much less appeal to, the sturdy religious instincts that continue to animate the great majority of the American people. Yet that, alas, is precisely the kind of Left America has in the early twenty-first century: an unchastened Left, reinforced in its sense of righteousness and its sense of political entitlement by the 2008 presidential election.

In retrospect, perhaps even President Obama ought to have understood that this kind of Left, which is hardly postideological and which had been chomping at the metaphorical bit since 1994, would be one of his chief burdens in office. He might have been better positioned to cope with that burden had he been more forthright about his own past dabblings in the shadow world of Sixties radicalism, and more critical of the unrepentantly stubborn moral blindness of some of his Hyde Park associates. As cool a customer as Barack Obama ought to have sensed potential danger when former SDS leader Todd Gitlin swooned on election night and declared that Obama's return to Grant Park—scene of riots during the 1968 Democratic Convention—meant that the new president stands "on the shoulders of the crowds of four decades ago."

G itlin was not the only swooner, of course. A young friend wrote me of a Toronto literary soiree that he, the author of a successful first novel, had attended five days before our election. There, he reported, "Otherwise intelligent, professionally ironic people—academics, writers, journalists—were going on and on and on: 'He's like nothing I've ever seen before.' 'Seriously, I think he really is a messiah figure for America.' 'You know his inauguration would happen within three weeks of Lincoln's [200th] birthday.' 'When I think of what we were hoping for in the Sixties, this is it.' 'He's going to change things here and everywhere; all over the world people want this to happen.' 'I know a lot of people in New York who are finally believing in America again.' 'The morning after the election, I'm going to wake up and feel like I'm in heaven.'"

That last effusion came from a retired academic, who seems to have retained at least some vestigial reference points from the biblical consciousness that was once a hallmark of Canadian culture. But chiliastic enthusiasm was by no means confined to Canada. Indeed, for many of the professionally ironic and skeptical members of the American commentariat, November 5, 2008, was a day of vapors:

- E. J. Dionne, Jr., of the *Washington Post*: "Yes, it is time to hope again."
- George Packer of the *New Yorker*: "We will have a President who can think and feel and speak; we will have a grownup who will treat us like grownups."
- Nancy Gibbs of *Time*: "Some princes are born in palaces. Some are born in mangers. But a few are born in the imagination, out of scraps of history and hope. Barack Obama never talks about how people see him: I'm not the one making history, he said every chance he got. You are. Yet as he looked out Tuesday night though the bulletproof glass . . . he had to see the truth on people's faces. We are the ones we've

been waiting for, he liked to say, but people were waiting for him . . . ."

Some of this was funny. But, coupled with the "Yes, we can" rhetoric of the campaign, it should also have been deeply troubling. Reinhold Niebuhr, the great American theologian of the ironies of history, got his quadrennial dusting-off in 2008, with Barack Obama, among others, averring a deep intellectual debt to Niebuhr. Well, Mr. President, I know something about Reinhold Niebuhr; and neither you, nor your more perfervid followers, nor your journalistic admirers, are Reinhold Niebuhr. Or anything remotely resembling Reinhold Niebuhr. If anything, the secular millenarianism that pervaded the Obama campaign—the yearning for the redemption-of-a-fallen-world-through-politics—was a pluperfect example of the kind of utopianism that Niebuhr, with his profound sense of the contingencies of history and the self-delusory capacities of human beings, spent three decades warning against. A definition of democracy? "Democracy is finding proximate solutions to insoluble problems"—that is Reinhold Niebuhr, not the Obama campaign. And can anyone seriously imagine a convinced Obama enthusiast praying Niebuhr's famous prayer: "God grant me the serenity to accept the things I cannot change, the courage to change the things I can, and the wisdom to know the difference"? If we are the change we have been waiting for, and "Yes, we can" is our creed, then Niebuhr's prayer for humility, bravery, and prudence is a non sequitur, for there is nothing we cannot change.

Many members of the commentariat found "those faces" at Invesco Field (where Obama accepted the Democratic nomination) and in Grant Park inspiring. I found them a little frightening. For the extraordinary expectations Obama raised were bound to remain unmet, for there were wrenchingly difficult, and in some cases, insoluble problems facing any American administration in both domestic sand international politics, and the realization of that in the cold light of reality was bound to produce disappointment, even bitterness, among the true believers in "Yes, we can." Conspiracy theories about reactionaries standing in the way of progress were bound to follow, as surely as night follows day.

B ut that is to leave the matter at the level of politics. The real question raised by the chiliasm of the 2008 Obama campaign is the question of American public culture. Americans once prided themselves on a combination of self-reliance and realism. Yet a considerable number of our countrymen have now accepted a governmental role in their daily lives that would have been inconceivable to their grandparents—and many seem eager for more. As for realism, does the uncritical acceptance of the politics of redemption suggest a national disconnect from some hard home truths about the human condition? Have we learned nothing from the bloody history of twentieth-century political messianism?

In the wake of Barack Obama's victory, more than one friend or colleague took down from the bookshelf a tattered copy of Robert Hugh Benson's 1904 apocalyptic novel, *Lord of the World*, and remembered the story of a previously unknown, superbly articulate figure from the American heartland who achieves great power in a postreligious world, not by brutality but by appealing to, and seeming to embody, universal virtue in a world without sin. This reach for a Bensonite analogy to the phenomenon of Barack Obama struck me as a bit over-the-top. Yet it does reflect a sensible, historically verifiable intuition: the passionate investment of inchoate utopian hopes in a political leader is almost always bad news, even if the bad news stops short of the apocalypse. For the real audacity of hope in politics is to know that our fondest hopes will not be realized through politics. Indeed, if our fondest hopes are such that they can be realized by politics, then our hope is a disordered hope.

If political messianism was one disturbing cultural undercurrent of the 2008 presidential election cycle, faux populism was another. Faux populism is a perennial American political temptation, brilliantly captured in our fiction by Robert Penn Warren's classic, *All the King's Men*. As a general rule, it has been more a Democratic temptation than a Republican one. In 2008, however, Republicans showed themselves just as susceptible to its siren songs, particularly when "Wall Street" became a convenient whipping boy for the nation's economic and financial woes—and "Joe the Plumber" became a kind of instant Republican mascot.

To those with longer memories and more political scar tissue, both campaigns' attempts to position their candidates as folks who were just as good as the American people set off alarm bells warning of a potential reprise of the late 1970s, when Jimmy Carter promised us "a government as good as the American people" and delivered a government as inept as the 1962 New York Mets. At several points in the 2008 campaign—those points at which Barack Obama, John McCain, Sarah Palin, and Joe Biden were straining every political muscle to appear as "just folks" as possible—the United States badly needed the wisdom of a James Madison, who in Federalist 51 famously reminded Americans of every generation that the very necessity of governance, even democratic governance, was "the greatest of all reflections on human nature," because "if men were angels, no government would be necessary." Such wisdom would have led to some of the necessary truth-telling that was notable for its absence from the scoundrel time of 2008.

None of the four principals in this drama was prepared to tell some hard truths to the American people about the American people. Such as the truth that irrational and self-defeating popular reactions to the initial financial crunch of mid-September 2008 were making matters worse in the markets. Or the truth that both management and labor had done everything possible to make the American automobile industry economically unviable. Or the truth that the business cycle has not been repealed, which means that there will be downturns as well as upturns in the economy. Or the truth that China owns a dangerously large amount of our national debt, which is itself the product of profligate spending to please "the people," or some politically adept subset thereof.

The people, in other words, get it wrong sometimes. Prudent statecraft—such as FDR's slow, steady education of an isolationist populace in the realities of world politics in 1939 and 1940—recognizes that. And rather than appeasing the wrongheaded, prudent statecraft uses the arts of persuasion to change minds and hearts. Lincoln's Second Inaugural Address is often described as the greatest of American political speeches; but how many of our fellow countrymen remember that the Second Inaugural was a sharp reminder to the entire nation that our common life stands under judgment, and that getting the Big Questions wrong can have terrible costs?

Then there is the question of the national or mainstream media and the culture of American public life: another key factor in assessing what the 2008 election cycle taught us about the health of our political culture. Conservatives and Republicans complained loudly, frequently, and often justifiably about media bias during the 2008 campaign. That there was no aggressive media investigation of Barack Obama's connection to Bill Ayers and the mad, radical wing of the post-Vietnam American Left manifested an undeniable double standard. For, to return to the analogy I used earlier, had John McCain been involved with Timothy McVeigh-types at some formative point in his political career, you may be sure that those linkages would have been investigated and reported *ad infinitum*, and indeed *ad nauseam*.

The same double standard was apparent when the campaign decisively shifted in mid-September. At that point, it seemed not only possible, but likely, that John McCain would win, and perhaps win by a substantial margin. That changed within two weeks, in no small part because of McCain's own fumbling reactions to the melt-down in the credit markets. But at no point during that period did the national media explain to the American people the relationship between the credit crunch and the housing policies of the Carter and Clinton administrations, or the cozy relations that had built up between current Democratic Congressional leaders and the senior management of the about-to-crumble Fannie Mae and Freddie Mac. Again, were the partisan shoe on the other foot, it is unlikely, bordering on inconceivable, that serious investigative reporting would not have ensued.

The indictment could, of course, be extended. Joe Biden's gaffes-of-the-day went unreported, while Sarah Palin was savaged from sea to shining sea. The truth of the Democratic Party's commitment to the most extreme abortion regime went unexplored and unreported, while considerable attention was lavished on Catholic intellectuals who tried to square the circle and defend Barack Obama as the true pro-life candidate—an exercise in sophistry that was breathtaking even by contemporary academic standards. As Edward Whelan pointed out, frequently and eloquently (and, as it turned out, presciently), some of a President Obama's Federal judiciary nominees would come from the farther reaches of the academic-legal Left, which boded poorly for the future of American constitutionalism; yet the national media failed to explore any of this, thereby reinforcing the brilliantly contrived stealth characteristics of the Obama campaign.

Conservatives and Republicans blame too many of their trials and tribulations on the mainstream media, and no doubt some of that displacement was going on in the 2008 election cycle. Moreover, the new, conservative alternative media—and particularly conservative talk radio—too frequently yielded to the temptation of faux populism in 2008: understandable from a ratings point of view, but yet another sign of trouble in our political culture. And yes, it is true that the 2008 cycle dramatically democratized the flow of information and commentary in our politics, largely through the impact of the Internet—just as it is true that this democratization has dramatically cut into, not just the profits, readerships, and viewership of the mainstream media, but into its influence as well.

Nonetheless, it is surely of some consequence for the health of our political culture that the summary judgment on the national media in the 2008 election cycle must be that it largely failed at its primary task, which is not to prescribe but to inform—and to inform accurately. That there was an empirically measurable "Obama tilt" in the reporting of 2008 was frankly conceded by no less than the *Washington Post's* ombudsman, Deborah Howell, in an unintentionally hilarious column published five days *after* the election. To which one wanted to say: Look, confession is always good for the soul, but avoiding sin in the first place is far better.

For if morally serious and intelligent debate is the lifeblood of democracy, then accurate information, widely disseminated, serves the same function in democracy as red blood cells do in the human body: accurate information is the oxygen supply that allows the organs of democracy to perform well. The Framers knew this; that is why they afforded such robust constitutional protections to the press, protections that have been strengthened over time. The United States cuts the press far more slack than any other stable democracy, precisely because we place such a high value on the free, fair, and accurate flow of information. Thus when the national media fails to provide accurate information and transforms itself into an organ of instruction, it misconceives its responsibilities, and creates imbalances in the constitutional order. This is a serious problem.

Despite the effusions of E. J. Dionne, Todd Gitlin, and Co., the 2008 presidential election did not mark an unmistakable turning point in American public life. Neither did it mark some great new achievement in the quest for racial justice. Barack Obama didn't create the change in America that made his election possible. He—and the rest of us—benefited from the profound transformation of American racial attitudes that has unfolded over the past five decades. And that change—which is truly change we can believe in—was not the product of government (although government had to play its role, in the endgame). The transformation of the United States of America into the most racially egalitarian society in human history was the moral and cultural accomplishment of American civil society, in which America's religious communities played indispensable roles. If there was a historical lesson to be teased out of the 2008 presidential cycle, that is the lesson to be drawn, not the lesson that Dionne, Gitlin, and other celebrants of the Sixties would have us draw.

Truths Still Held?
John Courtney Murray's
"American Proposition," Fifty
Years On

2 010 marked the golden anniversary of Father John Courtney Murray's *We Hold These Truths: Catholic Reflections on the
American Proposition*—arguably, the most important such reflection
composed in modern times, and perhaps in any time. Its publication landed Father Murray, an urbane New York Jesuit, on the cover
of *Time*, in the days when that distinction, like the Nobel Peace
Prize, actually meant something. Reviewing the book in the January 28, 1961, issue of *National Review*, William F. Buckley, Jr., described Murray and his work in these glowing terms: "A man with
commanding knowledge and piercing intuition who . . . speaks to
his . . . fellow Americans from breathtaking heights whence he sur-
veys the American and the world scene, creating thought and analysis which leave the reader stunned with admiration and pleasure, as
only the contact with a great thinker and a fine writer can do." Murray's reputation was such that Cardinal Francis Spellman of New
York brought him to the Second Vatican Council as a *peritus*, or
official theological adviser, so that Murray's historical and political-
philosophical work on Church-state theory could help shape the
Council's deliberations on religious freedom—which it did, if not
quite as decisively as some have suggested (or in precisely the way
Murray would have wished).

Murray's book was not without its critics, then or later. Some
argued, then and later, that Murray's account of the American

Founding massively underplayed the role of biblical religion, and especially Calvinist thought, on the national consensus that produced the new republic. Others, more later than then, suggested that Murray's theory of democracy was based on an excessively Neo-Scholastic (meaning, specifically, Suarezian) reading of the relationship between nature and grace—a charge denied by Father Francis Canavan, S.J., who argued that Murray was writing a politics, not a theology. Some scholars accept Canavan's distinction but argue that Murray's theory of democracy was too much beholden to John Locke. Still others find in Murray's address to specific questions of public policy in the mid-1960s the opening wedge to what might be called Cuomoism among Catholic public officials—a charge that, in the final analysis, does a disservice to Murray even as it gives an undeserved intellectual gloss to Mario Cuomo and those Jesuit theologians and lawyers who helped turn Clan Kennedy and other ill-catechized Catholic public officials into advocates for "reproductive choice."

For a man who was America's most prominent Catholic public intellectual in 1965, when Vatican II adopted the Declaration on Religious Freedom his work had helped make possible, Murray went into strikingly rapid eclipse after his death in 1967 from a longstanding heart ailment. A younger generation drinking deeply from the Kool-Aid of the Sixties rather than from Murray's favorite "Beefeater martini, desperately dry," jettisoned Murray as impossibly old hat, claiming, as one put it, that "we know so much more than Murray did." After twenty years of neglect however, Murray was resurrected in the mid-1980s by Catholic thinkers seeking materials from which to build a religiously informed public philosophy for the American experiment in ordered liberty (as the inaugural editorial in the journal *First Things* described the project). This, in turn, led to an effort, perhaps not surprising, to reclaim Murray for "progressive" Catholicism—a project risible to anyone familiar with the (often hilarious) stories of Murray's contempt for some of the woollier-headed notions being circulated at Woodstock College in the years before his death (and Woodstock's demise).

The question to be explored here, however, is not Murray's analysis of the Founding, and still less his metaphysics and epistemology. Rather, my purpose is to review the "American Proposition" he sketched in *We Hold These Truths* as a template for measuring the health of the American republic and its public culture in the second decade of the twenty-first century. That template has its own validity and utility, irrespective of where one stands on the questions of Murray-as-historian-of-the-Founding or Murray-the-Neo-Scholastic.

The opening paragraphs of Murray's book both summarize its argument and give the flavor of his cool, dry literary style:

> It is classic American doctrine, immortally asserted by Abraham Lincoln, that the new nation which our Fathers brought forth on this continent was dedicated to a "proposition."
>
> I take it that Lincoln used the word with conceptual propriety. In philosophy a proposition is the statement of a truth to be demonstrated. In mathematics, a proposition is at times the statement of an operation to be performed. Our Fathers dedicated the nation to a proposition in both of these senses. The American Proposition is at once doctrinal and practical, a theorem and a problem. It is an affirmation and also an intention. It presents itself as a coherent structure of thought that lays claim to intellectual assent; it also presents itself as an organized political project that aims at historical success. Our Fathers asserted it and most ably argued it; they also took to "work it out," and they signally succeeded.
>
> Neither as a doctrine nor as a project is the American Proposition a finished thing. Its demonstration is never done once for all; and the Proposition itself requires development on penalty of decadence. Its historical success is never to be taken for granted, nor can it come to some

absolute term; and any given measure of success demands enlargement on penalty of instant decline. In a moment of national crisis Lincoln asserted the imperiled part of the theorem and gave impetus to the impeded part of the project in the noble utterance, at once declaratory and imperative, "All men are created equal." Today, when civil war has become the basic fact of world society, there is no element of the theorem that is not menaced by active negation, and no thrust of the project that does not meet powerful opposition. Today therefore thoughtful men among us are saying that America must be more clearly conscious of what it proposes, more articulate in proposing, more purposeful in the realization of the project proposed.

This "American Proposition," as Murray understood it, was less a revolution than a conservation-by-development of the political dimension of the Western civilizational project that had emerged over the centuries from the fruitful interaction of Jerusalem, Athens, and Rome: that is, of biblical religion, Greek rationality, and Roman law. As such, the Proposition rested on a realist epistemology: there are truths built into the world and into us; we can know those truths through the arts of reason; knowing those truths, certain obligations, both personal and civil, are laid upon us. To be sure, those truths had to be "held, assented to, worked into the texture of institutions," in order for there to be a "true City, in which men may dwell in dignity, peace, unity, justice, well-being, [and] freedom." But that never-to-be-taken-for-granted quality of the truths of the American Proposition simply underscored the fact that the United States was an experiment: an experiment in ordered freedom.

That could be said, I suppose, of any democracy; and the perils attending any democracy's failure to live by the moral truths we can know to be true about the ordering of our life together were chillingly demonstrated by Weimar Germany and, less horribly, by the French Third Republic. What was, and is, distinctive about American democracy, however, is that our very nationhood depends on our purchase on the truths to which the Founders pledged their lives, fortunes, and sacred honor. The German nation remained, after the collapse of the Weimar Republic; France remained France under the Vichy regime. America was different, Murray argued. For America's native condition was plurality and the American people—the American nation—had to be constructed, not out of the old materials of blood and ethnicity and language and soil and common religious conviction, but out of the new materials of adherence to truths in the civic order. The survival of America, as both theorem and project, rested on the American ability to create *pluralism* out of plurality: to transform the native cacophony of ethnic and religious difference into an orderly conversation about public goods, the "order" being provided by common allegiance to the elementary truths of the Proposition.

Murray's theory of democracy, while seeming thin to some of his critics, was thus far thicker than the theory of democratic functionalists today, whose sole concern is to get the machinery of governance right. Murray, by contrast, thought of politics, not as machinery, but as deliberation—common deliberation, among men and women who were citizens and not merely bundles of desires; common deliberation about public goods, using the arts of reason in order to apply agreed-upon first principles of truth in the civic order to the exigencies of governance amidst the flux of history. In this conception of democracy, civility and tolerance were moral accomplishments, not poses, attitudes, or pragmatic accommodations. Tolerance meant not differences ignored but differences engaged. Civility was the achievement of a measure of order (and thus a measure of clarity, and perhaps even charity) in the public conversation.

Nor, contrary to others of his critics, was Murray's democratic theory overly dependent on a Hobbesian or Lockean construal of civil society:

> We no longer believe, with Locke or Hobbes, that man escapes from a mythical "state of nature" by an act of will, by a social contract. Civil society is a need of human nature before it becomes the object of hu-

man choice. Moreover, every particular society is a creation of the soil; it springs from the physical soil of earth and from the more formative soil of history. Its existence is sustained by loyalties that are not logical; its ideals are expressed in legends that go beyond the facts and are for that reason vehicles of truth . . . nevertheless, the distinctive bond of [civil society] is reason, or, more exactly, that exercise of reason which is argument.

Argument, in turn, gave form to a distinctive kind of association in the American democratic experiment. Jacques Maritain might have called it "civic friendship." A generation after Murray, John Paul II would call it "solidarity." It was, Murray wrote, a "special kind of moral virtue, a thing of reason and intelligence, laboriously cultivated by the [disciplining] of passion, prejudice, and narrow self-interest." This was not the friendship of David and Jonathan, or the fierce inclusiveness of the clan or tribe; it was not the bond of charity that binds disciples within the Church. It was a solidarity, a civic friendship, born of a common passion for justice, with the requirements of justice—what is owed by the City to the citizenry, and what citizens owe the City—understood according to the canons of public reason. And in the pursuit of justice would be found the perfecting of civility.

The bonds of this civic friendship or solidarity in America reinforced that founding consensus that gave philosophical content to Murray's American Proposition. This consensus was, in Murray's words, "an ensemble of substantive truths, a structure of basic knowledge, an order of elementary affirmations" that reflect the truths we can and must know by reason about how we ought to live together. No true City, and certainly no true democracy, is possible if everything is in doubt. If there is to be genuine argument, and not just cacophony or the will-to-power, there must be, Murray wrote, "a core of agreement, accord, concurrence, acquiescence," because only if certain truths are held can there be genuine arguments. Much of modernity, Murray knew, had this exactly backwards, thinking that argument ends when agreement is reached. The opposite is more fundamentally true, in both the sciences and the humanities: real argument is only possible within a pre-existing context of agreement on certain truths.

This may sound daunting, but we need not discover these truths by our own labors alone. Rather, the truths that form the moral-cultural foundations of American democracy come to us as a pat-rimony—an inheritance to be honored and cultivated—from the civilizational project of the West as it emerged over millennia: that inheritance that Pope Leo XIII, founder of modern Catholic so-cial doctrine, called the *patrimonium generis humani.* It was not a finished thing, this patrimony; it had, Murray argued, a "growing end." But the development that we, the inheritors, were to cultivate through civil argument had to be rooted in the inheritance of truth that gave distinction (in both senses of the term) to the Western civilizational project.

W hat were the inherited truths on which the American experiment rested and by which the American civil ar-gument was structured? According to Murray's analysis, the Ameri-can Proposition rested on the foundation of four such constituting truths.

I. A Nation Under Judgment

The first truth of the consensus that gave content to the Ameri-can Proposition was a truth that "lies beyond politics . . . [and] imparts to politics a fundamental human meaning": the truth that God is sovereign over nations as well as over individuals. Here, like Edmund Burke, Murray distinguished the Anglo-American political tradition from the Jacobinism of continental European po-litical philosophy. The latter began its thinking about politics with autonomous human reason; the former looked "to the sovereignty of God as to the first principle of its organization." The American experiment, in other words, was an experiment under transcendent judgment: the judgment of the God of the Bible; the judgment of those moral truths inscribed by nature's God in nature—that is, in the world and in us—as a reflection of the divine creative purpose.

That "natural law," which we can know by reason, gave government the authority to command, even as it limited the powers of the governors. The constitutional agreement by which the people, through their representatives, ratified the basic instruments of American governance and amended that agreement as circumstances required was a process, as Murray understood it, by which "the people define the areas where [public] authority is legitimate and the areas where liberty is lawful." Thus the U.S. Constitution and the various state constitutions both enumerated rights and laid out plans by which those rights might be lived in solidarity.

II. The Centrality of Consent

The second foundational truth of the American proposition also grew out of the Christian civilization of the Middle Ages, rather than from the autonomy project of the continental Enlightenment: the principle that all just governance is by and with the consent of the governed. On this reading of Western history, rather different from the Whig rendering, royal absolutism and its parallel union of altar-and-throne were the aberration; the rich social pluralism of the Middle Ages and the assumed limits on princely authority both reflected, in Murray's view, "the premise . . . that there is a sense of justice inherent in the people." (Contemporary Catholic social doctrine uses the term "subsidiarity" to express this premise by honoring mediating institutions or voluntary associations as comprising the "subjectivity" of civil society and by asserting that decision-making should be left at the lowest possible level of society—that is, the level closest to those effected by the decision—commensurate with the common good.) This principle of consent, and its premise that the people can know the moral truths by which we ought to live together, again stands in sharp contrast to the Jacobin tradition in continental Europe and its twentieth-century manifestation, totalitarianism, which proposed governance by elite vanguards. The principle also assumes that there are truths to be known and truths that we can know in common to be true, rather than postmodernism's "your truth" and "my truth." But that is to get ahead of ourselves a bit.

The principle of consent and the premise of the people's sense of justice framed Murray's understanding of human rights, which posed another challenge to an autonomy-based theory of democracy:

> In the American concept of them . . . [the] institutions of [free speech and a free press] do not rest on the thin theory proper to eighteenth-century individualistic rationalism, that a man has a right to say what he thinks merely because he thinks it. The American agreement was to reject political censorship of opinion as unrightful, because unwise, imprudent, not to say impossible. However, the proper premise of these freedoms lay in the fact that they were social necessities. . . . They were regarded as conditions essential to the conduct of free, representative, and responsible government. People who are called upon to obey have the right first to be heard. People who are to bear burdens and make sacrifices have the right first to pronounce on the purposes which their sacrifices serve. People who are summoned to contribute to the common good have the right first to pass judgment on the question, whether the good proposed be truly good, the people's good, the common good.

In the American Proposition, in other words, rights were not trumps recognized as such by the sheer fact of their assertion. Rights were rooted in the dignity of the human person as capable of rational moral choice and considered political judgment. Rights were acknowledged in law to facilitate the promotion and defense of the common good, not simply to protect individual "choice."

III. The Priority of Society

The third truth of the American Proposition also challenged both absolutism and the Jacobinism that sought to replace it, setting in motion the path toward totalitarianism: and that was the truth that, as Murray put it, "the state is distinct from society and limited in its offices toward society." Or, to put it in slightly different language, society exists prior to the state, ontologically as well as historically, and the state exists to serve society, not the other way around.

Here, too, was another ground for such basic civil rights as free speech and a free press: "the principle of the incompetence of government in the field of opinion." This retrieval of the medieval distinction between *studium* and *imperium*, the order of culture and the political order, would have large consequences for Murray's Church-state theory and indeed for Vatican Council II, which agreed with Murray's contention that the state was incompetent in theological matters, such that religious freedom is a fundamental human right grounded in both the dignity of the person and the natural limits of the rightly-ordered state. For our purposes, however, the salient point, as Murray put it, was that government, rightly understood, "submits itself to judgment by the truth of society; it is not itself a judge of the truth in society." Nor, *mutatis mutandis*, is government the judge of the truths inscribed in nature, which give rise to what Murray called "the truth of society." Rightly-ordered government submits itself to the judgment of those truths built into the world and into us, and if it attempts to redefine those truths, it has acted unjustly and illegitimately. The Polish bishops' heroic 1953 *"Non possumus!"* ["We cannot!"], spoken in defiance of an attempt by Poland's communist regime to make the Catholic Church a subsidiary of the party-state was one modern example of resistance to this attempted arrogation of illegitimate power by the state; other such attempts are close at hand, and will be discussed presently.

IV. Freedom and Virtue

The fourth component of the American Proposition was "the profound conviction that only a virtuous people can be free." There were no guarantees about the success of freedom, Murray knew; freedom could dissipate into license, private license could lead to public decadence, and decadence could lead to the chaos out of which a new authoritarianism would emerge. "It is not an American belief," Murray wrote, "that free government is inevitable, only that it is possible." Moreover, "its possibility can be realized only when the people as a whole are inwardly governed by the recognized imperatives of the universal moral law." Freedom and moral truth, Murray wrote in anticipation of the teaching of John Paul II in *Centesimus Annus*, are inextricably bound together: freedom must be tethered to truth and ordered to goodness if freedom is not to become its own undoing.

Murray applauded the ways in which the American cultural instinct for freedom (which had been forged from multiple sources— biblical, medieval, Puritan, and so forth) had succeeded over time in placing limits on the sphere of government within a functioning democracy. Both in personal moral decision-making, however, and in sustaining civil society, the American demand for freedom could "be made with the full resonance of moral authority only to the extent that it issues from an inner sense of responsibility to a higher law." Thus the American idea and the American ideal was *ordered* freedom: freedom ordered to goodness because tethered to truth. "Men who would be free politically must discipline themselves," Murray wrote; "political freedom is endangered in its foundations as soon as the universal moral values, upon whose shared possession the self-discipline of a free society depends, are no longer vigorous enough to restrain the passions and shatter the selfish inertia of men." Democracy, in other words, could not be reduced to a matter of political mechanics; democracy was "a spiritual and moral enterprise."

So: the sovereignty of God and of transcendent moral truth over nations as well as individuals, acknowledged through the people's possession of the truths of the natural moral law that bear on governance; the principle of consent, with its cousin, the principle of participation, grounded in the conviction that the people have within them an inherent sense of justice and giving rise to a thick notion of rights linked to both human dignity and civic responsibility; the priority of society over the state; the linkage between freedom and virtue and the ideal of *ordered* freedom—these were the consensus ideas that, in John Courtney Murray's view, informed and shaped the American Proposition as both a proposal and a project in history. How did Murray imagine them being held in his day, at the midpoint of the twentieth century?

He did not think the Proposition could be carried any longer by the primary institutions of its transmission between the colonial period and the Second World War: the Christian communities of the old Protestant mainline. The theological chaos in those quarters was such that no coherent account of the Proposition was likely to issue from, much less be transmitted by, the communities arrayed in what was then a formidable institution, the National Council of Churches. (Moreover, Murray suggested, the "seeds of dissolution" were already present in what became the Protestant mainline when it came to colonial America, as its left wing, following Ockham, substituted the voluntarist idea of law-as-will for the classical and older medieval idea of law-as-reason—thus unwittingly laying some of the groundwork for the contemporary autonomy project.)

Nor would the falling torch be picked up by the American academy, which had "long ago bade a quiet goodbye to the whole notion of an American consensus, as implying that there are truths that we hold in common, and a natural law that makes known to all of us the structure of the moral universe in such wise that all of us are bound by it to a common obedience." Pragmatism and utilitarianism, then dominant on prestigious American campuses, could not give a compelling account of the Proposition. (Murray could not, of course, have anticipated the contemporary dominance of the academy by postmodernism's epistemological skepticism, metaphysical nihilism, and moral relativism: but it is not difficult to imagine the odds he would have given on that intellectual dog's breakfast being able to give a persuasive account of the American Proposition—or indeed any other proposition.)

Murray's suggestion—a striking one at a historical moment when considerable swaths of the American Protestant leadership believed that the United States had been and must be a Protestant country, and held to that belief with a passion at least as fervent as Francisco Franco's convictions about the essential Catholicism of Spain—was that the originating and constituting consensus that had made America itself was still possessed by, and in fact might be revived by, the Catholic community in the United States.

That revitalization was not to happen, as the Catholic Church lurched into the fever swamps of the Sixties and Seventies in what seems in retrospect to have been an attempt to catch up with the Protestant mainline, just as it was becoming the Protestant oldline en route to becoming the liberal Protestant sideline. The brakes were put on, eventually, not so much by ecclesiastical disciplinary measures but by the lucid and luminous social doctrine of John Paul II and its promulgation in the United States by various of the late pope's disciples. But the opportunity Murray saw in the late Fifties and early Sixties was another victim of the immediate post-Vatican II silly season—although if we listen carefully, we can hear echoes today, and sometimes more than echoes, of the consensus ideas of the American Proposition in the pro-life advocacy of the Catholic Church in the United States and its new allies among the more thoughtful leadership of evangelical Protestantism. (This recent alliance would likely have come as something of a shock to Father Murray, but from his present station in the communion of saints he would, I think, appreciate both the ironies involved and the new possibilities of civil argument opened up by the rise of a new ecumenism.)

When, on the first page of *We Hold These Truths*, Father Murray referred to "civil war . . . [as] the basic fact of world society," he was thinking of the contest between imperfect democracies and the pluperfect tyranny of communism. The latter was sent onto the trash heap of history some twenty years ago, by brave men and women, often inspired by Christian faith, who had come, by their own hard and distinctive path, to an understanding of the "elementary affirmations" within the American Proposition as both truths to be affirmed and truths to be instantiated in history—thus demonstrating, I should note, the fact of a natural moral law that is universal in character. Yet the civil war continues; it is now prosecuted through what we call the American "culture war" and its analogues throughout the West. Murray, who did not use that term "culture war," clearly anticipated its possibility when he penned the following warning:

> Perhaps the dissolution, long since begun, may one day be consummated. Perhaps one day the noble many-storeyed mansion of democracy will be dismantled, leveled to the dimensions of a flat majoritarianism, which is no mansion but a barn, perhaps even a tool shed in which the weapons of tyranny may be forged. Perhaps there will one day be wide dissent even from the political principles which emerge from natural law, as well as dissent from the constellation of ideas that have historically undergirded those principles—the idea that government has a moral basis; that the universal moral law is the foundation of society; that the legal order of society—that is, the state—is subject to judgment by a law that is not statistical but inherent in the nature of man; that the eternal

reason of God is the ultimate origin of all law; that this nation in all its aspects—as a society, a state, an ordered and free relationship between governors and governed—is under God. The possibility that widespread dissent from these principles should develop is not foreclosed.

Indeed not, for that possibility is now manifestly with us. But the foreclosure need not be completed, and the dismantling of the house of freedom can be resisted. That, however, requires facing squarely the degree to which Murray's truths, the truths of the American Proposition, are, and are not, firmly held among us, more than two centuries after the Founding.

I t might seem that the first truth of the Proposition—the sovereignty of God over nations as well as individuals, with its parallel conviction about the universal moral law inscribed in nature and accessible to reason—would be most gravely threatened by the so-called "new atheism." But as David Bentley Hart bracingly demonstrated in *Atheist Delusions: The Christian Revolution and Its Fashionable Enemies*, the attacks of Richard Dawkins ("the zoologist and tireless tractarian who—despite his embarrassing incapacity for philosophical reasoning—never fails to entrance his eager readers with his rhetorical recklessness"), Christopher Hitchens ("whose talent for intellectual caricature somewhat exceeds his mastery of consecutive logic"), the "extravagantly callow" Sam Harris, and Daniel Dennett (whose "argument consists in little more than the persistent misapplication of quantitative and empirical terms to unquantifiable and intrinsically nonempirical realities"), and their down-market cash-out in Dan Brown's *Da Vinci Code* ("surely the most lucrative novel ever written by a borderline illiterate"), do not get us to the true root of the problem, which is not the historically ill-informed and philosophically embarrassing "new atheism," but rather what Romano Guardini used to call the "interior disloyalty of modern times," which is a betrayal of what Murray termed "the structure of reality itself."

This betrayal is most powerfully embodied, not by such relative lightweights as Dawkins, Hitchens, Dennett, Harris, et alia, but by postmodernism's skepticism about the human capacity to know the truth of anything with certainty, a skepticism that, as mentioned above, yields, on the one hand, metaphysical nihilism, and, on the other, moral relativism. Indeed, according to a trenchant reading of modernity by the French philosopher Rémi Brague, nihilism may be the defining challenge of this cultural moment in the West. For in Brague's analysis, the twenty-first century will be the century of being-and-nothingness, as the twentieth century (defined by the contest with totalitarianism) was the century of true-and-false and the nineteenth (defined by the "social question" emerging from the Industrial Revolution) was the century of good-and-evil. The metaphysical question—the question of loyalty to being itself—is the bottom of the cultural bottom line today, and in a way not seen since metaphysics emerged from the labors of Greek philosophy in the classical period.

In 1955, Flannery O'Connor wrote that, "if you live today you breathe in nihilism." Those who once found that complaint a bit extravagant might ponder the reality of contemporary nihilism through one of its recent public manifestations—the claim that the natural moral law we can know by reason is, in truth, a form of irrational bigotry and extremism. That claim was adduced on October 30, 2009, in the lead editorial of the *Washington Post*, written to cripple a candidate for attorney general of Virginia, Ken Cuccinelli, whose defense of natural law as an instrument for formulating public policy was decried by the sometimes-sensible editors of the nation's leading political newspaper as a "retrofit (of) the old language of racism, bias, and intolerance in a new context." That the "new context" in question was the gay insurgency and its demands that the state recognize gay unions as "marriages" was, in a sense, beside the point (although it illustrated the degree to which the abandonment of any natural law approach to the question of what constitutes a marriage soon leads to intellectual meltdown); the same charge of irrational bigotry could have been adduced had the issue been the first principle of justice that tells us that abortion and euthanasia are morally wrong.

But, for our purposes here, as we assay the health of twenty-first-century American political culture through the template of Murray's American Proposition, what was truly stunning about the *Post's* editorial assault on natural law was its implicit willingness to throw out Jefferson's claims in the Declaration of Independence, Lincoln's claims in the Gettysburg Address, and Martin Luther King, Jr.'s claims in his "Letter from Birmingham Jail," all of which appealed to a natural moral law that was a reflection of the eternal and divine law. To deny that such a moral law exists, and to compound that intellectual error by the moral crime of labeling those who still adhere to the first truth of the American Proposition as bigots, brought to mind, in this golden anniversary year, Murray's cautions of the threat we currently face:

> Barbarism is not . . . the forest primeval with all its relatively simple savageries. Barbarism . . . is the lack of reasonable conversation according to reasonable laws. Here the word "conversation" has its twofold Latin sense. It means living together and talking together.
>
> Barbarism threatens when men cease to live together according to reason, embodied in law and custom, and incorporated in a web of institutions. . . . Society becomes barbarian . . . when the ways of men come under the sway of the instinctual, the impulsive, the compulsive. When things like this happen, barbarism is abroad, whatever the surface impressions of urbanity.
>
> Barbarism likewise threatens when men cease to talk together according to reasonable laws. . . . Argument ceases to be civil . . . when defiance is flung to the basic ontological principle of all ordered discourse, which asserts that Reality is an analogical structure, within which there are variant modes of reality, to each of which corresponds a distinctive

method of thought that imposes on argument its special rules. When things like this happen, men cannot be locked together in argument. Conversation becomes merely quarrelsome or querulous. Civility dies with the death of the dialogue.

Barbarism masquerading as a defense of tolerance: that was what greeted readers of the *Washington Post* editorial page on the morning of October 30, 2009. That greeting was one ominous measure of the condition of the first truth in Murray's American Proposition.

O ne might think that the second truth of the Proposition— the centrality of consent, which reflects the conviction that the people have an inherent sense of justice, and which is allied to the principle of participation that provides an account of the nature of our civil and political rights—is in rather better shape. Elections in America take place regularly, however vulgarly. Public officials are rotated in and out of office, if not as often as some would like. Initiatives and referenda repair the damage that the people's inherent sense of justice tells them has been done to the common good by legislatures or courts. Free speech and freedom of the press are robust, if too often shallow. But the barbarians are among us on this front, too.

The most obvious instance of an assault on the principle of consent is what a *First Things* symposium termed, in 1996, the "judicial usurpation of politics." This violation of a constituting truth of the American Proposition was most egregious in *Roe v. Wade*; the degree to which the Supreme Court got it colossally wrong in *Roe* can be measured by the degree to which the effects of *Roe* have roiled our public life ever since (just as, in the past, the Court's colossal mistakes in *Dred Scott* and *Plessy v. Ferguson* distorted our public life for decades). By the same token, of course, the people's refusal to acquiesce to what their inherent sense of justice tells them is the fundamental injustice embodied in *Roe*'s virtually unfettered abortion license—a refusal that launched and sustains the pro-life movement—expresses the vitality of the second truth of the Proposition. Yet it is not easy to see how the mistake the Court made in *Roe* can be finally remedied until our public culture gains a firmer grip on the first truth of the Proposition. Until that day, there is important work to be done in mitigating the effects of *Roe*, as there will doubtless be efforts to reverse a grave error in constitutional judging. Both are welcome. Neither, however, will suffice to create an America in which every child is welcomed in life and protected in law. That requires a reclaiming of the truth that innocent life, at whatever stage and in whatever condition, has an intrinsic dignity and value that the law must acknowledge and protect. Meanwhile, the work of resistance to judicial usurpation—which effects our public life on virtually every front—will and must continue, in defense of the second truth of the Proposition.

It should also be noted, however, that there is a new assault on the second truth that bears careful watching in the early twenty-first century, and to which resistance must be mounted: the censorship of rationally defensible moral judgment in the name of laws banning what some deem "hate speech." Such censorship, enforced by coercive state power, is already underway in Canada (where Christian ministers have been assessed significant fines for preaching classic biblical morality in the matter of homosexual acts) and in Europe (where the most widely circulated quality Catholic magazine in Poland was recently convicted by both a European human rights court and a Polish court of violating a woman's "rights" by reporting, accurately, that she had sought an abortion on grounds of that bearing her child would threaten her eyesight; this was deemed by two courts an expression of hate speech). We need not doubt that similar attempts to censor the truths of the Proposition will cross the 49th parallel heading south, and the Atlantic Ocean heading west. The degree of resistance that can be mounted to these efforts will be an important measure of the degree to which the truth of the principle of consent is still held in these United States.

T hat the third truth within the Proposition—that the state exists to serve society, which is ontologically and historically antecedent to the state—has become attenuated in its grip on our public culture seems clear from two recent controversies.

The first involved President Obama's commencement address in May 2009 at the University of Notre Dame. It is beyond the scope of this essay to explore the question of whether Notre Dame violated its own commitments as a Catholic institution of higher learning by holding up this president as an exemplar and by granting him an honorary doctorate of laws; my focus here is on what the president said, which was most remarkable, and most disturbing.

Controversies over the doctrinal and moral boundaries of communities of faith have been a staple of American life for centuries. The State of Rhode Island is the by-product of one of those controversies. Trinitarians battled Unitarianism within Congregationalism. Missouri Synod Lutherans and Wisconsin Synod Lutherans battled other kinds of Lutherans. Reform Judaism sought to distinguish itself dramatically from Orthodox Judaism, and Conservative Judaism and Modern Orthodox Judaism sought to distinguish themselves from both (and from each other). Baptists have been notably fissiparous over the centuries, as have the heirs of John Calvin in American Presbyterianism. The Anglican Communion's recent difficulties are familiar enough. Into none of these controversies, however, had the president of the United States ever injected himself and his office—until May 2009, when President Obama did precisely that at Notre Dame. There, the president leapt into the middle of a decades-long ecclesiological debate within the Catholic Church in the U.S. by suggesting that the good Catholics—the real Catholics—were men like Father Theodore Hesburgh and the late Cardinal Joseph Bernardin, and indeed all those Catholics who supported the Obama candidacy in 2008 and agreed with the president on the nature of the common ground to be sought in American public life. President Obama, in other words, would be the arbiter of authentic Catholicism in America.

The Catholic Church can take care of itself, and will do so in the twenty-first century. What must be underscored here is the gravity of the threat that the president's Notre Dame commencement address posed to the fabric of religious freedom in America—which is one constitutional expression of the third truth of the American Proposition and its understanding of the relationship of society and the state. The White House likely thought it was simply playing wedge politics, strengthening its grip on certain Catholic constituencies while driving a wedge between those Catholics and their bishops. But there was nothing simple about this. Here was the state, embodied by the president, claiming a purchase in what had for centuries been understood to be the inviolable territory of society. To be sure, President Obama is not the Holy Roman Emperor Henry IV; he is not contesting with the pope for the legal authority to appoint bishops. But whether he knew he was doing this or not, the president in his Notre Dame address was usurping the bishops' right to define the doctrinal and moral boundaries of the Catholic community. That this astonishing act was not recognized for what it was is an important, and chilling, measure of the degree to which the priority of society over the state is, at best, tenuously held these days.

Then there is the marriage debate. There is no need to rehearse this at length. Marriage is one of those societal institutions (like the parent-child bond) that antedate the state historically and are prior to the state ontologically and morally. It is not within the competence of the state to define marriage as the union of two men or two women, any more than it is within the state's competence to define marriage in polygamous or polyandrous terms. Any state that does so has breached the border between society and state in a way that gravely endangers civil society and the common good. Any state that does so is engaging in what Cardinal Ratzinger called, on April 18, 2005, the "dictatorship of relativism": the use of coercive state power to compel recognition of what is neither true nor good, in the name of a nihilist insouciance toward the true and a relativist concept of the good. Such dictatorships will, sooner or later, lead to what the late John Paul II described as "open or thinly disguised totalitarianism."

As to the fourth truth within Murray's American Proposition—the truth that only a virtuous people can be free—the challenges from which it is under assault are so obvious as to need little exposition. Theories of democracy that reduce the democratic experiment to a matter of political mechanics chip away at the linkage between freedom and virtue by consigning virtue to the sphere of private life. The mantra of "choice," the unassailable trump in our contemporary public discourse, deliberately avoids the question of the good: Choose *what*? The reduction of public virtue to an ill-defined "tolerance" with no tether to what is objectively good erodes our sense that civil society is built on numerous virtues. The vulgarities of contemporary popular culture; the demeaning of women by a multi billion-dollar pornography industry; the casual brutality of some aspects of our sports; the eroticism of so much advertising—all of these challenges to virtue are also challenges to freedom rightly understood. Decadence and democracy cannot indefinitely coexist. If the American experiment constantly requires new births of freedom, then the nativity that we need in the early twenty-first century would tether freedom once again to both the true and the good.

Within months of what they at first imagined to have been their Waterloo-like rout of the advocates of classical biblical morality and classical Western political philosophy in November 2008, the proponents of the dictatorship of relativism in American public life were forced to concede that there had been no Waterloo, and that the American culture war continued. Yet the early over reach of the Obama administration and the counter-reaction may be considered a part of the natural ebb and flow of American politics. Amidst that ebb and flow, it is crucial that we maintain a focus on long-term trends in our political culture, and at the deeper level of analysis suggested by Father Murray.

In the early decades of the twenty-first century, many thoughtful Americans, looking inward and outward (and especially at Europe) have come to believe that the second decade of this new millennium will be a defining moment in our national life: roads are indeed diverging in the wood, and the choices taken will have much to do with whether the United States at its tercentenary in 2076 will be a political community in recognizable moral and cultural continuity with its Founding. One more citation from Father Murray may help us grasp precisely what is at stake in the question of whether Americans still hold these truths, and how their grip on them might be strengthened by the Catholic community in America:

> What is at stake is America's understanding of itself. Self-understanding is the necessary condition of a sense of self-identity and self-confidence, whether in the case of an individual or in the case of a people. If the American people can no longer base this sense on naïve assumptions of self-evidence, it is imperative that they find other more reasoned grounds for their essential affirmation that they are uniquely a people, uniquely a free people. Otherwise the peril is great. The complete loss of one's identity is, with all propriety of theological definition, hell. In diminished forms it is insanity. And it would not be well for the American giant to go lumbering about the world today, lost and mad.

Rescuing *Gaudium et Spes*: The New Humanism of John Paul II

O n August 7, 1945, the day after the world's first atomic bomb was dropped at Hiroshima, Norman Cousins wrote an impassioned editorial for *Saturday Review*, a political weekly firmly anchored on the liberal side of the American opinion spectrum. Entitled "Modern Man Is Obsolete," Cousins's editorial gave voice to the deep anxieties of many in the early days of the Cold War: modern technology, it seemed, had produced threats to the human future to which Technological Man had few, if any, answers. As Cousins wrote, "Man stumbles fitfully into a new age of atomic energy for which he is as ill-equipped to accept its potential blessings as he is to counteract or control its present dangers."

Seventeen years after Cousins sounded the alarm about the obsolescence of "modern man," the Second Vatican Council formally opened on October 11, 1962. Four days later, President John F. Kennedy was shown definitive photographic evidence that the Soviet Union was surreptitiously emplacing offensive nuclear missiles in Cuba, missiles whose warheads could destroy Washington, New York, and every other major city on the east coast of the United States in a matter of minutes. It has rarely been remarked that the first three weeks of Vatican II—weeks of high ecclesiastical drama in which John XXIII called the Church to a new evangelical activism in the modern world, and the Fathers of the Council sought to wrest control of the Council's agenda from the Roman Curia—coincided with the Cuban Missile Crisis: by all accounts, the closest the world ever came to a nuclear holocaust in which "modern man," rather than being rendered obsolete, would be annihilated. Yet here was a coincidence with consequences.

That juxtaposition of the Council's opening with the terrifying high point of the Cold War had its effects in the Church's life in the years immediately following. The experience of the Cuban Missile Crisis, which threatened to preclude the work of the Council before the Council had really begun, accelerated the Holy See's quest for a new *Ostpolitik*, which would be designed and implemented by Agostino Casaroli during the pontificate of Paul VI. The strange coincidence of a world "one minute from midnight," and the opening of a Council intended to create the conditions for the possibility of a new Pentecost throughout the world Church, was undoubtedly one motive behind John XXIII's April 1963 encyclical on the imperative of peace, *Pacem in Terris*. It just as certainly formed part of the historical, even psychological, background from which emerged one of Vatican II's most controversial documents, known during its developmental phase as *Schema XIII*.

Schema XIII had distinguished ecclesiastical parentage: John XXIII himself; Cardinal Giovanni Battista Montini of Milan (later Pope Paul VI); and the Belgian Cardinal Leo Jozef Suenens, one of the Council's four moderators. These churchmen wanted the Council to initiate a pastoral dialogue with modernity—with "modern man," full of confidence in his new scientific and technological powers, yet fearing his obsolescence (as that quintessential modern man, Norman Cousins, had put it in 1945). *Schema XIII* was also intended to be the model of a new style of ecclesiastical rhetoric: the rather formal (some might say, petrified) rhetoric of neoscholastic propositions would give way to a more conversational tone, in which the Church would make respectful proposals to the "modern world," aimed at eliciting a dialogical response from rapidly secularizing societies and cultures.

After four years of gestational travail (in which the archbishop of Kraków, Karol Wojtyła, played a significant role as one of many midwives), *Schema XIII* was finally born at the end of the Council's fourth period and christened *Gaudium et Spes* [hereafter, *GS*]. The Pastoral Constitution began with an introductory reflection on the human situation in the contemporary world, which was followed by two lengthy parts, "The Church and Man's Vocation" (which continued the analysis of the introduction) and "Some More Urgent Problems" (which addressed a cluster of specific issues). The structural organization of this second part anticipated the teaching of John Paul II in *Centesimus Annus* by describing a tripartite modern society in which politics, culture, and economics are in vigorous interaction; this scheme cleared the path in the development of Catholic social thought to John Paul II's teaching on the free and virtuous society as one composed of a democratic polity, a free economy, and a vibrant public moral culture, with the last being crucial to the proper functioning of the other two. It is the portrait of the "modern world" running through *GS* on which I wish to concentrate here, however. For in addition to analyzing specific issues, the Council Fathers highlighted what seemed to them the principal signs of the times—the chief characteristics of modernity, if you will—to which the proclamation of the Gospel had to attend.

GS is a complex document containing many enduring insights. But, read from the perspective of the second decade of the twenty-first century—a mere two generations after it was written—the Pastoral Constitution also seems curiously, even strangely, dated. *GS* is a photographic still, a snapshot, of the "modern world," and the image is true enough for that time. But what the Council Fathers describe as the "modern world" turns out to have been a modernity that would soon self-destruct because of internal tensions and contradictions the Council did not address—a modernity that would produce, not obsolescent modern man living under the shadow of global nuclear war, but postmodern man. And postmodern man is beset by more, and arguably graver, dangers than Norman Cousins and the Fathers of Vatican II imagined, when they pondered a modernity imperiled by its own artifacts and bereft of satisfying answers to the questions its accomplishments raised.

There is no need here to belabor the worthy insights in *GS*: the sympathetic treatment of the contemporary human quest for freedom; the dialogical approach to the challenge of modern atheism; the celebration of the genuine achievements of science and democracy; the ecclesiology and missiology of a Church that proposes, but does not impose; the touching description of conscience as "the most secret core and sanctuary of man . . . [where] he is alone with God, Whose voice echoes in its depths." Above all, the Council Fathers grasped the nub of the modern dilemma and the root of the modern possibility in their focus on philosophical anthropology—the idea of the human person—as the crucial question of the day. These insights remain entirely pertinent to our situation, more than two generations after the Pastoral Constitution was promulgated, and we should remain grateful for them.

Nevertheless, and in that spirit of gratitude, I would like to focus for a moment on the things that *GS* did *not* see or did not anticipate, with an eye to rescuing the Pastoral Constitution from an undeserved obsolescence. For it is only when we identify these missing pieces that we can begin to understand why the challenge of postmodernity is even greater than the challenge of late modernity. And it is only from *that* understanding that we can begin to grasp why the new humanism of John Paul II—which is embedded in telegraphic form in key sections of *GS*—remains essential for the rescue of the Pastoral Constitution and for the New Evangelization of the twenty-first century.

So, to put the matter bluntly: What did *GS* miss, in its portrait of what we now call late modernity? And what are the contemporary realities that *GS* did not anticipate, but which are crucial components of the postmodern circumstance in which much of the developed world finds itself in the first years of the twenty-first century?

GS recognized that a revolution in human self-understanding had followed Darwin and Freud, just as dramatic changes in our understanding of the cosmos and our place in it had followed the discoveries of Einstein and the other great twentieth-century physicists. The introductory section even suggested that humanity has, *pace* Feuerbach, passed through a "fiery brook," on the far side of which religious conviction must be a matter of personal decision, rather than a matter of understandings and practices inherited from one's ancestors and one's culture. The Pastoral Constitution did not, however, take the full measure of the effects of the discovery of the DNA double helix by James Watson and Francis Crick, and the new genetics that would follow. Thus the Pastoral Constitution did not anticipate that biology and the other life sciences would rapidly displace the hard sciences (such as physics) as the source of Promethean threats to the human future—and to man's self-understanding.

GS depicted a world in which the chief philosophical challenges to the Christian worldview and to the Christian view of man are Marxism and existentialism of the Sartrean variety. Yet Marxism was in the ash can of history within a generation of the Pastoral Constitution's promulgation, and in the twenty-first century Sartrean existentialism is studied, if at all, as a matter of antiquarian interest. Moreover, in surveying the intellectual-cultural landscape, *GS* does not seem to have discerned that another philosophical challenger, the utilitarianism of Jeremy Bentham and his followers, would mount a more forceful challenge to the Christian view of the human person (and to the possibility of a truth-centered public moral discourse) than Sartre ever managed.

GS welcomed the new roles that women were assuming throughout the world, and has important things to say about marriage and the family. But the Pastoral Constitution did not anticipate the harder-edged forms of the new feminism that would break out into mainstream Western culture a few years after Vatican II. Nor does *GS* seem to have expected the emergence of the two-worker family (in which both parents are wage-earners) and the changes that would effect in family life. Nor did the Pastoral Constitution anticipate the global plague of abortion (a practice closely linked in the West to radical feminism). Nor did it anticipate the "gay rights" movement and what would become a worldwide and historically unprecedented struggle over the very definition of marriage.

In short, *GS* gave us few, if any, hints that a new gnosticism, teaching the radical plasticity of human nature, was about to hit the Western world like a cultural tsunami: a gnosticism that, married to the biotechnological revolution produced by the new genetics, proposes to remake the human condition by manufacturing (or re-manufacturing) human beings. Focused in part on the destructive capabilities of modern weaponry, *GS* does not anticipate the threat to the human future embodied in the "immortality project" of the new genetics and the new biotechnologies, despite the warnings that had been raised by Aldous Huxley thirty-some years before. The Pastoral Constitution does acknowledge that "it is in the face of death that the riddle of human existence grows most acute," and suggests that "the prolongation of biological life is unable to satisfy" the deepest desires of the human heart. But the Council Fathers do not seem to have anticipated that this "prolongation" was on the verge of becoming virtually infinite, a technological development with the most profound consequences for human self-understanding and for society.

GS sympathetically explored modern man's crisis of religious faith, and rightly suggested that the Church's failures must be taken into account when analyzing the roots of modern agnosticism and atheism But *GS* did not anticipate the demise of the secularization hypothesis: that once-taken-for-granted claim that modernization inevitably leads to secularization, which has now been empirically falsified in every part of the world except the North Atlantic community and its former colonies in Australasia. *GS* does not, in other words, imagine a world that is becoming *more* religious, and in which religious conviction is having a determinative effect on world politics. Yet that is the world in which we live, a world in which, *inter alia*, radical forms of Islamism like jihadism have changed the way each of us lives, works, and travels.

The Council Fathers noted that population growth was putting social, economic, and spiritual pressures on many societies and tried to respond in a pastorally sensitive way. But there is no hint in *GS* that "overpopulation" (whatever that means, for the term is essentially undefinable) would turn out to be a myth. Nor is there any suggestion that one of the gravest problems of the twenty-first century would be a precipitous drop in fertility across the globe, led by a Europe for whose lack of children a new demographic term had to be invented: "lowest low fertility." The Council Fathers were not, of course, antinatalist scientific charlatans like Paul Ehrlich, whose 1968 book, *The Population Bomb*, did much to popularize the "threat" of "overpopulation." But *GS* depicted a world in which too-many-people-with-too-few-resources is the norm and projected that norm into the foreseeable future; the Pastoral Constitution did not anticipate what seems likely to be the mid-twenty-first-century reality, which, in the aggregate, will be one of too few people in some parts of the world, and that world one of expanding wealth.

Moreover, that wealth will be expanding because of something else that *GS* did not anticipate: the silicon revolution, the rise of the Internet and other new communications media, and indeed the entire phenomenon of communications-driven "globalization." That the world would soon become, for economic purposes, a single time-zone world in which virtually everyone is in real-time communication with everyone else, is not something a reader of *GS* in 1965 would have learned. *GS* did not anticipate that vast numbers of human beings would in fact lift themselves out of poverty in the late twentieth century, such that by the first decade of the twenty-first century some 5/6 of the world would be un-poor, or well on the way to being un-poor—while the "bottom billion" would be mired in abject poverty, in considerable part because of something else that GS did not anticipate: the fantastic corruption and incompetence of postcolonial governments in the Third World.

In light of the revolutionary upheavals of the late eighteenth, nineteenth, and early twentieth centuries, and mindful of the charge (however false) that the Church of 1789 was essentially a department of the *ancien régime*, the Council Fathers recovered a Gelasian theme from the distant past of the Church's teaching about civil authority and lifted up the legitimate autonomy of the secular in *GS*. But the Pastoral Constitution did not anticipate the emergence of a radical secularism that would seek to enforce a public arena shorn of religious and moral reference points, to the point of imposing what Cardinal Joseph Ratzinger called, on April 18, 2005, the "dictatorship of relativism."

Then there was the Council Fathers' call for a new intellectual synthesis focused on the cultivation of wisdom: surely a worthy goal. Yet within a decade and a half, the very idea of "synthesis" in the world of learning would be displaced by theories of the inevitable fragmentation and incoherence of knowledge. Similarly, the Council Fathers had some kind things to say about modern art, seemingly innocent of any concern that the avant-garde might soon collapse into new forms of decadence.

In terms of international affairs, *GS* suggested that economic inequality would be the primary *casus belli* between nations in the future. Yet it is hard to think of very many wars caused by economic inequality or the desire to plunder resources since 1965. Rather, the world's wars in the decades following *GS* would be caused by ideological conflict and passion, ancient ethnic, racial, and tribal hatreds, and/or distorted religious conviction—aided and abetted by the failures of the United Nations (in which *GS* reposed considerable confidence) and the disinclination of the former colonial powers to impose a measure of the tranquillity of order in the places they once ruled (like Rwanda and Sudan) or that were once their close neighbors (such as Yugoslavia).

Perhaps most tellingly, *GS* suggested that an intellectually assertive atheism would continue to pose a particularly sharp challenge to the Church, when in fact a massive religious indifferentism—described by the Orthodox scholar David Bentley Hart as "metaphysical boredom"—would soon descend over Christianity's European heartland like a thick, choking fog. *GS* anticipated the possibility of a new, respectful dialogue between belief and unbelief; it did not anticipate that Catholic proposals would be received with a yawn of indifference in cultures whose deepest civilizational subsoil was once tilled by the Church. *GS* argued that "atheism must be accounted among the most serious problems of this age"; yet the problem would in fact be much worse. Boredom in both its spiritual and metaphysical forms—a debonair indifference to the question of God, and a stultifying lack of awe and wonder at the very mystery of being—would turn out to be a far more lethal, and far more effective, challenge to the biblical view of man than "scientific atheism" or existentialism ever was.

And the net result, in the Western world at least: not an obsolescent "modern man" of the sort imagined by both a secular analyst like Norman Cousins and the Fathers of Vatican II, but postmodern man—metaphysically indifferent, spiritually bored, demographically barren, skeptical about the human capacity to know the truth of anything with certainty, rigorously relativistic in morals, willing to impose that relativism on others through coercive state power, and determined to live according to the conviction that personal autonomy is the highest expression of the human.

Modern man may have been "obsolete" in 1945 or 1965. What came next was even worse.

W hat, then, are we to make of these multiple failures to read accurately the signs of the times? Do they suggest a certain naivete about modernity, as Pope Benedict XVI suggested several times in his prepapal commentary on *GS*? Was the very idea of a document like *GS* misbegotten, as Tracey Rowland and others in the camp of "radical orthodoxy" imply? Is *GS* hopelessly antiquated?

Read from the vantage point of today, *GS* does suffer from a kind of historical myopia. The document's description of the key cultural challenges of the "modern world" sheds some light on the situation in the period 1945–1965, but that analysis does not anticipate, much less describe, the end of late modernity and the rise of postmodernity that followed the flashpoint of "1968." Yet the Pastoral Constitution's analysis is both correct (for its time) and prescient (with reference to the impending future) on what is perhaps *the* crucial point: in both the late modern world of Vatican II and the postmodern world of today, *the anthropological question is fundamental.*

And that, interestingly enough, is the question Bishop Karol Wojtyła wished the Council to address, right from the beginning.

The first volumes of the *Acta* of Vatican II make fascinating reading, being a collection of submissions to the conciliar Ante-Preparatory Commission, which was charged with formulating an agenda for the Council and asked the world bishops, seminary faculties, and religious superiors (of men!) for ideas. Some submissions to the Ante-Preparatory Commission show genuine insight into the Church's condition, *ad intra* and *ad extra*; they reflect a sense that a good, self-critical stock-taking, and serious pastoral reform, were in order in the Catholic Church. Other submissions, perhaps the majority, suggest that many of the world's bishops expected a brief, virtually *pro forma* Council, focused on matters of internal ecclesiastical housekeeping: thus the bishops would come to Rome for a few months, ratify a few adjustments in Church practice, and return home by Christmas, their business done. The tensions between these two visions of what Vatican II should be were the matrix, of course, of some of the high drama in the Council's opening weeks; as one of the curially experienced reformers among the Council Fathers, Cardinal Montini, put it to a friend on the night that John XXIII announced his intention of summoning an ecumenical council: "This holy old boy doesn't realize what a hornet's nest he's stirring up."

Like other bishops, the young auxiliary bishop of Kraków touched on pastoral matters in his submission to the Ante-Preparatory Commission: the possibility of vernacular liturgy; a new urgency in ecumenism; the need for Christian education of the laity; a reform in the intellectual and cultural formation of priests, before and after ordination. Yet the heart of Wojtyła's response to the queries from Rome was a kind of philosophical essay. What, he asked, was the human condition today? What do people expect to hear from the Church, and what do they need to hear from the Church?

What the modern world needed, Wojtyła suggested, was an integral vision of the human person, nobler and more comprehensive than other understandings of man then on offer. The Western humanistic project, he argued, had gone off the rails in recent centuries. Defective, truncated, even demonic ideas of human nature, human community, human origins, and human destiny were everywhere; the most lethal of those false ideas created the cultural conditions for the possibility of the civilizational catastrophes of the first half of the twentieth century. Why, Wojtyła asked, had a century that had begun with such high expectations for the human future produced two world wars, a Cold War that threatened the very survival of humanity, oceans of blood, mountains of corpses, the Gulag, Auschwitz, and the greatest persecution of Christianity in two millennia—and all between 1914 and 1960? The abattoir of the twentieth century, Wojtyła proposed, had been made possible by desperately defective ideas of who man is, which had led to distorted human aspirations and grotesque political projects.

Others knew that the anthropological question was central, Wojtyła acknowledged, even if their answers were deficient. Scientific positivists, dialectical Marxists, and literary existentialists all imagined themselves humanists; each thought that his method and his insight could lead humanity to a genuine liberation. What did the Church have to say to all of this? After two millennia, the world had questions to put to the Church: What is the Church's idea of man? What is Christian humanism? How does it differ from the many other humanisms in the modern world? Can Christian humanism answer the burning questions that naturally arise in the human heart—questions that are part and parcel of the struggles of a material creature with intense spiritual longings?

Bishop Karol Wojtyła, in other words, proposed that the entire project of Vatican II be organized around the anthropological question. The Council was meeting in the middle of a century that prided itself on its humanism. Yet humanism was manifestly in crisis, and had been for decades. The promise of salvation through ultra-mundane humanism had led to grief and slaughter, time and again; accepting the Great Commission (Matthew 28:16–20) in these circumstances meant nothing less than mounting a cultural rescue operation. Thus Wojtyła suggested that the Church's central task at Vatican II was to think through a Christian anthropology adequate to the demands of Christian humanism in an age in which humanism's decay had had lethal consequences.

To this task, Wojtyła brought the philosophical anthropology he had developed over two decades of reflection, teaching, and writing. Wojtyła's "new humanism" grew from three sources, and at the risk of oversimplification, its sources and main ideas can be summarized as follows.

From his readings in St. John of the Cross, Wojtyła took the view that the distinctive characteristic of human existence is man's interiority, which has its roots in the origins of every being—in God. Thus for Wojtyła, modernity's "turn to the subject," properly understood, is a turn toward God. Cartesian subjectivity—at least as understood by Descartes' most influential followers, such as Hume—led only to the self. Wojtyła's concept of subjectivity was such that the "turn" need not bracket (or dismiss) the transcendent dimension, or the question of God; rather, the "turn to the subject," rightly taken, opens up the question of God.

From Thomas Aquinas, Karol Wojtyła took a realistic ontology that would secure the epistemological foundation of his new humanism. His philosophical anthropology was built on a trust in human experience, and on rationally defensible convictions about the human capacity to get at the truth of things, however incompletely. Thus it posed a challenge to the post-Kantian and (especially) post-Humean hermeneutics of suspicion, which had had such a corrosive effect on the humanistic project. From Aquinas, Wojtyła also learned that philosophical anthropology was a matter of both/and: *both* the old masters of the Western philosophical tradition *and* contemporary questions and questioners are to be in play in a Christian reflection—indeed, in any serious philosophical reflection—on the question of man. Thus Wojtyła's new humanism would reject the self-regarding "presentism" of too much contemporary thought; by contrast, the new humanism would practice the ecumenism of time. Finally, Wojtyła took from Aquinas a determination not to be reductive: the task of philosophical anthropology was to see, probe, and understand man in his full complexity. Thus the spiritual dimension of human experience must be part of any genuinely humanistic account of the human condition.

Finally, from Max Scheler and others in the early phenomenological movement, Wojtyła learned that feeling and sensibility can disclose metaphysical and moral truths—and that this, too, was part of dealing with man "in full."

Wojtyła deepened his exploration of philosophical anthropology in his graduate-level "Lublin Lectures" during the mid- and late-1950s. These lectures involved a transtemporal dialogue with some of the great thinkers of the past: Plato, Aristotle, Augustine, Aquinas, Kant, Hume, and Scheler. (Interestingly enough, as if in anticipation of one the challenges of postmodernity cited above, Wojtyła also analyzed Bentham and utilitarianism during this period.) And if there was a focal point around which Wojtyła's explorations in philosophical anthropology pivoted, it was the question of freedom. This was a question with a certain existential urgency, of course, given the realities of life in Poland in the immediate post-Stalin period; here, Wojtyła honed his claim that communism's economic and political failures were based on a fundamental anthropological error. At the same time, Wojtyła sharpened his philosophical understanding of human freedom by analyzing the defects of the moral theories of Kant (deformed by a certain rationalistic reduction) and Scheler (deformed by a certain emotivist reduction). The net result was a Thomistically grounded, yet thoroughly contemporary, ontology and phenomenology of freedom that was positioned to challenge both the false humanisms of late modernity and the postmodern reduction of freedom to a matter of individualist, autonomous "choice."

Thus for Wojtyła, a truly human freedom is "freedom for excellence"(to borrow a phrase from the moral theologian Servais Pinckaers, O.P.): freedom is a matter of freely choosing what we can know to be good, and doing so as a matter of moral habit. Against the assumptions of postmodernism (which, as Pinckaers shows, are actually rooted in an Ockhamite voluntarism), freedom is not to be understood as a free-floating faculty of choice that can legitimately attach itself to anything; this, for Wojtyła, is a dehumanizing concept of freedom. Rather, freedom is a capacity into which individuals, cultures, and societies grow. On this analysis, what postmodernity would come to call "autonomy" is in fact a prison, with bars of solipsism and locks of ignorance. Because of that, the postmodern "autonomy project" leads to both auto-enslavement at the personal level and relativism-imposed-by-authoritarianism at the societal level.

This rich theory of freedom is at the heart of Wojtyła's new humanism, and it is crystallized in the two most-quoted passages from *GS* in the magisterium of John Paul II: *GS* 22 ("[I]t is only of the Word made flesh that the mystery of man truly becomes clear. . . . Christ the Lord, Christ the New Adam, in the very revelation of the mystery of the Father and his love, fully reveals man to himself and brings to light his most high calling"), and *GS* 24 ("[M]an can discover his true self only in a sincere giving of himself"). These two passages from *GS*, in which it is reasonable to speculate that Wojtyła had an authorial hand, encapsulate what Wojtyła would call, in a 1974 lecture at an international symposium on the seventh centenary of the death of Thomas Aquinas, the "Law of the Gift." And the Law of the Gift was at the center of the moral, indeed ontological, truth about man: we are made for freedom, which means that our lives must be lived as the gift-for-others that life itself is to each of us.

For Wojtyła-the-Christian, the ultimate ground of the Law of the Gift was the interior life of the Holy Trinity, which imprints itself *ad extra* on the human person as the *imago Dei*. Yet Wojtyła-the-philosopher was persuaded that one could get to the Law of the Gift, rationally and reasonably, through a serious reflection on human moral agency: a turn to the subject that did not lead to solipsism and "autonomy," but to love and responsibility. Freedom, lived according to its proper dignity, is always freedom tethered to truth and ordered to goodness.

Pope John Paul II would develop this concept of freedom, and deepen the new humanism encoded in *GS* 22 and *GS* 24, throughout his pontificate.

Freedom for excellence, for example, is the central organizing idea of the 1991 social encyclical, *Centesimus Annus*, an encyclical that not only looks back at the heritage of post-Leonine Catholic social doctrine but looks ahead to the postmodernity of the immediate future—and presciently anticipates some of the major challenges of a world in which history has clearly not ended.

John Paul II's "Theology of the Body," laid out in his Wednesday catecheses from 1979 through 1984, is perhaps the Church's most compelling response to the new gnosticism of postmodernity; it challenges postmodern man to rediscover his sacramentality and the sacramentality of the world. Not only does the Church take our human embodiedness as male and female far more seriously than post-modern gnostics, John Paul II suggests; the Church's sacramental vision of human embodiedness, linked to freedom-for-excellence, sheds important light on some of the most deeply controverted issues of our time.

In *Veritatis Splendor*, John Paul challenged the moral relativism that is central to the autonomy project by an appeal to the dignity of conscience as central to human dignity.

In *Fides et Ratio*, John Paul challenged postmodern man to grow up: to leave the sandbox of metaphysical and epistemological skepticism and, in doing so, to break through to a new, genuinely mature humanism that would be proof against the temptations of spiritual boredom.

Then there is the new catechism, promulgated by John Paul in 1992 with the Apostolic Constitution *Fidei Depositum*. The very existence of *The Catechism of the Catholic Church*, as Cardinal Christoph Schönborn, O.P., has pointed out, is a challenge to postmodernism's insistence on the incoherence of knowledge. Here, the Church proposes, is a comprehensive and coherent account of what we believe, how we pray, and how we think we ought to live. And with the *Catechism*, the Church proposes a question to the world: Which of these two alternatives strikes you as the more deeply humane, the Church asks postmodern man—the vision of human nature and possibility we propose, or a life in which material wealth is coupled with spiritual boredom and moral insouciance?

Finally, mention should be made of the impact of John Paul's new humanism or personalism on key theological themes of the pontificate: his Christology, as evidenced from the beginning in *Redemptor Hominis*; his ecclesiology and his theory of Christian mission in *Redemptoris Missio*; his sacramental theology in *Novo Millennio Ineunte* and *Ecclesia de Eucharistia*; his dialogical approach to ecumenism (*Ut Unum Sint*) and interreligious dialogue (*Redemptoris Missio*, again); his treatment of the priesthood (*Pastores Dabo Vobis*); and his theory of Catholic higher education (*Ex Corde Ecclesiae*). Personalism, the new humanism, and freedom for excellence were also decisive factors in the social doctrine of John Paul, beginning with his innovative theology of work in *Laborem Exercens*, continuing with the definition of a "right of economic initiative" in *Sollicitudo Rei Socialis*, and culminating in his empirically sensitive treatment of the dynamics of the free economy in *Centesimus Annus*.

The new humanism of John Paul II is a living thing, a growing body of thought that must be nurtured and developed by the late pope's intellectual disciples in the decades ahead, if the Church is to respond adequately to the anthropological question that lies at the heart of so many postmodern dilemmas. Such a development must reckon with some of the serious questions that have been put to John Paul's personalism by sympathetic critics and faithful Catholics.

Granted that Wojtyła's personalist approach to a new humanism works well in promoting an integral vision of the human person, in giving content to the notion of "human dignity," in catechizing the sacraments, in unpacking questions of sexual ethics, in fostering ecumenical interreligious dialogue, and even in explicating doctrines such as the Trinity, does the personalist approach "work" quite as well when issues of state power are engaged? What, for example, does the new humanism have to say when international conflicts become simply intractable, and further negotiation is both futile and dangerous?

Does John Paul's new humanism lead to a functional pacifism that retains the Church's tacit adherence to the just war tradition while de facto putting the Church in opposition to virtually every imaginable use of armed force? Is a dignitarian-personalist opposition to capital punishment the last word to be said on that difficult subject?

Theologians sympathetic to John Paul's personalism have also raised concerns about its methodological effects in moral theology. Pastoral experience suggests that a personalist approach to the central teaching of *Humanae Vitae* is far more successful than the Thomistic teleology in which Paul VI framed that teaching; yet does such an approach tend, over time, to weaken the Church's sense of the ontological dimensions of the moral law? Christological and eschatological questions are also engaged: could the late pope's stress in his magisterium on the person of the Christ, whose ministry embodies in a perfect way the Law of the Gift, lead to a kind of ecclesial forgetting of the sovereignty of the Risen Lord, who is the world's judge as well as its servant? Or, in a related matter: does the purification in purgatory stressed by the pope's personalism minimize the penal dimension of that purification—so beautifully expressed, for example, in elements of the funeral liturgy and in Dante's *Purgatorio*?

Grappling with these questions will not vitiate, but rather strengthen, the claim that the new humanism of John Paul, manifest in both his philosophical and theological personalism, is a uniquely valuable resource for responding to the anthropological question that, as the Fathers of Vatican II saw, was central in parsing the human condition in the modern world. It is just as valuable a resource for the postmodern world that *Gaudium et Spes* seems not to have seen, hovering just beyond the immediate horizon. The philosophical and theological anthropology of John Paul II, developed and refined, is thus the key to the rescue of the Pastoral Constitution on the Church in the Modern World from the imprisonment in the dungeon of the Sixties to which some of its critics have consigned it.

Blair, Benedict, and Britain

Two weeks before Pope Benedict XVI's September 2010 visit to the United Kingdom, former British Prime Minister Tony Blair's memoir, *A Journey: My Political Life*, was published in the United States. At first glance, the two events might seem disconnected, even juxtaposed: a politician's memoir, with its inevitable score-settling, and a bishop's pastoral visit, stressing unity amidst contention. On closer inspection, however, Blair's book and Benedict's pilgrimage turned out to have a lot to do with each other. For *A Journey: My Political Life* helped illuminate, if indirectly and inadvertently, the ferocity of the Christophobic campaign against Catholicism and the pope mounted in Britain prior to the papal visit. What Blair had to say about twenty-first-century Britain, and, by extension, twenty-first-century democracies around the world, was also in striking contrast to the analysis of contemporary democratic public life offered by the bishop of Rome in Glasgow, London, and Birmingham.

Tony Blair was an engaging public figure and in that respect his memoir is precisely what one might have expected: articulate, energetic, clever in argumentation—and decidedly postmodern (hence the book's title, a staple of postmod "spirituality"). Blair was often accused, not without reason, of being a master of spin. Yet in *A Journey*, he is admirably frank about both politics and personalities, although his candor on the latter front can be, serially, bracing, jarring, and weirdly confessional.

Thus Blair-the-bracing on his longtime communications chief, Alastair Campbell: "In my experience there are two types of crazy people: those who are just crazy, and who are therefore dangerous; and those whose craziness lends them creativity, strength, ingenuity, and verve. Alastair was of the latter sort." Or Blair-the-jarring on his wife: "Cherie didn't always help herself, and as I have remarked before she had this incredible instinct for offending the powerful . . . " Or Blair-the-self-scrutinizer, in confessional mode: "By the standards of days gone by I was not even remotely a toper, and I couldn't do lunchtime drinking except on Christmas Day, but if you took the thing everyone lies about—units per week—I was definitely at the outer limit . . . I was aware it had become a prop." Such self-conscious bluntness does keep one turning the pages; but it also makes one wonder about the author's sense of propriety.

At least some of Blair's American readers would likely have been moved (as many of Blair's fellow Britons manifestly were not) by the former prime minister's love affair with the United States, his confidence in the essential goodness of the American democratic experiment, and his respect for American power. And no one familiar with the increasingly vulgar folkways of the Fourth Estate could challenge Blair's contention that the 24/7 news cycle, with its relentless hunt for the spectacular and scandalous, its capacity to destroy the reputations of the innocent, and its inability to take policy argument seriously, has become a serious problem for all democracies. Then there is Blair's openness about the emotional costs of high office, including his profound sense that decisions he made cost some men and women their lives, and made sorrow a staple in some families.

Blair-haters (and Bush-haters) certainly found his defense of the stalwart support he gave George W. Bush after 9/11 stomach-churning; both gangs could not have been happy, either, with Blair's praise of Bush's intelligence and decency. But the fair-minded reader would have noted that Blair could be critical of those Americans with whom he was in basic agreement on post-9/11 issues in world affairs. And only the willfully obtuse will deny that Blair was right in his convictions that radical Islamist jihadism is a mortal threat to the civilization of the West, and that the West's self-defense is imperiled by sentiments of "malaise, decline, impotence, challenges unmet, promises unfulfilled."

Participants in the ongoing debate over just war and the Iraq War will have to contend with Blair's contention that Iraq fell into bloody chaos after the deposition of Saddam Hussein, not because of culpably inept postwar planning by American and British strategists, but because of the bloody-minded determination of Iraq's remaining Baathists, al-Qaeda in Iraq, and Iran to turn Mesopotamia into a central battlefield in the jihadist war against the West. Blair's recollection of those events also makes a powerful case against Michael Walzer and those Catholic just war theorists who argued in 2002–2003 that a "small war" (i.e., intensified sanctions and a countrywide no-fly zone) would eventually bring Saddam's regime to its knees. In marshaling evidence against this claim, Blair gives a lucid explanation of the definitive Duelfer Report on Iraqi weapons of mass destruction; he also provides a useful reminder that, while the report's first conclusion has been set in concrete in the public mind (Iraq destroyed its WMD after the 1991 Gulf War), its critical second conclusion remains virtually unknown: that Saddam had retained the human and technological infrastructure to ramp up his WMD programs once he had gotten out of the sanctions box, and would undoubtedly have done so. Blair is also forceful in his argument that the U.N. sanctions regime would have eventually crumbled in the face of Iraqi intransigence, although he is less sharp than George W. Bush's memoirs were on the subjects of French president Jacques Chirac and German chancellor Gerhard Schroeder.

A Journey provides a compelling account of the peace negotiations in Northern Ireland, in which Blair was admirably indefatigable (and, by his own account, notably dishonest at one point, in order to keep the negotiation going). But with the exception of his defense of his policies on Iraq, he is most passionate in defending his creation of "New Labour": a party disentangled from its platform's

hitherto sacrosanct Clause 4 (a relic of Marxist antiquity about
common ownership of the means of production); a party comfortable with middle-class aspiration; a party no longer in thrall to trade
union obtuseness and leftist intellectual abstraction; a party tough
on crime but bullish on empowering the poor; a party that, by appealing to a broad constituency, could become Britain's natural
party of governance, rather than its natural party of opposition. It
was a grand aspiration but a truncated one. And its shortsighted-
ness helped create the kind of Britain that would eventually turn on
a reasonably successful prime minister like Tony Blair—and pour
venom on a pope.

A Journey is also rife with judgments that even those who
admired Blair's steadfastness as an ally will find, well,
strange. Bill Clinton, who never got 50 percent of the popular vote
in the two presidential elections he contested, is nevertheless "the
master," a "brilliant president" who "ran a good economy" and
"made big reforms." Barack Obama, similarly, is "brilliant," a "man
of genius." Long after a raft of contrary evidence was readily at hand,
Blair suggests that Russia's increasingly brutish domestic and foreign
policies in the first decade of the new century were the by-products,
not of Vladimir Putin's nationalism and KGB background, but of
Putin's sense of not getting enough respect from George W. Bush;
Blair even avers a certain sympathy for the paranoid Russian reaction to proposed U.S. missile defense emplacements in central
Europe, "which, in a sense understandably, they saw as aimed at
them." The same Blair who could be tough as nails on the need
to use military force to repel the genocidal Slobodan Milosovic in
Kosovo can, without blush, repeat the old, tired shibboleths about a
Palestinian state being the magic key that will unlock the minds and
hearts of Arabs unreconciled to the fact and legitimacy of the State
of Israel. As for climate change, well, that, for Blair, "is *the* global
challenge," the answer to which is a "global agreement," a "collective

bargain" that China, India, the United States, and Europe all recognize is in "their national interest."

If Tony Blair is right that the war against jihadism is the defining struggle of the early twenty-first century between the West and the rest, he is spectacularly wrong about the defining battle *within* the West, which John Paul II defined as the contest between a "culture of life" and a "culture of death," and which Benedict XVI has described as a struggle against the "dictatorship of relativism." Blair's otherwise comprehensive account of his ten-year premiership is strangely silent on these issues: there is no account given of his government's support for embryo-destructive stem cell research, for abortion-on-demand being recognized as a universal human right, for sex education programs that now require eleven-year olds to demonstrate familiarity with the use of condoms, or for the withdrawal of nutrition and hydration from patients deemed beyond the reach of medical science (or too much of a drain on the budget of the National Health Service, or both).

Alastair Campbell famously said of New Labour that "we don't do God." However one might parse what the great spinmeister meant by that glib line, *A Journey* is notably reticent about religious conviction, as either a personal matter or a factor in public life. There is nothing about Blair's own path from Anglicanism to Catholicism (completed, to be sure, after he left 10 Downing Street); but we are informed that "religion starts with values that are born of a view of humankind," which perhaps explains a later reference to the "inestimable Hans Küng." The name "Rowan Williams" does not appear in the book's index, although Dr. Williams's appointment as archbishop of Canterbury took place during Blair's second term (and may be seen, in retrospect, as the appointment that put paid to the Anglican Communion as it has been known for centuries). George W. Bush, in conversation in the Oval Office in 2007, described the funeral Mass of John Paul II on April 8, 2005, as one of the three most moving and important days of his life; Tony Blair's spare narrative of what NBC's Brian Williams called, that day, "the human event of a generation," is dominated by recollections of his efforts to avoid being photographed sitting next to Zimbabwean dictator Robert Mugabe. Blair's description of New Labour stresses that "progressive" politics should be about strengthening "community—i.e., [the notion that] people owed obligations to each other and were social beings, not only individuals out for themselves"; but he betrays no familiarity with Catholic social doctrine, with its balanced emphases on the person and the common good, subsidiarity and solidarity. And his concept of religious communities as crucial components of democratic civil society seems largely confined to their being delivery vehicles for social services.

B lair's recounting of the death and funeral of Diana, Princess of Wales, brings into clearest focus the hollowness at the heart of the Britain he and New Labour helped midwife into being. That this was a crucial moment for Blair personally, and for his premiership, seems evident from the fact that he devotes an entire chapter to the tale. Diana, he writes, was "an icon" who "captured the essence of an era and held it in the palm of her hand"; she was, in the Alastair Campbell/Tony Blair phrase, "the people's princess." Her state funeral, the prime minister decided, "had to be dignified; it had to be different; it had to be Diana." What it didn't have to be, at least by Blair's account, was Christian, despite its being held in Westminster Abbey, "hard by the shrine of St. Edward the Confessor and the sacring place of the kings of England," as Evelyn Waugh once wrote. Somehow, according to Blair, "Elton John singing 'Candle in the Wind' and doing it rather brilliantly" was "in keeping with Westminster Abbey." Well, yes, if Westminster Abbey is simply a stage, a shrine to the Real Absence on which any romance may be produced.

There is something rather sad about the fact that Tony Blair, an intelligent man, grasps far less of the truth about Diana, Princess of Wales, than celebrity journalist and editor Tina Brown, whose 2007 biography, *The Diana Chronicles*, shattered a lot of the Diana mythology to which Blair seems stuck like a fly in amber. Yes, as Blair contends, Diana was "hunted down" by the paparazzi and the editors who paid huge sums for pictures of her and her lover, Dodi Fayed. Yes, she was a devoted mother to her two sons, and yes, her royal husband was a callous, self-absorbed bore of dubious metaphysics and equally dubious morals.

But as Tina Brown amply demonstrated, Diana was also a wildly ambitious, poorly educated, shallow, and vindictive woman who came close to bringing down the British monarchy in a fit of pique over their unwillingness to integrate her Sloan Ranger style into the royal family. That this woman's death, however tragic, sent an entire country into a nervous breakdown says something deeply disturbing about the culture of contemporary Britain. That Tony Blair perceived this national crack-up as "a tide that had to be channeled" rather than a nonsense that had to be confronted suggests that he is not quite the Churchillian figure some of his American admirers would like to remember him as being. Imagine Churchill dealing with his fellow Britons in June 1940 the way Blair dealt with his fellow Britons in September 1997, and you can begin to imagine the royal family, led by the heirs of the Nazi-sympathizing Duke of Windsor, reverting to its surname of Saxe-Coburg-Gotha and speaking German.

This shallowness is of a piece with Blair's surprisingly superficial view of the West he wishes to defend against jihadists. How is the West to confront the self-destructive cultural malaise of which Blair rightly warns if he can only define the West as a set of political and economic arrangements agreed to on essentially utilitarian grounds? (And how does the former prime minister expect the West to get a grip on itself in the face of this threat if he couldn't bring himself to tell Britain to get a grip after a beautiful and troubled young woman was killed in a cruel accident in a Paris tunnel?)

Cardinal Cormac Murphy-O'Connor, who was archbishop of Westminster from 2000–2009, never made any pretensions to being an intellectual. But, in a 2001 conversation, he offered an analysis of the cultural crisis of Tony Blair's Britain that cut much deeper into the truth of the matter than the analysis forwarded by New Labour. I asked the then sixty-nine-year-old archbishop, who had come to Westminster late in life, what his pastoral priorities were in the years he likely had left as head of the Catholic Church in England and Wales. The cardinal responded that he had to "make [John Paul II's encyclical] *Veritatis Splendor* come alive" in British public life, "where we have no idea today of absolute moral norms." In twenty-first-century Britain, Murphy-O'Connor said, "the 'doable'" trumps everything else, especially when it's a question of "deferring to science" on issues like stem cell research.

Tony Blair would claim that he is a man of principle who met John Paul II's standard for a serious statesman: he was willing to lose his office over something he believed was right. Yet Blair's tone-deafness to urgent questions of the moral-cultural foundations of democracy suggests that Murphy-O'Connor perceived the hollowness in the soul of the New Labour project in a way that escaped that project's progenitor and embodiment. In the face of old Labour's bewitchment by Marxist shibboleths and class struggle, and after eighteen years of Tory governance under Margaret Thatcher and John Major, New Labour crafted an electoral formula that would prove winning for more than a decade. As Blair admits, the party now insisted with an "emphasis bordering on the religious" that "what counts [is] what works." But that crass (if swinging) utilitarianism failed to address the cultural crisis of a Britain that had largely come unstuck from its historic Christian foundations. And into the hollow soul of Britain during the Blair years roared any number of demons.

Like the kind of demons that could, with no fear of public retribution, describe the eighty-three-year-old bishop of Rome as a former Nazi who ought to be arrested on arrival in the United Kingdom as the central figure in an international criminal conspiracy of child rapists and their abettors.

G iven that antipopery was a crucial ideological component of nation-building in sixteenth century England, it is not altogether surprising that, 181 years after Wellington's Catholic Emancipation Act, pope-baiting remains a popular blood sport in twenty-first-century Britain. Previously militant-Protestant (think "Ian Paisley"), it is now militant-secularist in character. But even by local standards, the torrent of vitriol visited on the Catholic Church and Pope Benedict XVI in the months prior to the pope's September 2010 visit was astonishing. As the *Spectator* put it, in a leader published just before Benedict arrived, protests against the papal visit "far exceed[ed] those that greet the state visits of blood-drenched dictators." But then blood-drenched dictators don't embody all that Britain's Christophobic high culture loathes.

The first to garner extensive British media attention prior to the pope's visit were the paladins of the New Atheism, Richard Dawkins and Christopher Hitchens, who, in league with transplanted Australian barrister Geoffrey Robertson, proposed in April that Benedict be clapped in irons on arriving in Britain and charged with enabling child abuse. That baseless indictment was relentlessly repeated by the chattering classes for the next four months, with the BBC serving as a tax-supported megaphone for calumny. Three days before Benedict landed in Scotland, Channel 4 aired an hourlong "documentary" in which British LGBT activist Peter Tatchell claimed that Catholic teaching on artificial contraception is a prominent factor in global poverty, that Catholic teaching on the appropriate ways to combat the scourge of HIV/AIDS has caused untold deaths, that Catholic teaching against embryo-destructive stem cell research are cruel and "dogmatic," and that, of course, the Catholic Church is a global criminal conspiracy of child abusers. (As Scottish Bishop Philip Tartaglia pointed out, Tatchell's ignorance of the facts about poverty, AIDS prevention, and the curative possibilities of stem cell research was matched by a certain implausibility in his self-presentation as a defender of the innocence of the young: in a 1986 book, Tatchell, a campaigner for lowering the age of consent, had argued that "not all sex involving children in unwanted, abusive, and harmful.") A few days earlier, Geoffrey Robertson added to Britain's fund of ignorance about the Catholic Church by claiming, in a lecture at the London School of Economics, that the Holy See (which was involved in diplomatic exchange centuries before the United Kingdom existed) ought not to enjoy the privileges of sovereignty, which functioned as a blind behind which criminal popes evaded the reach of domestic and international law. (Mr. Robertson, his eyes on what he imagines to be the Croesus-like wealth of the Vatican, moved from the Antipodes to the Mother Country to try to bring the joys of American liability law into the British legal system.)

The pile-on continued in the op-ed pages, with the *Independent*'s Julie Burchill bawling that "a Church which rails against abortion and then spends decades covering up the most appalling degree of child abuse obviously has no problem with holding two opposing ideas at once." But, wrote Burchill, "at least the opposition to termination now makes perfect sense, with hindsight. All those unborn children that could have been molested—what a waste!" Three days later, fifty prominent British intellectuals and writers published a joint statement in the *Guardian* that claimed that "Pope Ratzinger should not be given the honor of a state visit" to Britain because "the organization of which he is head has been responsible for opposing the distribution of condoms and so increasing large families in poor countries and the spread of AIDS; promoting segregated education; denying abortion to even the most vulnerable women; opposing equal rights for lesbians, gays, bisexual, and transgender people; [and] failing to address the many cases of abuse of children within its own organization." Then, having acknowledged in their preamble that the pope is a "head of state," the signatories rejected "the masquerading of the Holy See as a state and the pope as a head of state as merely a convenient fiction to amplify the international influence of the Vatican."

The secularists' anti-Benedictine campaign was given tacit support by the feckless British Catholic Left. A former Blair counselor and former public affairs adviser at the Archdiocese of Westminster, Sir Stephen Wall, G.C.M.G., L.V.O., took to the op-ed page of the *Financial Times* to propose that the "demonstrations of hostility" that would greet the pope had "everything to do with opposition to the Roman Catholic Church as a political entity," by which Wall meant a community that had not bent its moral teaching to the prevailing sentiments of the chattering classes. For the Church to regain a foothold in the West, Sir Stephen wrote, it must recognize that "individuals have their own values" and that a "changing moral code is a normal part of social evolution."

There was some pushback to this torrent of disinformation, slander, and deep theological confusion. One *Guardian* journalist, albeit unnamed, told his paper's ombudsman that his colleagues had "an instinctive hostility to religion" which led them to "stroke our readers' prejudices and reinforce them. . . . Over the last five to ten years we have adopted a pompous, self-satisfied triumphalism." The redoubtable David Quinn, a hardy campaigner against the secularist wave washing over Ireland, made a telling comparison in the Irish *Independent*: "*Newsnight* on BBC-2 last week ran an interview with former Conservative politician Chris Patten, who is helping to oversee the arrangements for the imminent visit of the pope to Britain. The interviewer treated the strident objections to the visit as perfectly reasonable and understandable. Patten did his considerable best to answer. The very next item covered the objection of a majority of Americans to the building of a mosque near the site of Ground

Zero in New York. These objections were treated by the reporter as manifestations of 'Islamophobia.' [Thus] criticisms of Catholicism, no matter how extreme, are now treated as mainstream and acceptable, but criticisms of Islam are seen as indications of bigotry." A week before the pope arrived, Edinburgh's Cardinal Keith O'Brien unloaded on the BBC, charging it with an "institutional bias" against Christianity and describing the forthcoming Tatchell "documentary" as a "hatchet job."

But no such broadsides issued from Archbishop's House in Westminster, which seemed more concerned to distance Archbishop Vincent Nichols from the comments of an archdiocesan staffer who described Britain to the ZENIT News Service as "the geopolitical epicenter of the culture of death" and a country beset by an "ever-increasing commercialization of sex"—sharply stated judgments, to be sure, but not substantively different from the pro-life advocacy of Cardinal Murphy-O'Connor during his years in Westminster.

Sir Stephen Wall warned that, given Benedict XVI's intransigent "conservatism," the papal visit would see the pontiff "whistle into a wind that threatens to blow him, in the U.K. at least, into irrelevance if not ignominy." A week later, at the pope's departure, Prime Minister David Cameron described the papal pilgrimage as an "incredibly moving four days" and thanked the pope for raising "searching questions" that challenged "the whole country to sit up and think." The winds of irrelevance and ignominy, it seemed, had blown in a direction other than that taken by the Popemobile.

From September 16 through September 19, the numbers of those gathered to see the pope, pray with him, or listen to him were consistently higher than predicted. One hundred twenty-five thousand people lined the streets of Edinburgh to cheer Benedict XVI on September 16, and while a combination of aggressive governmental security measures and

inept work by Catholic trip-planners made getting to the papal
venues difficult, hundreds of thousands greeted the pope in London and some eighty thousand attended an evening vigil in Hyde
Park on September 18. (London antipapal activists claimed to
have turned out twenty thousand protesters that afternoon; the
police estimated their number at two thousand.) Anger had been
the dominant emotion prior to Benedict's arrival. But as Bishop
Tartaglia put it, the pope's "grace and intelligence" changed the
atmosphere among those willing to maintain an open mind, and
encouraged all those Catholics whom the secularists (and self-
marginalizing Catholics like Stephen Wall) had written off as rel-
ics of a lost past. Good humor, even amidst long waits at papal
venues, prevailed—as did the British taste for curious expressions
of affection: One poster along the pope's route as he entered
Crofton Park in Birmingham for the beatification of John Henry
Newman read, "We ❤ U Papa More Than Beans on Toast."

Benedict intended John Henry Newman, who got rather short
shrift amidst the pre-visit polemics, to be the symbolic centerpiece
of history's second papal pilgrimage to Britain: Newman, who embodied modernity's quest for religious truth amidst skepticism and
uncertainty; Newman, revered by both Anglicans and Catholics;
Newman who (like Joseph Ratzinger) had a way of doing theology outside the classic Thomistic channels; Newman, for whom the
truth of faith was grasped when heart spoke to heart. Thus, while
the Episcopal Conference of England and Wales proposed that the
papal visit would be about reaffirming religion's place in the democratic public square, Benedict XVI (who indeed warned against the
dictatorship of relativism and the marginalization of religious voices
in democratic public life) focused intently on holiness and friendship with the crucified Lord as his key themes.

In that respect, the most winsome of the pope's addresses was to
a gathering of students at Twickenham on September 17, which was

linked via television to Catholic schools throughout the country. His brief remarks were vintage Joseph Ratzinger—over a half-century of scholarship distilled into a compelling catechetical message:

> It is not often that a pope, or indeed anyone else, has the opportunity to speak to the students of all the Catholic schools of England, Wales, and Scotland. And since I have the chance now, there is something I very much want to say to you. I hope that among those of you listening to me today there are some of the future saints of the twenty-first century. What God wants most of all for each one of you is that you should become holy. He loves you much more than you could ever begin to imagine, and he wants the very best for you. And by far the best thing for you is to grow in holiness. . . .
>
> When I invite you to become saints, I am asking you not to be content with second best. . . . Happiness is something we all want, but one of the great tragedies in this world is that so many people never find it, because they look for it in the wrong places. The key to it is very simple— true happiness is to be found in God. . . .
>
> As you come to know him better, you find you want to reflect something of his infinite goodness in your own life. . . . You want to come to the aid of the poor and the hungry, you want to comfort the sorrowful, you want to be kind and generous. And once these things begin to matter to you, you are well on your way to becoming saints.

At Westminster Cathedral the next day, Benedict addressed the sin and crime of sexual abuse in its appropriate context: as an evil that can be overcome by the power of the Cross. Directing the congregation's attention to "the great crucifix dominating the [cathedral's] nave, which portrays Christ's body, crushed by suffering, overwhelmed by sorrow, the innocent victim whose death has reconciled us with the Father and given us a share in the very life of God," the pope proposed that it was here that we find the courage to address "the immense suffering caused by the abuse of children, especially within the Church and by her ministers." And address it Benedict did, bluntly: "I express my deep sorrow to the innocent victims of these unspeakable crimes, along with my hope that the power of Christ's grace, his sacrifice of reconciliation, will bring deep healing and peace" to broken lives. Acknowledging the "shame and humiliation" felt by serious Catholics because of the scandal of abuse and episcopal malfeasance, Benedict asked that the Church offer that shame and humiliation "to the Lord with trust that this chastisement will contribute to the healing of the victims, the unification of the Church, and the renewal of her age-old commitment to the education and care of young people."

That afternoon, Benedict addressed the political and cultural leaders of Britain in historic Westminster Hall, the oldest part of the Palace of Westminster and, as he reminded his audience, the place where St. Thomas More was tried (having been abandoned by the British establishment, a point the pope discreetly omitted). Here, Benedict put a crucial question on the table: What are the moral foundations of democracy, and of the democratic commitment to civility, tolerance, and the rule of law? Can there in fact be democracy "if the moral principles underpinning the democratic process are themselves determined by nothing more solid than social consensus?" Would this not lead to a condition of "fragility" that could, in time, lead to democratic crack-up—and either the imposition of a dictatorship of relativism, or surrender to another cultural project (such as that of militant Islam) with a very different view of the political future?

The pope continued with a plea for reason, and reason's role in understanding the irreducible moral dimension of public policy. While warning against "distortions of religion [that] arise when insufficient attention is given to the purifying and structuring role of reason within religion," the pope nonetheless proposed that people of faith can, with the aid of revealed truth, "help purify and shed light upon the application of reason to the discovery of objective moral principles" for the guidance of public policy. Faith and reason, he concluded, "need one another and should not be afraid to enter into a profound and ongoing dialogue, for the good of our civilization."

It was likely an accident but it was not without poignancy that, on the sixty-fifth anniversary of the death of Dietrich Bonhoeffer, Benedict should have reminded those praying in Hyde Park the night before Newman's beatification about the opposite of cheap grace: Newman's life taught us, the pope said, "that passion for truth, intellectual honesty, and genuine conversion are costly." Moreover, Benedict noted, "Newman reminds us that . . . we are created to know the truth, to find in that truth our ultimate freedom and the fulfillment of our human aspirations." It was a pointed, if tacit, re-buke to a political culture that, as Tony Blair put it in his memoirs, places an "emphasis, bordering on the religious," on the notion that "what counts [is] what works."

S hortly before the pope arrived in Scotland, the choice be-fore the Catholic Church in Britain was made unmistak-ably clear in a single story in the *Scotsman*, in which Bishop Joseph Devine of Motherwell and Bishop Philip Tartaglia of Paisley were interviewed. The impact of the papal visit wouldn't be "great," Bishop Devine said, because "we have known Benedict XVI for a very long time, or at least the clergy have . . . [so] I don't anticipate that [the visit] will have a long, lasting effect. No, I don't think so." Bishop Tartaglia, a man of a different generation and a differ-ent ecclesial sensibility, had a strikingly different prognosis: "Let me tell you that with this pope there will be no lack of insightful, encouraging, and challenging reflections on the Christian message and the condition of humanity today, and I think this will help Catholics and other Christians and people of faith and goodwill understand better the period of history they are living in, in which faith is not the default position of society, when Parliament enacts laws which stand Christian conviction on its head, when fundamental teaching on the sanctity of human life and the nature of marriage are not just rejected but actually considered subversive in our liberal society."

Thus the choice that the remarkable success of Benedict XVI's pilgrimage to the U.K. has put before British Catholics: institutional maintenance amidst downsizing, with a modest place in the public square being accepted as recompense for not being too pushy on Those Issues; and an evangelically assertive Catholicism, unapologetically and persuasively offering friendship with Jesus Christ and proclaiming the truths that can be known by reason as essential to sustaining free and virtuous societies capable of defending their democratic commitments. How that choice would come down in the decades after Benedict's visit would, clearly, be shaped by another set of choices: the choices of bishops that Benedict and his successors make for the United Kingdom.

As one lucid observer put it in the aftermath of the papal visit, "The British hierarchy didn't do much wrong on this visit, but they did contain their enthusiasm until the secular press declared it a success, and then they joined in." Five days after Benedict left, Archbishop Nichols of Westminster reflected on the visit in an article in *L'Osservatore Romano* and suggested that the thread uniting the pope's various talks in the U.K. was that "faith in God plays an important role in modern pluralist societies." That role should be played, the archbishop continued, with sensitivity, openness, and courtesy. All of this, he concluded, amounted to a "new agenda" for the Church in Great Britain.

Unobjectionable if not inspired, one might say. But Archbishop Nichols's summary did seem to underplay several of the points that Benedict stressed in Britain. The first was the imperative of seeking holiness in truth, and speaking the truth in love. Then, and only then, will the Church's place at the table of public conversation mean anything. Then there was the pope's pointed comment in a press conference on his plane en route to Britain: "[A] Church that seeks above all to be attractive is already on the wrong path." In other words: a Church that takes the edge off the truth it bears will be evangelically unattractive and publicly useless.

And there was that business about cheap grace and costly grace, at the nocturnal vigil before Newman's beatification: Will the "new agenda" of the British hierarchy include a call to bear the costs of a "passion for truth, intellectual honesty and genuine conversion"?

That, one might suggest, is the only appropriate strategy in addressing the spiritual hollowness of the Britain the Tony Blair left behind: a Britain whose early twenty-first-century cultural crisis seemed less well understood by a former prime minister than by the German pope who thanked the people of the U.K. for winning the Battle of Britain.

Pope Benedict XVI
and the Future of the West

A s Pope Benedict XVI was being assailed by the British opinion
establishment prior to his September 2010 visit to the United
Kingdom, the suggestion that he might in fact have something important to say about twenty-first-century public life would likely
have struck some as counterintuitive, implausible, even absurd:
Why would an octogenarian German theologian with little practical experience of political and economic life have anything interesting or important to say about the future of the West? Pope Benedict
XVI's Westminster Hall address on September 17, 2010, ought to
have put paid to at least some of that cynicism. For as many Britons
conceded after the 2010 papal visit, the elderly German theologian
had indeed given the U.K., and the rest of the West, a lot to think
about in his reflections on the relationship between the health of a
culture and the health of the democratic institutions that culture
must sustain.

And that, in turn, should focus attention on the font of wisdom from which Benedict drew in analyzing the current cultural situation of the Western democracies: the social doctrine of
the Catholic Church as it has developed from Pope Leo XIII—
the last pope of the nineteenth century and the first pope of the
twentieth—through John Paul II, the last pope of the twentieth century and the first pope of the twenty-first. Benedict has, of course,
made his own distinctive contributions to this evolving body of
thought; but before exploring those themes, a brief sketch of the Catholicism that has emerged during the period following Leo XIII, and
that is struggling to come to full maturity today, will help orient the

distinctively Benedictine reflections on society, culture, politics, and economics that follow.

J ohn Paul II and Benedict XVI represent the full flowering of a renaissance in Catholic thought that began with Leo XIII, who, after his election to the papacy in 1878, sought an engagement with modern intellectual and cultural life through distinctively Catholic methods. The Leonine Catholic renaissance flourished in the mid-twentieth century in philosophical, theological, liturgical, historical, and biblical studies. Those studies in turn paved the intellectual way to the Second Vatican Council, and shaped its deliberations between 1962 and 1965. The Second Vatican Council was unique, however, in that it did not provide keys for its proper interpretation: it wrote no creeds, legislated no canons, defined no doctrines, condemned no heresies—all the things other ecumenical councils had done. Absent such keys, the nature and terms of Vatican II's achievement were sharply, even bitterly, contested in the years immediately following the Council's conclusion. As a result, the evangelical energy that Blessed John XXIII had intended his Council to ignite—the determination to bring the Gospel of God's passionate love for the world *to* the world through a dialogue with the world—was dissipated.

Then came the Wojtyła-Ratzinger years. Since October 16, 1978, the Second Ecumenical Council of the Vatican has been given an authoritative interpretation by two popes who, as young men, had both been influential participants at Vatican II. And with that authoritative interpretation, which synthesized the achievements of Catholic intellectual life since the Leonine revival of the late nineteenth century, a decisive moment was reached in the history of the Catholic Church: the catechetical-devotional Catholicism of the Counter-Reformation began to be replaced by what may be called Evangelical Catholicism.

Evangelical Catholicism takes its ecclesiology, its idea of the Church, from *Lumen Gentium* [Light of the Nations], Vatican II's Dogmatic Constitution on the Church, as interpreted by John Paul II's 1991 encyclical *Redemptoris Missio* [The Mission of the Redeemer]. In this ecclesiology, the Church does not so much *have* a mission (as if "mission" were one among a dozen other things the Church does); the Church *is* a mission. Everything the Church does, the Church does to propose Jesus Christ as the answer to the question that is every human life. Everything the Church does, the Church does in order to offer friendship with Jesus Christ as the true means of satisfying the deepest longings of the human heart. Evangelical Catholicism takes to heart John Paul II's injunction in the 2001 apostolic letter *Novo Millennio Ineunte* [Entering the New Millennium]: it sets sail from the stagnant shallows of institutional maintenance into the deep waters of postmodernity, preaching the Paschal Mystery as the central truth of the human condition, while building communities of integrity, decency, solidarity, and compassion—Eucharistic communities of supernatural charity capable of nurturing genuine human flourishing.

Evangelical Catholicism is thus both culture-forming and counter-cultural. It is culture-forming, in that it takes the formation, nurturance, and maturation of a distinctive culture—the Church—with utmost seriousness. And it does not look to the ambient public culture for suggestions as to how this distinctive ecclesial culture, this distinctive mode of life called "Christian," is to be structured and lived. Thus it is no accident, as the Marxists used to say, that the emergence of Evangelical Catholicism has been concurrent with the liberation of the Catholic Church from the Babylonian captivity of ecclesial establishment, with its evangelically unbecoming nexus between the power of the state (however that state might be organized politically) and the life of the Church. This liberation has been a fruit of Vatican II and its Declaration on Religious Freedom [*Dignitatis Humanae*]; it has been codified in ecclesiastical law by Canon 377, which bars governments from any direct role in the nomination of bishops. Evangelical Catholicism is, then, post-Constantinian Catholicism. It does not seek the favor of the state. Rather, it asks of the state, and if necessary it demands of the state, the free space in which to be itself: a community of Eucharistic worship, evangelical proclamation, and charity. And it does so in order to ask the state (and society, and culture, and economics) to consider the possibility of their redemption.

This last suggests at least one facet of Evangelical Catholicism's countercultural character. This side of the Kingdom of God, the Church will always be challenging the principalities and powers (be they political, social, economic, or cultural) to admit that the actions of states, economies, societies, and cultures do stand under the judgment of moral norms that do not emerge from within themselves. Rather, the moral norms applicable to constructing and sustaining states, economies, societies, and cultures, that foster the conditions for the possibility of genuine human flourishing are transcendent; they reflect the inalienable dignity and value of the human person—a dignity and value that is inherent, not conferred. Those moral norms stand in judgment on us; we do not construct them or tailor them to our own requirements.

At a moment in the cultural history of the West when utilitarianism is the default moral position in public life, Evangelical Catholicism insists that "Will it work?" is not the only question. "Is it right?" is the prior question, and the answer to that question, Pontius Pilate, the *New York Times*, and the *Guardian* notwithstanding, can be known by the arts of reason, properly deployed.

E vangelical Catholicism, in the line of development that runs from Leo XIII through Benedict XVI, thus takes a rather different stance toward public life than the Catholicism of Christendom (whose conception of Church-and-state—or, more broadly, Church-and-society—long outlasted the sixteenth

century fracturing of Christendom). Evangelical Catholicism de-
clines the embrace of state power as incompatible with the proclamation of the Gospel: the Gospel is its own warrant, and the power
of that warrant is blunted when coercive state power is put behind
it, however mildly. Evangelical Catholicism is also wary of a direct
role for the Church, as institution, in the affairs of the state. There
may be moments when a robustly evangelical Church must speak
truth to power, directly and through its ordained episcopal leadership, bringing the full weight of their unique form of authority to
bear on a matter in public dispute. But the normal mode of the
Church's engagement with public life will not be that of another
lobbying group. Rather, Evangelical Catholicism takes its lead from
Vatican II's Decree on the Laity [*Apostolicam Actuositatem*], and
from John Paul II's teaching in the encyclicals *Redemptoris Missio*
and *Centesimus Annus* and the postsynodal apostolic exhortation
Christifideles Laici: it seeks to form the men and women who will, in
turn, shape the culture that creates a politics capable of recognizing
the transcendent moral norms that should guide society's deliberations about the common good.

Within the Anglosphere, this facet of Evangelical Catholicism
will necessarily cause some re-examination of consciences and
political alignments. In the United States, it has already caused a
major, and in some cases wrenching, re-examination of the traditional Catholic affinity for the Democratic Party, as that party has
embraced what John Paul II called the "culture of death" in the
party's radical commitment to an unfettered abortion license. In
Great Britain, the emergence of Evangelical Catholicism will likely
cause a similar re-examination of traditional Catholic alignments
with Labour, although it is not clear, from the western shores of the
Atlantic at least, where, in practical terms, such a realignment might
eventually lead. But as the life issues and the challenge of lifestyle
libertinism continue to define the great fault lines in the domestic
politics of the West, Evangelical Catholicism—which follows John

Paul II (in *Evangelium Vitae*) and Benedict XVI (in *Caritas in Veritate*) in insisting that the life issues are basic social justice issues—will find itself, irrespective of voting patterns, in a profoundly countercultural position, much as the evangelical-Wesleyan opponents of the slave trade found themselves in a countercultural position in early nineteenth-century Britain.

The Evangelical Catholicism that has been struggling toward maturity in the pontificates of John Paul II and Benedict XVI is also a Catholicism with a distinctive public voice—or perhaps I should say, voices. Within the household of faith—inside the distinctive culture that is the Church—that voice is a Gospel voice, and the deepest warrants for the Church's defense of life, of religious freedom, and of the dignity of the human person are found in the Church's sacramental life, and in Scripture and Tradition as interpreted by the Church's authentic magisterium. In addressing the wider culture and society, and in the give-and-take of the democratic political process, the public voice shaped by the culture of Evangelical Catholicism is a voice that makes genuinely public arguments, deploying a grammar and vocabulary that those who are not of the household of faith can engage.

That voice, it should be added, is primarily the voice of truly converted disciples: lay men and women, bringing the universal moral truths learned within the household of faith to bear in their workplaces, their voluntary associations, their cultural activities, and their political lives. The voice of the pastors is not, and cannot be, the only voice of the Church in the public square. The pastors' voice ought to be heard when questions of first principles are at issue (as, to be sure, they are, and not infrequently these days). But when there are legitimate differences of prudential judgment on how the principles of the Church's social doctrine are to be driven into the hard soil of political reality, the principal voices in those debates should be lay voices. The pastors have graver matters to which they must attend.

W hat have been Benedict XVI's contributions to the emergence of Evangelical Catholicism and to its interface with the public life of the West?

A profound and compelling synthesis of Benedict XVI's contribution to the development of Evangelical Catholicism may be found in the second volume of his projected three-volume study, *Jesus of Nazareth*, which was published in 2011. In this middle panel of his Christological triptych, in which the pope analyzes the biblical texts that deal with Holy Week and Easter, the Evangelical Catholic project is laid out with scholarly insight and catechetical power. For Benedict's intent is nothing less than to bring his readers into a personal encounter with the world-transforming power of the Paschal Mystery through his reflections on the Passion narratives and Easter accounts: the axial moment of human history in which the human drama finds its climax in the suffering, death, and resurrection of the Son of God. Here, a lifetime of scholarship is sifted and distilled in service to the essential Christian *kerygma*: the proclamation of Jesus Christ, crucified and risen, as Lord. It is a hard heart indeed that does not read Benedict on Holy Week and Easter without sensing the power of God at work in history, bending history toward redemption.

As for the interface between this unapologetically Evangelical Catholicism and the principal questions of public life in the West today, the first, and perhaps most important, of Benedict XVI's contributions has been his challenge to the West to recover the full richness of its cultural patrimony. Here, as in so many other ways, Benedict XVI's magisterium is in dynamic continuity with that of his predecessor (which of course should be no surprise, as both men's thought emerges out of the great tradition of the Catholic Church). We remember John Paul II's insistence, during the 2003–04 debate over the preamble to the European Constitutional treaty, that the New Europe of an expanded twenty-five member

European Union ought to acknowledge Christianity as one of the sources of contemporary Europe's commitments to human rights, democracy, and the rule of law. Benedict XVI has continued to press this theme while sharpening it in his gentle, scholarly way. The civilization of the West, he regularly reminds us, is the product of the interaction of three great cultural forces: biblical religion, Greek rationality, and Roman law. Or, if you will, what we know as "the West" emerged from the mutually fruitful interaction of ancient Hebrew convictions about the God of the Bible (who comes into history as a liberator freeing humanity from the often bloody-minded whims and caprices of the pagan gods); the Greek conviction that there are truths embedded in the world and in us, truths that we can know by reason; and the Roman conviction that the rule of law is superior to the rule of brute coercion in public life.

Absent any of these three supports, the entire Western project in history begins to teeter, and may eventually collapse. Twentieth-century high-cultural postmodernism—with its principled epistemological skepticism and metaphysical nihilism ("there may be your truth and my truth, but there is no such thing as *the* Truth")—followed readily from the abandonment of the God of the Bible in the name of human liberation: a nineteenth-century project Henri de Lubac analyzed in great depth in the 1944 study, *The Drama of Atheistic Humanism*. So with the God of the Bible gone, the foundation stone of the Western civilizational project labeled "Greek rationality" began to crumble, the first signs of decay being the irrationalism that shattered European political life in the two great mid-century wars. In the twenty-first century, the situation is perhaps even more perilous: for absent both biblical religion and the arts of reason (to which postmodernist skepticism and nihilism can hardly be said to contribute), the foundation stone of Western civilization marked "law" has begun to crack and may crumble under the pressure of political correctness (a lame substitute for moral reason), such that mere coercion will be the order of the day in democratic lawmaking.

This unhappy prospect is the situation often described by Benedict XVI as the "dictatorship of relativism": absent agreed moral references points that can be rationally known, defended, and deployed in public life, coercive state power is deployed to impose the canon of moral relativism—in the definition of marriage, in the resolution of debates over the life issues, in the legal understanding of religious freedom—on entire societies. When couples are declared incompetent to be foster parents because their Christian convictions compel them to teach the truth about men and women and the ethics of human love, the dictatorship of relativism is at work. When doctors are threatened with the loss of professional accreditation because they will not perform procedures that are immoral, or because they will not facilitate behaviors that endanger both health and morals, the dictatorship of relativism is at work. When the state imposes a definition of "marriage" that is incoherent in itself and that has no standing in the history of the West—or, even worse, when the state requires ministers of religion to cooperate in confecting such unions—the dictatorship of relativism is at work. In all these cases, democracy is threatened, because a false idea of freedom-as-willfulness is being imposed by coercive state power and the virtues that make democratic self-governance possible are being attenuated.

The Evangelical Catholicism of Vatican II, John Paul II, and Benedict XVI thus brings a thicker idea of democracy to bear in public life than the thin, indeed anorexic, concept of procedural democracy that dominates political science departments in the universities of the West. Thin democracy is democracy unmoored from its historic moral-cultural foundations in biblical religion, Greek rationality, and Roman notions of law. The democracy that can lead to genuine human flourishing in the twenty-first century—the democracy that can defend the West against other civilizational projects with very different views of what constitutes "human flourishing"—is a democracy that has re-established the linkage between the forms of democratic governance and the cultural foundations of democratic civilization: a democracy that understands that it takes a certain kind of people, possessed of certain virtues, to make the adventure of democratic self-governance work.

This brings us to another of Benedict XVI's signature challenges to those who care about the future of the West: his distinctive understanding of how the Church might help the West meet the challenge of jihadist Islam, a challenge that was by no means resolved by the death of Osama bin Laden and that reflects a deep conflict within Islam itself about Islam's relationship to modernity. In Benedict's view, the Church will help facilitate a useful conversation between Islam and the West, and thus help shift the correlation of forces within Islam away from the jihadist radicals, not by being acquiescent and "understanding," but by posing challenges—politely, to be sure, but challenges nonetheless.

The pope laid out these challenges in his 2006 Regensburg Lecture—an event that may take the gold medal for comprehensive media incomprehension (which would be no small accomplishment). Rather than the "gaffe" that it was immediately assumed to be, the Regensburg Lecture, and the Holy Father's subsequent exegesis of it in his Christmas 2006 address to the Roman Curia, correctly identified the two challenges facing Islam in the twenty-first century, within its own house and in its interaction with those who are "other." The first challenge is to understand religious freedom (which necessarily includes the right to convert to another faith) as a universal human right that can be known by reason and thus lays moral obligations on everyone. The second challenge for Islam is to find, within its own intellectual and spiritual resources, Islamic warrants for a clear distinction, in theory and in practice, between religious and political authority in a twenty-first-century state.

Benedict XVI also suggested that the Catholic Church might be of some assistance to genuine Islamic reformers interested in advancing these developments of Islamic self-understanding. Why? Because the Church itself had taken almost two centuries to find a Catholic understanding of religious freedom and political modernity that did not represent a rupture with, but a development of, classic Catholic understandings of the act of faith and the nature of political society. This process did not involve a wholesale, uncritical embrace of Enlightenment thought. Rather, it involved the recovery of classic Catholic notions of the distinction between sacerdotal and imperial authority, and the development of those ideas in light of the emergence of the political institutions created by the Enlightenment.

Retrieval and renewal, Benedict XVI proposed, was the way ancient religious traditions engaged political modernity without losing their souls. It remains to be seen whether the pope's offer to reframe the Catholic-Islamic dialogue along these lines is taken up by Islamic scholars, legal authorities, and religious leaders. But an offer like Benedict's does seem more congruent with the demands of both faith and reason than a supine acquiescence, in the name of "toleration," to the agenda of those who would impose on Western societies the social mores and cultural standards of seventh-century Arabia.

Two other themes have been prominent in Benedict XVI's commentary on the contemporary challenges facing the civilization of the West. The first is his distinctive papal environmentalism. While there is a sense in which Benedict is the first "green pope," in that concern for environmental quality is a regular feature of his public commentary, the full meaning of that papal environmentalism is often missed by the global media. For as the pope insisted in the 2009 encyclical *Caritas in Veritate*, a truly humanistic environmentalism does not limit its concerns to clean air, water, and soil, nor does it deny to men and women the dominion over the natural world that is the gift of the Creator. Rather, a truly humane environmentalism will pay equal, if not greater, attention to what the pope called "human ecology": the moral-cultural environment of civilization, which, like rivers and seas, belts of black earth and the jet stream, can also be poisoned. And among the toxic wastes threatening the human environment of the West, the pope relentlessly points out, are the practices of abortion and euthanasia, which a poisoned moral-cultural environment imagines to be technological "solutions" to situations in which the human protagonists have been reduced to the dehumanized status of problems-to-be-solved. The decline of the family in the West is another facet of the ecological crisis of the twenty-first century, the pope has taught, as is the demographic winter that Europe has brought upon itself.

Benedict's public commentary has also embraced economic questions where, like John Paul II, the pope takes an antilibertarian or anti-Benthamite view by insisting that the free economy, like democratic politics, is not a machine that can run by itself. The free economy, like the democratic polity, is bound by moral norms that transcend it. Those norms emerge from a careful and rational reflection on the dignity of the human person as an economic actor who is the subject, not merely the object, of economic processes.

Twenty-first-century economic life should thus value the entrepreneurial creativity built into humanity by God the Creator, and revalue the fruits of economic activity as what we might call "profit-plus." Thus, in Benedict's vision, business, making its own distinct contribution to the common good, will sustain private- and independent-sector philanthropies that educate and empower the poor, that care for those who are unable to care for themselves, and that give expression to a vibrant culture of life in a society of solidarity. (Implicit in this view, of course, is the judgment that the social-welfare responsibilities of society are not exhausted by, and indeed ought not be dominated by, the state—a

judgment sustained by the bedrock Catholic social-ethical principle of subsidiarity.)

W hat chance does this Catholic challenge to the twenty-
first-century West have to be heard? It has been mounted
in an intellectually impressive way by two popes in whom the Second
Vatican Council, and indeed the entire Leonine reform, have come
to full flower. If it has the wit and will to seize them, the Church
has unprecedented opportunities to get its message out, through
the new media that have broken the chokehold of the mainstream
global press (much to the fury of Miss Polly Toynbee, Ms. Maureen Dowd, and other cultured despisers of orthodox Christianity).
So both message and medium would seem to be properly aligned
for Evangelical Catholicism to advance the "New Evangelization"
of which John Paul II and Benedict XVI have spoken so often. Yet
there are two major obstacles to the flourishing of the New Evangelization that should be identified.

One is the phenomenon that the international constitutional
legal scholar Joseph Weiler (himself an Orthodox Jew) dubbed
"Christophobia" during the 2003–04 debates over the European
Constitutional Treaty. It was on raw and ugly display in the months
preceding Benedict XVI's visit to the United Kingdom in September 2010, and while the pope's self-evident humanity and decency—as well as the power of his message—drew a lot of the poison
out of the air, the broader problem of Christophobia remains. This
irrational and, let it be said frankly, deeply bigoted refusal to concede that Christian moral ideas have any place in the public square
(even when "translated" into genuinely public language) is evident
throughout the Western civilizational orbit. It is evident in the attacks on Christian orthodoxy and classic Christian morality that are
now a regular feature of the European Parliament and other E.U.
bodies. It is evident when the Star Chambers known in Canada as
"human rights commissions" or "human rights tribunals" lay severe
monetary penalties on evangelical Protestant pastors who dare teach

publicly the biblical understanding of marriage. The measure of its potency and its potential for wickedness may be taken from the remark of a senior member of the Catholic hierarchy in the United States, a man of deep learning, who has said privately that, "I will die in my bed; my successor will die in prison; and his successor will die a martyr." The formulation was deliberately provocative, but it does not take an especially lurid political imagination to construct scenarios in which precisely such a history unfolds. The pressures from the dictatorship of relativism—which is one political expression on Christophobia—could become that severe. And in those circumstances, the public impact of the New Evangelization will be severely impeded, even halted, because Evangelical Catholicism will have become an underground religion.

This fate is not inevitable, although its possibility may illustrate what Hans Urs von Balthasar called (as only German-language theologians can name things) the "theological law of proportionate polarization": the more God's presence is felt within history, the more opposition that presence elicits; the more vigorously the Gospel is preached, the more those forces determined to deny the divine love will intensify their efforts. This is the rhythm of salvation history: it is evident in the intensifying opposition to Jesus as he goes up to Jerusalem for the last time; it is described in spectacular world-historical imagery in the Book of Revelation. Yet we know, in faith, the way the story will end. And so we can live within history with an eye to the vindication of God's purposes in the end of history and the coming of the Kingdom in its plenitude.

And because of that, we can, here and now, take heart from what Edmund Burke taught the Anglosphere two centuries ago: that the immediate triumph of evil here and now is possible only if good men do nothing. Burke's dictum has an unintended but unmistakable implication for the Catholic Church of the twenty-first century in the West. For if Christophobia is one major obstacle to the flourishing of a New Evangelization that will be a culture-healing presence in all of society, so is ecclesiastical pusillanimity. And by that term I mean a timid response to the challenges of Christophobia and the dictatorship of relativism, married to a less-than-fervid embrace of the New Evangelization, both born of an internalized sense of marginality to the tides of history as they are flowing in the twenty-first century. This is the timidity from which Blessed John Paul II and Pope Benedict XVI have been calling the Church throughout the Western world. This is the timidity to which the antidote is the courage to be Catholic: vibrantly, compellingly, evangelically Catholic, not out of some cranky wish to re-create the old regimes (however we imagine them), but out of an apostolic passion to bring the Gospel to the world—and in so doing, to create conditions for the possibility of free and virtuous societies.

Thus the New Evangelization requires radically converted disciples, and it requires bold leaders who call the timid to the fullness of conversion. It requires disciples and leaders who are unfailingly pro-life, and who are capable of rebutting the spurious charge that to be pro-life is to be anti-woman. It requires disciples and leaders who are prepared to defend religious freedom in full, and who refuse to concede that religious freedom can be whittled down to freedom of worship. It requires disciples and leaders who are pro-family and pro-marriage, and who are prepared to defend their advocacy against the charge that they are "homophobic." It requires disciples and leaders prepared to speak truth to power, especially when coercive state power is deployed to impose the agenda of the dictatorship of relativism.

And to form these disciples and leaders, the demands of the New Evangelization require the Church throughout the Anglosphere to learn the lesson that Blessed John Henry Newman tried to teach more than a century ago, and that the sad fate of liberal Protestantism and the disintegration of the Anglican Communion illustrate in our time: that "religion as mere sentiment . . . is a dream and a mockery." Religion as "mere sentiment" is our search for God, which inevitably ends up in the sandbox of our own self-absorption, where anything may be countenanced as an expression of my "authenticity." Biblical religion, by contrast, is about God's search for us, and our learning to take the same path through history that God is taking: a journey guided, Catholics affirm, by the doctrines of the Church and the *regula fidei*, the rule of life that is the sacramental system. The New Evangelization requires teachers who teach that, pastors who support that, and disciples who believe that—and believe it, not as a personal lifestyle option, but as the revealed truth of the world, which has been given into our completely unworthy and often trembling hands.

T he late French journalist André Frossard was a convert to Catholicism from the fashionable atheism of his class, an atheism that was once a Parisian intellectual fad but that has now taken on a much harder, Christophobic edge across the twenty-first-century Western world. When Frossard saw John Paul II at the Mass marking the beginning of the pope's public ministry on October 22, 1978, he wired back to his Paris newspaper, "This is not a pope from Poland; this is a pope from Galilee." It was a brilliant metaphor, and it still speaks to us today.

For that is where the Leonine revival that has reached its fulfillment in John Paul II and Benedict XVI, heirs and authentic interpreters of the Second Vatican Council, is inviting us: to Galilee, and then beyond. We are being invited to meet the Risen Lord in the Scripture, the sacraments, and prayer, and to make friendship with him the center of our lives. We are being invited to think of ourselves as evangelists, and indeed to measure the truth of our lives by the way in which we give expression to the human decency and solidarity that flows from friendship with Christ the Lord. We are being invited, through the New Evangelization, to make our distinctive, Catholic contribution to the renewal, and perhaps the saving, of the civilization of the West, which is beset from within by the corrosive forces of the dictatorship of relativism and from without by the passions of jihadist Islam.

Through the witness of John Paul II and Benedict XVI, and by the teaching of the Second Vatican Council, we are being invited to have the courage to be Catholic. Whether we accept that invitation or not, God's purposes will be vindicated. But a lot of what happens to the West over the balance of this century will depend on whether a critical mass of men and women embrace the Gospel in full, and have the courage to take the Gospel beyond Galilee and out to the nations.

Part II

Men of Letters

St. Evelyn Waugh

More than one novelist has had an intricate, even prickly, personality. In Evelyn Waugh, however, nature and grace contrived to fashion an exceptionally complex character; understanding him in full would require the combined skills of an archaeologist, a psychiatrist, and an old-school spiritual director. It would be a mistake, though, to miss the subtleties of Waugh's art or the depth of his novelist's vision by focusing exclusively on his personal quirks and eccentricities, amusing or appalling as they may be.

Who was Evelyn Arthur St. John Waugh, born in the Hampstead area of London in 1903, the younger son of a literary critic and publisher? He was, touching but the surface of his art, a brilliant satirist—one of the funniest writers of the twentieth century. The humor was combined, however, with a literary craftsmanship unsurpassed among his contemporaries (although Waugh himself would make an exception here in favor of P. G. Wodehouse). To take but one comparison: Tom Wolfe's *Bonfire of the Vanities* is a splendid dissection of late-twentieth-century American manias: race, sex, money, status; but for all its wit and insight, the scalpel of Wolfe's wit in *Bonfire* cuts nowhere near the heart of American materialism's particular darkness so cleanly or deeply as did Waugh in his little novella, *The Loved One*. Nor does it involve any diminution of Wolfe's accomplishments to suggest that the difference between these two wildly funny authors is rather easily stated: Wolfe is a brilliant writer, but Waugh was a genius, and (at least at his work) a disciplined genius to boot. Indeed, Waugh was a master craftsman of English prose, a man incapable of writing a dull sentence—arguably the finest craftsman in the Anglosphere since Henry James.

Waugh was also a world-class eccentric, and it is to this dimension of his personality that many of his biographers have been drawn. The fascination is understandable—Waugh's personality encompassed an astonishing range of idiosyncracies. But if he was an eccentric, he was not a crank. Yes, Evelyn Waugh reveled in being politically incorrect (and in the most outrageous ways). Yes, he could be terribly self-centered and, at times, selfishly cruel. Yes, he lived a considerable part of his adult life in auto-constructed physical and psychological enclaves intended to keep the world at bay—including, sometimes, the world inhabited by his six children. Yes, he was a "displaced person" by nature, as one of his biographers, Martin Stannard, put it.

To file Waugh away under the category "gifted eccentric," however, would be a bad mistake; no one imagines that the literary gifts of a Herman Melville or a Henry James can best be understood through the oddities of their personalities. Or to take another writer, one whom Waugh admired: no serious student of Flannery O'Connor's distinctive fiction would suggest that we get to the essence of her inner life and its impact on her novels and short stories by pondering her fondness for guinea fowl. By the same token, it doesn't make much sense to think that we can get to the core of Evelyn Waugh by contemplating his affectation of a Victorian ear-trumpet in his later years—or by remembering that he once asked a briefing officer during World War II whether it was true that "in the Romanian Army no one beneath the rank of Major is permitted to use lipstick."

A great comic writer? Yes. An eccentric whose personal crotchets gave his fiction and his journalism a distinct tang? To be sure. Beneath and beyond all this, however, Evelyn Waugh, as he understood himself, was a Christian pilgrim—a Catholic with an intensely sacramental apprehension of reality, a craftsman with a profound belief that writing was his vocation, not simply his career. Waugh himself admitted that he was a very bad Christian, a man to whom neither prayer nor charity came easily; as he was famously reported to have said to a society matron who had complained about his boorish manners, "Madame, were it not for the Faith, I should scarcely be human." At the same time, few novelists have explored with more profundity than Evelyn Waugh the mysterious workings of grace in the humanizing of a disparate cast of characters.

In *The Life of Evelyn Waugh: A Critical Biography*, a magisterial work that sets the gold standard for Waugh criticism, Douglas Lane Patey demonstrates that an earlier conception of the "essential Waugh" was mistaken: his soul was not formed (or, more accurately, deformed) in the Oxford of the bright young things that Waugh memorialized as "Arcadia" in Part One of *Brideshead Revisited*. To be sure, this early Waugh, the aesthete turned chronicler/satirist of the flapper era, leaped out of literary and social obscurity by limning his generation's follies in *Decline and Fall* and *Vile Bodies*. But these early works were in fact but the literary—and—more important, moral—prologue to Waugh's identity as a mature novelist: the prologue to Waugh as our most acute literary pathologist of the crisis of modernity.

To recognize that Waugh's literary genius was driven by a profound moral (and religious) insight into modernity and its discontents does not require, and in fact probably precludes, treating him with the well-intentioned *pietas* of his first biographer, his friend Christopher Sykes. For Waugh was many other things, including a shameless social climber, particularly in his early years. But the traumatic experience of being cuckolded and then divorced by his first wife, Evelyn Gardner, right on the cusp of his early fame, led Waugh, not into terminal cynicism, but to the conviction that (as biographer Stannard put it) "decline and fall were no longer the subject for jokes."

At first, Waugh experienced the disaster of his divorce in deeply personal terms: as he wrote Harold Acton, "I did not know it was possible to be so miserable [and] live. . . ." But his betrayal by "She-Evelyn" eventually crystallized in Waugh a broader and more literarily fruitful, if no less dramatic, vision: about his times, and about himself.

As for the times, by 1930 Waugh had come to believe that "civilization, and by this I do not mean talking cinemas and tinned food, nor even surgery and hygienic houses, but the whole moral and artistic organization of Europe—has not in itself the power of survival. It came into being through Christianity, and without it has no significance or power to command allegiance. . . . It is no longer possible, as it was in the time of Gibbon, to accept the benefits of civilization and at the same time deny the supernatural basis on which is rests. . . . Christianity . . . is in greater need of combative strength than it has been in centuries."

As for himself, Waugh chose a place in what he regarded as the front trench of the cultural battle line: rejecting both the comfortable agnosticism of his literary and social friends and the vestigial Anglicanism of his parents, he entered the Catholic Church on September 29, 1930, under the spiritual direction of the legendary English Jesuit Martin D'Arcy. As Father D'Arcy himself would note, Waugh's was a singular conversion:

Few [converts] can have been so matter of fact as Evelyn Waugh. As he said himself, "On firm intellectual conviction but with little emotion I was admitted to the Church." All converts have to listen while the teaching of the Church is explained to them—first to make sure that they do in fact know the essentials of the faith and secondly to save future misunderstandings. . . .

Another writer came to me at the same time . . . and tested what was being told him by how far it corresponded with his experience. With such a criterion, it was no wonder that he did not persevere. Evelyn, on the other hand, never spoke of experience or feelings. He had come to learn and understand what he believed to be God's revelation, and this made talking to him an interesting discussion based primarily on reason.

Waugh was thus under no romantic illusions when he became a Catholic. Given his divorce, he believed he was abandoning any hope of future marriage (a belief that proved mistaken). He knew he would suffer the prejudices the English establishment subtly (and not so subtly) visits on papists. He was leaving the aesthetic pleasures of High Church Anglicanism, not for Chartres and the chant of Solesmes, but for the *declassé* rituals of (typically Irish) British Catholicism. But Waugh believed that he had found, not a piece of the truth, but the truth itself: "I reverence the Catholic Church because it is true, not because it is established or an institution." And that truth would become the centerpiece of his vision of the world—and thus the mainspring of his artistry—throughout the balance of his career. Dependence on a God who not only brought creation into being but sustained it with his loving care was not, Waugh once explained to the BBC, "a sort of added amenity to the Welfare State that you say, well, to all this, having made a good income, now I'll have a little icing on top, of religion." No, faith was "the essence of the whole thing."

Waugh is frequently accused of having practiced a snobbish Catholicism. And while it is true that he had no truck with what he regarded as the uncouthness of much of "liturgical reform," it would be unfair to suggest, as do some of his critics, that Waugh entered the Church because it was a more exclusive club than others that were available to him. Indeed, in his correspondence, Waugh reveals himself to be a man keenly aware of the Church as *ecclesia semper reformanda*; take, for example, a letter he wrote to Edith Sitwell on the occasion of her conversion:

> Should I as Godfather warn you of probable shocks in the human aspect of Catholicism? Not all priests are as clever and kind as Father D'Arcy and Father Caraman. (The incident in my book of going to

confession to a spy is a genuine experience.) But I am sure you know the world well enough to expect Catholic bores and prigs and crooks and cads. I always think to myself: "I know I am awful. But how much more awful I should be without the Faith." One of the joys of Catholic life is to recognize the little sparks of good everywhere, as well as the fire of the Saints.

The charge of "snob" is also leveled in light of Waugh's polemics against the "Age of the Common Man" (a notion he pillories throughout his World War II epic, the *Sword of Honor* trilogy). But while Waugh clearly preferred the company of some social classes to that of others, his mature concern was less social than moral: he feared (and not without good reason) that the "Age of the Common Man" meant an age of moral vulgarity, exemplified in the later novels by characters like Trimmer (the hairstylist turned bogus war hero) and Hooper: "blasé, half-educated, insensitive bores who converse only in slang," as Martin Stannard describes them.

These mass-produced moral cretins were not only offensive in personal intercourse (which, after all, could be avoided); they had created a public moral climate in which it was increasingly difficult for the West to recognize, much less resist, the tyranny-masquerading-as-humanism that lay just over the horizon of Western decadence: the tyranny that eventually murdered the Kanyis, a Jewish refugee couple, in Titoist Yugoslavia at the end of the war trilogy. Or as Waugh put it in 1946 in a preface to the American edition of his prize-winning biography of an Elizabethan Jesuit martyr, "We have come much closer to [Edmund] Campion" in the twentieth century. "In fragments and whispers we get news of other saints in the prison-camps of Eastern and Southern Europe, of cruelty and degradation more frightful than anything in Tudor England, and of the same, pure light shining in the darkness, uncomprehended. The hunted, trapped, murdered priest is amongst us again, and the voice of Campion comes to us across the centuries as though he were walking at our side." It was a voice to whose call Waugh believed the celebrated "Common Man" would prove largely insensate.

A lthough it would be wrong to regard him as a "Catholic novelist" (in the sense that Bernanos, for example, was a "Catholic novelist"), Waugh's Catholic imagination—a sacramental imagination, really, in which visible realities are the outward expressions of an interior and invisible grace—suffused much of his later work: and in far more subtle ways than Lord Marchmain's deathbed sign of the cross at the end of *Brideshead Revisited*.

One aspect of that imagination—its metaphysics, so to speak—was given voice by the protagonist of the war trilogy, Guy Crouchback, who, in the midst of a somewhat drunken revel, asks the regimental chaplain, "Do you agree that the supernatural Order is not something added on to the natural Order, like music or painting, to make everyday life more tolerable? It is everyday life. The supernatural is real; what we call 'real' is a mere shadow, a passing fancy. Don't you agree, Padre?" (Padre: "Up to a point.")

That conviction about the reality (and Presence) of the transcendent bore fruit, in turn, in the serenity and humility that Waugh never achieved in his own life, but which he sketched in his touching portrait of Guy Crouchback's father, Gervase, a kind of human guardian angel to his son throughout the trilogy. Knowing that he is close to death, and troubled by his son's preoccupations with politics, military affairs, and the future, Gervase defines the transcendent humanism of the Christian worldview in one brief sentence: "Quantitative judgments don't apply." And in pondering that homely phrase, Guy begins to discern the sources of his own spiritual aridity while kneeling at his father's funeral Mass:

> "I'm worried about you," his father had written in [a] letter . . . that Guy regarded as being in a special sense the conclusion of their rather reserved correspondence of more than thirty years. His father had been

worried, not by anything connected with his worldly progress, but by his evident apathy; he was worrying now perhaps in that mysterious transit camp through which he must pass on his way to rest and light.

Guy's prayers were directed to, rather than for, his father. For many years now the direction in the *Garden of the Soul*, "Put yourself in the presence of God," had for Guy come to mean a mere act of respect, like the signing of the Visitors' Book at an Embassy or Government House. He reported for duty saying to God: "I don't ask anything from you. I am here if you want me. I don't suppose I can be of any use, but if there is anything I can do, let me know," and left it at that.

"I don't ask anything from you." That was the deadly core of his apathy, his father had tried to tell him, and was now telling him. That emptiness had been with him for years. . . . Enthusiasm and activity were not enough. God required more than that. He had commanded all men to *ask*.

In the recesses of Guy's conscience there lay the belief that somewhere, somehow, something would be required of him; that he must be attentive to the summons when it came. . . . Even he must have his function in the divine plan. He did not expect a heroic destiny. Quantitative judgments did not apply. All that mattered was to recognize the chance when it was offered. . . .

The Evelyn Waugh of the flapper era and of that low decade, the 1930s, gave way to a maturity that seems no less dramatic when one considers Waugh's war service (recklessly brave and hopelessly undisciplined, in fairly equal proportions), his family life, his friendships, his nervous collapse under the influence of excessive ingestion of sleeping droughts (which eventually yielded the novelistic self-portrait, *The Ordeal of Gilbert Pinfold*), and Waugh's love-hate relationship with the United States. During this period, Waugh was not only a literary lion, but one of the most financially successful writers of the twentieth century. Moreover, he was also one of the most generous, handing over copyrights and stacks of royalty money to various charities, primarily religious ones. (Waugh's generosity was, to be sure, colored by his violent detestation of the income tax, and his determination to keep every penny possible out of the clutches of Her Majesty's Inland Revenue.)

Waugh's war experience not only provided him ample grist for his literary mill; it further hardened his contempt for modernity. Personal service in two of Britain's more ignominious wartime enterprises—the failed attack on the Vichy French garrison at Dakar and, far worse, the scuttle from Crete—led Waugh to conclude that "the English are a very base people. I did not know this, living as I do. Now I know them through and through, and they disgust me." That disgust was intensified by Waugh's service at the end of the war with Randolph Churchill's mission to the Tito partisans in Yugoslavia. Here, Waugh witnessed what he regarded as nothing less than the betrayal of yet another ally to the tender mercies of yet another totalitarianism. (And here, too, as critic Colin Walters once pointed out, Waugh abandoned his romantic desire to be a tough guy, a "hard man": When he got to Yugoslavia and met the genuine article in Josip Broz Tito and Fitzroy Maclean, the brigadier representing Churchill, "they shocked him with their toughness"—that is, with their utterly amoral ruthlessness.)

Then there was the United States. For all his incessant deprecation and mockery of America and Americans, Waugh was of two minds about the trans-Atlantic cousins. At one level, he was appalled by parts of the America he discovered in the course of a grand tour arranged by *Life* magazine. This was the America of materialistic, optimistic, Panglossian humanism that Waugh skewered in *The Loved One:* an America that was, on the one hand, afraid of life, and on the other, repelled by and in love with death. One suspects that Waugh could scarcely believe his own eyes when he read, in a tract entitled *Art Guide of Forest Lawn with Interpretation*, that "the cemeteries of the world cry out with man's utter hopelessness in the face of death. Their symbols are pagan and pessimistic.... Here, sorrow sees no ghostly monuments, but only life and hope." In truth, of course, here one saw that fact was more bizarre than the most lurid fiction. (As Waugh would wryly note in *Life*, "The Christian visitor [to Forest Lawn] might.... remark that by far the commonest feature of other graveyards is still the cross, a symbol in which previous generations have found more Life and Hope than in the most elaborately watered evergreen shrub.") This was the America that was the apotheosis (so to speak) of modernity: modernity raised up to bogus deity, and thus reduced, *ad absurdum*, to banal farce.

Oddly enough, though, it was from America that Waugh foresaw the launching of a spiritual renewal that might, just might, reverse the decline and fall of civilization. Waugh was, for example, the editor of the British edition of Thomas Merton's *The Seven Storey Mountain* (and reduced that overwritten book to a much tighter narrative); and during his travels in the U.S. in the late 1940s, he was deeply moved by the monastic renaissance then flourishing. "There is an ascetic tradition deep in the American heart which has sometimes taken odd and unlovable forms," Waugh wrote in his foreword to Merton (in an unmistakable swipe at Prohibition). "[But] here in the historic Rules of the Church lies its proper fulfillment...." Waugh was also touched and impressed by Dorothy Day, the co-founder of the radical Catholic Worker movement. After first twitting her by inviting her to lunch at what was then the best restaurant in New York, Waugh agreed to Dorothy's proposed compromise that they meet in a Greenwich Village trattoria, where a four-hour conversation ensured. Biographer Martin Stannard captured the unexpected symbiosis nicely: "Waugh encountered in Mrs. Day a personality as tough and autocratic as his own, yet infinitely less selfish—a disarming combination."

The result of his American tours was that Waugh became an early exponent of the notion that there might be a "Catholic moment" in American history and an "American moment" in the history of the Catholic Church. To be sure, Waugh's "Catholic moment" was not John Courtney Murray's (much less Richard John Neuhaus's). Waugh was essentially a monist in his vision of Church, culture, and state, and he would have regarded Murray's call for Catholic participation in the definition of a "public philosophy" capable of sustaining genuine pluralism as something of a low aim. On the other hand, Waugh was convinced that "Catholicism was not something alien and opposed to the American spirit but an essential part of it."

He knew that the Church had enemies in the United States, and that they were on the march, in however peculiar a form:

> The shops all over the country seek to substitute Santa Claus and his reindeer for the Christ-child. I witnessed, early in Lent, the arrival at a railway station of an "Easter Bunny," attended by a brass band and a posse of police. Just as the early Christians adopted the pagan festivals and consecrated them, so everywhere, but peculiarly in the United States, pagan commerce is seeking to adopt and desecrate the feasts of the Church. And wherever the matter is one for public authority, the State is "Neutral"—a euphemism for "unchristian."

Yet rather like Jacques Maritain, Waugh seemed to think that American "materialism" was not quite so ubiquitous, or so deeply ingrained, as the country's domestic cultured despisers or foreign critics believed. Forest Lawn was not the whole story—or even the heart of the matter. To those who looked to America, "half in hope and half in alarm"; to those whose understanding of American life was derived from "what they see in the cinema, what they read in popular magazines, what they hear from the loudest advertiser"; to those whose gratitude for the "enormous material benefits" they received from America was "tempered with distaste for what they believe is the spiritual poverty of the benefactor"; to all of these, Waugh had a simple, yet powerful, suggestion: come and have another look. For "it is only when one travels in America that one realizes that most Americans either share this distaste or are genuinely unaware of the kind of false impression which interested parties have conspired to spread."

Indeed, and in a manner that seems touchingly innocent in retrospect, Waugh concluded his essay on "The American Epoch in the Catholic Church" with a remarkable confession of confidence: "There is a purely American 'way of life' dreaded in Europe and Asia. And that, by the grace of God, is the 'way of life' that will prevail." And in the prevailing, American Catholicism would, by Providential design, assume "the historic destiny long borne by Europe" in defense of the faith.

W augh's extensive corpus lends itself to friendly arguments about which of his novels is the greatest. Two generations of critics have deplored both the piety and the lush, magenta pose of *Brideshead Revisited*; yet an argument can be made that *Brideshead* is singularly effective in tracing the divine twitch on the thread of human lives, calling us from lesser, easier, more self-centered loves to higher, truer, harder loves (as Douglas Patey demonstrates with great skill in his study of Waugh). Yet even those who defy critical convention and celebrate *Brideshead* will often be found stumping for the artistic superiority of *A Handful of Dust* as a cleaner, more sharply etched, more psychologically nuanced novel. Waugh's *Sword of Honor* trilogy (*Men at Arms*, *Officers and Gentlemen*, and *Unconditional Surrender*—known to Americans by the inferior title, *The End of the Battle*) arguably stands at the apex of his artistic achievement; these are, surely, the finest novels to come out of World War II, and their morally driven view of world politics, scorned in the 1960s, was proven remarkably prescient by the Revolution of 1989.

Evelyn Waugh's personal favorite among his works was none of these, however. It was *Helena*. When it was first published in 1950, critics paid it little regard, imagining it another exercise in Waugh's alleged snobbery, this time masquerading as piety. *Helena* has, at times, fallen out of print, a fate that has befallen none of Waugh's other novels. Yet he loved it; his daughter, Harriet, remembered that *Helena* was "the only one of his books that he ever cared to read aloud to the whole family." We can learn much about Waugh the artist (and the man) by learning why.

As for the artistry, Waugh was not modest in his claims for *Helena*. On the dust jacket of the first edition, he wrote, evidently without a blush, "Technically this is the most ambitious work of a writer who is devoted to the niceties of his trade." However that may be, there's something to be said for Waugh's pride in his craft here: the novel's spare narration, its crisp dialogue, its beguiling yet deceptive simplicity, the ongoing confrontation between myth and history that gives *Helena* its narrative line—all of this suggests an intriguing experiment, in the late 1940s, with a form of postmodern fiction.

At the same time, *Helena* was, and is, Waugh's most intentional statement about the truth of Christianity, and about vocation—the divine call to a specific work in life—as the heart of Christian discipleship. *Helena* is full of biting historical and theological commentary (including a hilarious put-down of Edward Gibbon's anti-Christian reading of Roman history). But, in the main, we are far, far away here from what one Waugh biographer calls the "jubilant malice" with which Waugh pilloried the California way of death in *The Loved One*. In *Helena*, Waugh explored, sparely but deeply, the question that shaped the last thirty-six years of his life—how does one become a saint?

In the course of his conversion to Catholicism, Evelyn Waugh came to the conviction that sanctity was not reserved for the sanctuary. *Every* Christian had to be a saint. And one of the hardest parts of that lifelong process of self-emptying and purification was to discover one's vocation: that unique, singular *something* that would, in accord with God's providential design, provide the means for sanctification. Helena's sense of vocation, and the Christian scandal of particularity to which her vocation bore witness, was what attracted Waugh to the fourth-century empress, whom the world remembers as the mother of the Emperor Constantine. Waugh later explained his choice in a letter to the poet John Betjeman, who confessed to being puzzled by the fact that, in the novel, Helena "doesn't seem like a saint":

> Saints are simply souls in heaven. Some people have been so sensationally holy in life that we know they went straight to heaven and so put them in the [liturgical] calendar. We all have to become saints before we get to heaven. That is what purgatory is for. And each individual has his own form of sanctity which he must achieve or perish. It is no good my saying, "I wish I were like Joan of Arc or St. John of the Cross." One can only be St. Evelyn Waugh (or St. Fill-in-the-blank)—after God knows what experiences in purgatory.

> I liked Helena's sanctity because it is in contrast to all that moderns think of as sanctity. She wasn't thrown to the lions, she wasn't a contemplative, she didn't look like an El Greco. She just discovered what it was God had chosen for her to do and did it. And she snubbed Aldous Huxley with his perennial fog, by going straight to the essential physical historical fact of the redemption.

W augh was never a proselytizer, and *Helena* is no more an exercise in conventional piety than Graham Greene's *The Power and the Glory*, whose hero is an alcoholic priest. But Waugh was a committed Christian apologist, and his apologetic skills are amply displayed in *Helena*. Thus *Helena* was not only addressed to those Christians who were trying to figure out the meaning of their own discipleship; it was also intended as a full-bore confrontation with the false humanism that, for Waugh, was embodied by well-meaning but profoundly wrong-headed naturalistic-humanistic critics of the modern world like Aldous Huxley and George Orwell.

More specifically, Waugh wanted to suggest that a familiar spiritual pathogen was lurking inside the hollowness of modern humanisms: gnosticism, the ancient yet durable heresy that denies the importance or meaningfulness of the world. So, to adopt a neologism from contemporary critics, *Helena* is, "metafictionally," an argument on behalf of Waugh's contention that modern humanistic fallacies are variants on the old, gnostic temptations exemplified by the Emperor Constantine and his world-historical hubris. And at the core of the gnostic temptation was, and is, the denial of the Christian doctrine of original sin—which is, in effect, a denial of some essential facts of life, including the facts of suffering and death. In *Helena*, the arrogantly ignorant Constantine puts it in precisely these terms to old Pope Sylvester, as the headstrong young conqueror heads off to his new capital on the Bosporus: "You can have your old Rome, Holy Father, with its Peter and Paul and its tunnels full of martyrs. We start with no unpleasant associations; in innocence, with Divine Wisdom and Peace."

And what was the answer to the gnostic fallacy, which produced in Constantine's time, as in ours, a kind of plastic, humanistic utopianism? For Helena, and for Waugh, it was what the aged empress went to find: the "remorseless fact of the lump of wood to which Christ was nailed in agony," as Stannard put it. This remorseless lump of wood reminds us of two very important facts: that we have been created, and that we have been redeemed. Helena believed, and Waugh agreed, that without that lump of wood, without the historical reality it represented, Christianity was just another Mediterranean mystery religion, a variant on the Mithras cult or some other gnostic confection. With it—with this tangible expression of the Incarnation and what theologians call the "hypostatic union" (the Son of God become man in Jesus of Nazareth)—a window was open to the supernatural, and the "real world" and its sufferings were put into proper perspective. For God had saved the world, not by fetching us out of our humanity (as the gnostics would have it), but by embracing our humanity in order to transform it through the mystery of the cross—the mystery of redemptive suffering, vindicated in the resurrection of Jesus from the dead.

Gnosticism, and the plastic utopianism that follows in its wake, is every bit as much a temptation in the twenty-first century as it was in Helena's day. Fish don't notice water; postmoderns don't notice gnosticism—even when it's celebrated in a bestseller like *The Da Vinci Code*. Audiences still find it amazing, even unbelievable, when told that, in the overwhelming majority of American universities today, very, very few members of the philosophy department will defend the claim that the reality we perceive discloses the truth of things. Somehow, the radical skepticism and relativism of the intellectual guilds hasn't penetrated down to the level of the people who sign the checks that allow the guild members to live in style. Or perhaps ordinary people—who think that they do, in fact, know some things—feel intimidated by the serpentine arguments of today's gnostic intellectuals.

Although set more than a millennium and a half ago, *Helena* is a bracing antidote to this contemporary gnosticism: this "bosh" and "rubbish," as Waugh's Helena would put it. From her childhood, Helena is determined to know whether things are real or unreal, true or false—including the claims of Christianity. For her, Christianity is not one idea in a world supermarket of religious ideas. Christianity is either the truth—the Son of God really became man, really died, and really was raised from the dead for the salvation of the world—or else it's more "bosh" and "rubbish." The true cross of Helena's search is not a magical talisman; it is the unavoidable physical *fact* that demonstrates the reality of what Christians propose, and about which others must decide.

W augh returned to these same themes of incarnation and vocation at the end of the *Sword of Honor* trilogy. In this case, the man who must discover his divinely mandated task in the world is the protagonist, Guy Crouchback, whose dreams of military glory have been overrun by events (and by the colossal incompetence of the military bureaucracy of the day, which Waugh lampoons as only he could do). But in the aptly named third volume, *Unconditional Surrender*, Guy discovers what his father's maxim—"Quantitative judgments don't apply"—means in his own life: he accepts paternal responsibility for the illegitimate child conceived by his philandering ex-wife, Virginia, and the embodiment of the Age of the Common Man, Trimmer, who has been turned into a fake war hero (and directed into Virginia's bed) by Ian Kilbannock, a sportswriter-peer turned military publicist. The decision is another form of the Christian scandal of particularity and historicity: "My dear Guy," Kilbannock's socialite wife, Kerstie, protests, "the world is full of unwanted children. Half the population of Europe are homeless—refugees and prisoners. What is one child more or less in all in all that misery?" Guy replies, "I can't do anything else about all those others. This is just one case where I can help. And only I, really. I was Virginia's last resort. So I couldn't do anything else. Don't you *see*?" "Of course, I don't," came the angry retort. "You're insane."

About which, Crouchback/Waugh can only reflect, "It was no good trying to explain. . . . Had someone said, 'All differences are theological differences?' He turned once more to his father's letter: 'Quantitative judgments don't apply.'"

O ne Waugh biographer suggests that the novelist's later years were marked by an agonizing spiritual quest for compassion and contrition. As for many of us, the contrition likely came easier than the compassion. But it is difficult to read *Helena* and

Brideshead and *Sword of Honor* without discerning in its author the capacity for a great compassion indeed—a compassion for the human struggle with the great questions that are raised in every life, in every age. Evelyn Waugh's comic energy once sprung from his pronounced power to hurt others, as a novel like *Vile Bodies* demonstrates. But in the mature Waugh, the farce has been transformed into comedy, and the comedy has become, for all the chiaroscuro shadings, divine.

Making Sense of H. L. Mencken

A s a son of the Baltimore middle class, I should like to be able to report that I first learned about the old hometown's most famous writer in a suitably dignified manner; that, say, my father lifted his head from his perusal of the *Sun* on the morning of January 30, 1956, and announced, with due solemnity, "Mencken is dead"—after which, the import of the occasion would have been explained to an earnest five-year old. Alas for the bourgeois propriety that the Bad Boy of Baltimore ironically cherished, my fascination with Henry Louis Mencken and my attempts to unravel the puzzle of his persona began not around the family board but in circumstances uncomfortably close to some that Mencken pilloried over the years.

If memory serves, it was 1971 and I was spending my summer months as a seminarian-intern at St. Mary Star of the Sea Church in South Baltimore—a rough part of town that Mencken disdained after covering it during his reportorial hazing in 1899. Even more improbably, the agent of my initiation into Menckeniana was Ab Logan, doctoral candidate in English (and thus in Menckenese, an "academic wizard") turned community organizer (and thus a practitioner of what Mencken derided as "uplift"), who sublet office space from the parish. It was Logan who left behind, in an office washroom, a copy of *The Vintage Mencken*, edited by Alistair Cooke. Here, I first read "The Baltimore of the Eighties," Mencken's jaunty, evocative re-creation of the world of my grandparents; here I got my first taste of Mencken, perhaps the best newspaper reporter ever, on "The Nomination of FDR"; and here I discovered "The Archangel Woodrow" (as in Thomas Woodrow Wilson), a book review at once brutal and yet wickedly, deliciously funny. Thus I became addicted to Mencken thanks to a professorially defrocked social worker. There are many ironies in the fire.

I suppose it is theoretically possible that my interest in Mencken might eventually have flagged. But as more than one Menckenian can attest, the master himself plotted to keep his fans hooked by a crafty gift to Baltimore's Enoch Pratt Library of papers and memoirs placed under a rolling series of time locks. As these materials have been opened, edited, and published, they have set loose a whole new series of Mencken controversies, decades after his death—just as Mencken, a preternaturally gifted publicist, knew they would.

The first explosion in this postmortem sequence came in 1989, when *The Diary of H. L. Mencken*, edited by Charles A. Fecher, was published by Knopf. Written between 1930 and 1948, the diary's end-of-the-day ruminations on persons and events gave considerable aid and comfort to those who had long believed Mencken a pathological personality. Mencken's own paper, the Baltimore *Sun*, took the lead in denouncing his alleged sundry bigotries, and editor Fecher himself stated, flatly, that "Mencken was an anti-Semite"—a charge carefully and, I believe, persuasively rebutted by Joseph Epstein.

Two years later, two other memoirs were released: *My Life as Author and Editor*, which Knopf published in 1993 in a volume superbly edited by Jonathan Yardley, and *Thirty-five Years of Newspaper Work*, issued by the Johns Hopkins University Press. *My Life as Author and Editor* covered Mencken's *Smart Set* period during the flapper era, the beginnings of his work with George Jean Nathan and Alfred Knopf (which later gave birth to the *American Mercury*), and his early relationships with Theodore Dreiser, Sherwood Anderson, Sinclair Lewis, F. Scott Fitzgerald, and Willa Cather. In addition to providing a brisk and amusing account of some of his adventures as a political reporter, *Thirty-five Years of Newspaper Work* also chronicles Mencken's efforts to turn the Baltimore *Sun* into the country's most influential paper—a notion that may seem bizarre now, but one that had real possibilities in the Roaring Twenties and the New Deal Thirties.

The release of Mencken's long-withheld papers also energized a bevy of biographers—Fred Hobson, Marion Elizabeth Rodgers, Terry Teachout—eager to use the newly available materials to craft a portrait of the Sage more comprehensive than the earlier efforts of William Manchester and Carl Bode. Cheek by jowl with all this attention, however, have come some of the sharpest attacks on Mencken's character ever written. The *Diary*, as noted, led to accusations of racism and anti-Semitism; but perhaps even more damning was Garry Wills's portrait of Mencken as a brutal Social Darwinist in Wills's revisionist reading of the Scopes "Monkey Trial," published in *Under God* in 1990.

All of which poses questions for this Menckenian. Why do I find Mencken's writing so irresistible, even as I become ever more aware of the deep shadows in his personality? Why was Mencken such a spectacularly gifted political reporter and such a singularly inept political prognosticator? How could a man with his legendary capacity for friendship, the scintillating conversationalist who was the center of any group before he was twenty-five, be so ugly toward some of his oldest associates in his private descriptions of them? Why have the attempts at serious philosophy in which Mencken put such stock—his *Treatise on the Gods* and his *Treatise on Right and Wrong*—been among his least enduring works, while his entertainments (notably *Happy Days, Newspaper Days*, and *Heathen Days*) seem certain to be read and enjoyed in the twenty-second century? Was Mencken, with his lusty disdain for both professional politicians—"the clowns in the ring"—and the "quacks" who ran the New Deal's social engineering shops, a precursor of what would come to be called neoconservatism? Or would his libertarian streak, his isolationism, and his eugenics have made him more at home on the farther reaches of the paleoconservative fringe?

Finally, and perhaps most intriguingly, what about Mencken and religion—which is to say, in the case of this lifelong agnostic, what about Mencken's general outlook on the human condition, his system of values, his basic character? Was Mencken, for all the felicity of his prose, really the Nietzschean monster drawn by Garry Wills? Or is Mencken another postmortem victim of the idiocies (including the moral idiocies) of political correctness?

A s Jonathan Yardley notes in his introduction to *My Life as Author and Editor*, Mencken's self-portrait as a man "born with an extraordinary amount of reserve energy" is altogether too modest a description for someone who lived a full, vigorous, and boozy social life while conducting a professional career—as newspaperman, newspaper executive, essayist, book reviewer, book author, magazine editor, philologist, correspondent, and camp counselor to two generations of American writers—"so busy and diverse as to stagger the imagination." And that fantastic energy, which seems to have derived in part from an insatiable fascination with the human comedy, spilled over time and again into Mencken's distinctive prose. Thus the irresistibility of Mencken is, to my mind, the easiest part of him to explain: Mencken is irresistible because he is compulsively readable, and he is compulsively readable because his writing is a lot of fun to read.

Indeed, it is not an exaggeration to suggest that, in his maturity, Mencken—a stylist as distinctively American as Mark Twain, his first literary hero—was virtually incapable of writing a dull sentence. Even when composing a rather straightforward historical narrative like *Thirty-five Years of Newspaper Work* (which he did not edit with the exquisite care that obviously went into crafting the *Days* books), Mencken nonetheless let fly with exhilarating regularity on almost every other page.

Thus, in 1920, the various aspirants to the presidency were "the candidates then preparing in their paddocks" for the race ahead.

A few months later, after her husband had grabbed the brass ring, reporters noticed a dramatic change in the self-presentation of Mrs. Warren G. Harding: "The last time most of us had seen her she looked like the president of the Christian Endeavor Society of Middletown, but now she almost suggested the Whore of Babylon." Hiram Johnson, who had loftily disdained an invitation to become Harding's running mate in 1920, thereby botching his best shot at the presidency, "became a sort of walking boil" in consequence. At the 1928 Republican Convention, Herbert Hoover, taking no chances, "had all the delegates he needed bought, paid for, and safe in his pens"; at the same Republicanfest, Mencken ran into Oswald Garrison Villard, editor of the *Nation*, who was "sweating his usual moral indignation." During the Scopes Trial, the Prohibitionists in Dayton, Tennessee, drank a corn whiskey "fermented in tubs set far back in the mountains, and all sorts of wild creatures, including squirrels, bats, and snakes, took nips of it, got drunk, and were drowned. The locals distilled the ensuing mess without removing the carcasses." At the 1936 convention of the Townsend old-age pensioners, Gerald L. K. Smith, formerly Huey Long's factotum in Louisiana, was much in evidence at the top of Townsend's "hierarchy of attendant wizards and visionaries." Compared to FDR and his "associated quacks," Alf Landon looked "like an honest horse-doctor beside Lydia Pinkham." In 1940, Mencken recalled, Wendell Willkie had been "put up to speak at the annual dinner of the American Newspaper Publishers' Association [and had] made a big hit with the assembled Barabasses"—perhaps by contrast with the insufferable "crooning" of FDR, Mencken's *bête noire*.

The multiple editions and supplements of *The American Language*, Mencken's pioneering philological investigation of the distinctiveness of spoken and written English in the United States, are similarly enlivened page after page by the vivacity of his prose. Take but one brief example: imagine the stultifying drivel to be found in such Modern Language Association convention papers as "Embodied Metaphor as a Cultural Construct: The Cultural Scene as Circle Metaphor in Jane Austen's *Emma*" (or, perhaps, "Redressing the Female Subject: Transvestite Saints' Lives and the Benedictine Reform"), and then savor the breezy yet historically precise way in which Mencken, opening *The American Language's* eight-hundred-page fourth edition, describes the beginnings, and the ultimate futility, of the British assault on the Americanization of English:

> The Jay Treaty of 1794 gave notice that there was still some life left in the British lion, and during the following years, the troubles of the Americans, both at home and abroad, mounted at so appalling a rate that their confidence and elation gradually oozed out of them. Simultaneously, their pretensions began to be attacked with pious vigor by patriotic Britishers, and in no field was the fervor of these brethren more marked than in those of literature and language. . . . [Yet] Americanisms are forcing their way into English all the time, and of late they have been entering at a truly dizzy pace, but they seldom get anything properly describable as a welcome, save from small sects of iconoclasts, and every now and then the general protest against them rises to a roar.

Mencken's prose is at its most dulcet in his *Days* books, written during the early 1940s under the urging of Harold Ross and Katherine White of the *New Yorker. Happy Days*, the memoir of HLM's boyhood in bourgeois German West Baltimore during the 1880s, begins with this fetching caveat emptor, which might with justice apply to the entire trilogy: "These casual and somewhat chaotic memoirs of days long past are not offered to the nobility and gentry as coldly objective history. They are, on the contrary, excessively subjective, and the record of an event is no doubt often bedizened and adulterated by my response to it. I have made a reasonably honest effort to stick to the cardinal facts, however disgraceful to either the quick or the dead, but no one is better aware than I am of the fallibility of human recollection. . . . As Huck Finn said of *Tom Sawyer*, there are no doubt some stretchers in this book, but mainly it is fact."

With Mencken, though, what you get is fact related through that inimitable prose, as when HLM is introducing us to his parents and their world:

> My early life was placid, secure, uneventful, and happy. I remember, of course, some griefs and alarms, but they were all trivial, and vanished quickly. There was never an instant in my childhood when I doubted my father's capacity to resolve any difficulty that menaced me, or to beat off any danger. He was always the center of his small world, and in my eyes a man of illimitable puissance and resourcefulness. If we needed anything he got it forthwith, and usually he threw in something that we didn't really need, but only wanted. I never heard of him being ill-treated by a wicked sweat shop owner, or underpaid, or pursued by rent-collectors, or exploited by the Interests, or badgered by the police. My mother, like any normal woman, formulated a large program of desirable improvements in him, and not infrequently labored it at the family hearth, but on the whole their marriage, which had been a love match, was a marked and durable success, and neither of them ever neglected for an instant their duties to their children. We were encapsulated in affection, and kept fat, saucy, and contented. . . . I was a larva of the comfortable and complacent bourgeoisie, though I was quite unaware of the fact until I was along in my teens, and had begun to read indignant books. To belong to that great order of mankind is vaguely discreditable today, but I still maintain my dues-paying membership in it, and continue to believe that it was and is authentically human, and therefore worthy of the attention of philosophers, at least to the extent that the Mayans, Hittites, Kallikuks, and so forth are worthy of it.

And so it continues for 313 singularly winsome pages of reminiscence, in which a small boy's life in the Golden Age of American cities is chronicled under such typically Menckenian headings as "The Caves of Learning," "Recollections of Academic Orgies," "Memorials of Gormandizing," "First Steps in Divinity," "In the Footsteps of Gutenberg," and "Recreations of a Reactionary."

The tempo changes from *andante* to *allegro con brio* in *Newspaper Days*, as the scene shifts from the row houses, alleys, and back yards of Union Square to the raucousness of the newsroom, and Mencken memorializes his adventures as police reporter, city hall reporter, and *Wunderkind* editor on the old Baltimore *Herald*. It was, Mencken believed, "the maddest, gladdest, damndest existence ever enjoyed by mortal youth. At a time when the respectable bourgeois youngsters of my generation were college freshmen, oppressed by simian sophomores and affronted with balderdash daily and hourly by chalky pedagogues, I was at large in a wicked seaport of half a million people, with a front row seat at every public show, as free of the night as of the day, and getting earfuls and eyefuls of instruction in a hundred giddy arcana, none of them taught in schools." The narrative of that experience, in which, as Mencken put it, he laid in "all the worldly wisdom of a police lieutenant, a bartender, a shyster lawyer, [and] a midwife," is one of the greatest invitations to journalism ever issued; it also includes, *en passant*, the social and political history of a major American city at the turn of the century, including an account of the Great Baltimore Fire of 1904, that is as uncannily accurate as it is amusing.

But it is when Mencken is "writing at the top of his lungs," as the editors of *Thirty-five Years of Newspaper Work* put it, that he is most, well, Menckenian. Our age fancies that it invented the newspaper op-ed page and the celebrity columnizer, but for more than forty years, Mencken was a columnist in the *Sun* and elsewhere, and some of his most irresistible prose is found in these gems of daily and weekly journalism.

Thus Mencken on "Gamalielese," the dotty language of Warren G. Harding's Inaugural Address:

> On the question of the logical content of Dr. Harding's harangue of last Friday, I do not presume to have views. . . . But when it comes to the style of the great man's discourse, I can speak with . . . somewhat more competence, for I have earned most of my livelihood for twenty years past by translating the bad English of a multitude of authors into measurably better English. Thus qualified professionally, I rise to pay my small tribute to Dr. Harding. Setting aside a college professor or two and half a dozen dipsomaniacal newspaper reporters, he takes the first place in my Valhalla of literati. That is, he writes the worst English that I have ever encountered. It reminds me of a string of wet sponges; it reminds me of tattered washing on the line; it reminds me of stale bean soup, of college yells, of dogs barking idiotically through endless nights. It is so bad that a sort of grandeur creeps into it. It drags itself out of the dark abysm . . . of pish, and crawls insanely up to the topmost pinnacle of posh. It is rumble and bumble. It is flap and doodle. It is balder and dash.

The *New York Times*, serenely unaware—as ever—of its terminal pomposity, countered editorially that "Mr. Harding's official style is excellent. Its merits are obvious. In the first place, it is a style that looks presidential. It contains the long sentences and big words that are expected. . . . In the president's misty language the great majority see a reflection of their own indeterminate thoughts." To which Mencken replied, "In other words, bosh is the right medicine for boobs."

Or, in a more mellow vein, try Mencken on Al Smith in 1928:

> It is difficult to make out how any native Marylander, brought up in the tradition of this ancient commonwealth, can fail to have a friendly feeling for Al Smith in the present campaign. He represents as a man almost everything Maryland represents as a State. There is something singularly and refreshingly free, spacious, amiable, hearty, and decent

about him. Brought up in poverty, and educated, in so far as he got
any education at all, in the harsh school of the city streets, he has yet
managed somehow to acquire what is essentially an aristocratic point of
view, the habit and color of a gentleman. He is enlightened, he is high-
minded, he is upright and trustworthy. What Frederick the Great said
of his officers might well be said of him: he will not lie, and he cannot
be bought. Not much more could be said of any man.

Or Mencken on the sorry life of presidents:

All day long the right hon. lord of us all sits listening solemnly to quacks
who pretend to know what the farmers are thinking about in Nebraska
and South Carolina, how the Swedes of Minnesota are taking the German moratorium, and how much it would cost in actual votes to let
fall a word for beer and light wines. Anon a secretary rushes in with the
news that some eminent movie actor or football coach has died, and
the president must seize a pen and write a telegram of condolence to
the widow. Once a year he is repaid by receiving a cable on his birthday from King George V. . . . There comes a day of public ceremonial,
and a chance to make a speech. Alas, it must be made at the annual
banquet of some organization that is discovered, at the last minute, to
be made up mainly of gentlemen under indictment, or at the tomb of
some statesman who escaped impeachment by a hair. A million voters
with IQs below 60 have their ears glued to the radio: it takes four days
hard work to concoct a speech without a sensible word in it. Four dry
senators get drunk and make a painful scene. The presidential automobile runs over a dog. It rains.

Or Mencken, declaring himself for Al Landon in 1936 (and
anticipating the circumstances of many Democrats forty-four years
later):

Nevertheless, and despite all Hell's angels, I shall vote for the Hon.
Mr. Landon tomorrow. To a lifelong Democrat, of course, it will be
something of a wrench. But it seems to me that the choice is one that

genuine Democrats are almost bound to make. On the one side are all the basic principles of their party, handed down from its first days and tried over and over again in the fires of experience; on the other side is a gallimaufry of transparent quackeries, puerile in theory and dangerous in practice. To vote Democratic this year it is necessary, by an unhappy irony, to vote for a Republican. But to vote with the party is to vote for a gang of mountebanks who are no more Democrats than a turkey buzzard is an archangel.

Or Mencken, firing back at the Eastern Shoremen who were threatening a business boycott of Baltimore because his *Evening Sun* column had condemned the lynching of a black prisoner in Salisbury, Maryland, as "a public obscenity worthy of cannibals."

A third item I lift from the celebrated *Marylander and Herald* of Princess Anne, a leader in the current movement to bust Baltimore by boycott: "One member of the mob took his knife and cut off several toes from the Negro's feet and carried them away with him for souvenirs." What has become of these souvenirs the *Marylander and Herald* does not say. No doubt they now adorn the parlor mantelpiece of some humble but public-spirited Salisbury home, between the engrossed seashell from Ocean City and the family Peruna bottle. I can only hope that they are not deposited eventually with the Maryland Historical Society.

Or Mencken, celebrating the rhetorical powers of the aforementioned Gerald L. K. Smith at the 1936 Townsend pensioners' convention:

His speech was a magnificent amalgam of each and every American species of rabble-rousing, with embellishments borrowed from the Algonquin Indians and the Cossacks of the Don. It ran the keyboard from the softest sobs and gurgles to the most ear-splitting whoops and howls, and when it was over the 9,000 delegates simply lay back in their pews and yelled.

Or, finally, Mencken on the culinary differences between barbaric New York and epicurean Baltimore, c. 1918:

> No civilized man, save perhaps in mere bravado, would voluntarily eat
> a fried oyster. . . . Down in Maryland, where the dish originated among
> the Negro slaves, it is to be had only in cheap lunchrooms and at what
> are called oyster-suppers, usually held in the cellars of bankrupt church-
> es. The first-class hotels would no more serve it than they would serve
> pig liver. . . .
>
> In New York, however, there is no such refinement of palate and dignity
> of feeling. I have seen fried oysters served in one of the most expensive
> hotels of the town, and the head waiter didn't even put a screen around
> the table—which would have been done in Baltimore had a United
> States senator, a foreign ambassador, or some other untutored magnifico
> insisted upon having them. And in the so-called seafood eating houses,
> so I hear, they are dished up without the slightest question, and all the
> year 'round. Imagine a Christian eating a fried oyster in the summer!
>
> Well, the people of New York do even worse; they eat Chesapeake soft
> crabs fried in batter! What is cannibalism after that? I'd as lief eat a
> stewed archdeacon.

In terms of sheer technical virtuosity, Mencken was arguably
at his most impressive as a political reporter working under
extreme deadline pressure during the "carnival of buncombe" (as
he once termed it) of a national political convention. Thus HLM
would look up from the press box in 1948, note the presence on
the platform of the "uniquely slim and smartly clad" Mrs. Dorothy Vredenberg, secretary of the Democratic National Committee,
murmur to his colleagues, "This is unprecedented," and write that
she had triumphantly defied the tradition that "lady politicians shall
resemble British tramp steamers dressed up for the king's birthday."
But my personal favorite is "The Wet Wets Triumph," the dispatch
Mencken sent to the *Sun* on June 30, 1932, describing the victory

of the anti-Prohibitionist forces at the Democratic National Convention—a splendid piece of raillery (and a wholly accurate account of what actually happened) that only Mencken's dourest enemies could resent:

> Since one o'clock this morning Prohibition has been a fugitive in the remote quagmires of the Bible Belt. The chase began thirteen hours earlier, when the resolutions committee of the convention retired to the voluptuous splendors of the Rose Room at the Congress Hotel. For four hours nothing came out of its stronghold save the moaning of converts in mighty travail. Then the Hon. Michael L. Igoe, a round-faced Chicago politician, burst forth with the news that the wet wets of the committee had beaten the damp wets by a vote of 35–17. There ensued a hiatus, while the quarry panted and the bloodhounds bayed. At seven in the evening the chase was resumed in the convention hall, and four hours later Prohibition went out the window to the stately tune of 934 3/4 votes to 213 1/4, or more than four to one. So the flight to the fastnesses of Zion began.

But even down there where Genesis has the police behind it, and an unbaptized man is as rare as a metaphysician, the fugitive is yet harried and oppressed. Only two states, Georgia and Mississippi, showed a solid dry front on the poll, and in Georgia there were plenty of wets lurking behind the unit rule. All the other great commonwealths of the late confederacy cast votes for the immediate repeal of the Eighteenth Amendment and the Volstead Act, led by Texas with its solid forty-six, and South Carolina with its solid eighteen. Even Tennessee, the Baptist Holy Land, went eighteen dripping wet to six not so wet. Taking all the Confederate states together, with Kentucky thrown in, they cast 165 votes for the forthright and uncompromising plank of the majority and only 123 for the pussy-footing plank of the minority. In the Middle West the carnage was even more appalling. Kansas voted 12–8 for the minority straddle, but Iowa went the whole hog with loud hosannas, and so did North Dakota, and so did Indiana and Illinois. Even Ohio, the citadel of the Anti-Saloon

League, went over to the enemy by 49–2, and Nebraska, the old home of
William Jennings Bryan, voted nearly two to one for rum and rebellion.

All of which suggests that Alistair Cooke was right that Mencken,
hunched over his battered Corona typewriter with an Uncle Willie's
cigar jammed into his mouth, was "the master craftsman of daily
journalism in the twentieth century," and that Mencken would be
best remembered as a great American humorist.

C ritics have argued for decades over the source of Menck-
en's distinctive imagery, rhythms, viewpoint, and vocabulary. Fred Hobson, Vincent Fitzpatrick, and Bradford Jacobs, three
Mencken scholars who edited *Thirty-five Years of Newspaper Work*,
suggest that HLM's principal inspirations and models were Mark
Twain, Finley Peter Dunne (of "Mr. Dooley" fame), George Bernard
Shaw, and Will Rogers. But, ultimately, Mencken's irresistibility is
a function of the fact that he was, and remains, a stylistic original.
Nothing that came before him was ever like him; and no one since
has been able to pull off the "Mencken style" quite like the master.
The impossibility of successfully imitating him (as demonstrated,
for example, by R. Emmett Tyrrell) is the best posthumous evidence
for Mencken's striking creativity as a writer.

Fred Hobson began his 1994 study, *Mencken: A Life*, by suggesting that Henry Louis Mencken, the man, has "never been adequately explained." Hobson's hopes—and similar aspirations by Marion
Elizabeth Rodgers and Terry Teachout—notwithstanding, I fear this
remains the case even after these three major Mencken biographers
strip-mined the materials unavailable to earlier scholars. Somewhat
like Ronald Reagan, H. L. Mencken defies the efforts of a biographer to fit him into any Procrustean bed.

Hobson did advance our understanding of Mencken's demons
(and energies) in one crucial respect, when he explored in sympathetic detail the adolescent struggle with his father that Mencken let

fall through the autobiographical cracks between *Happy Days* and *Newspaper Days*. August Mencken, a successful cigar manufacturer, was determined that his eldest son Henry should follow him into the family business—a trade for which HLM, who desperately wanted to be a newspaperman, was singularly ill equipped. Hobson reports that the seventeen-year-old Mencken once contemplated suicide in despair of ever breaking free of his father's will. (It seems to me more likely that he would eventually have rebelled, confronted August, and gone his own way—a possibility made moot by August's sudden death at age forty-four, when young Henry was eighteen.) But that Mencken's relationship with his father, whose basic political, social, and religious attitudes he shared, was a volatile compound of affection and deep resentment, Hobson seems to have established rather persuasively. It is an interesting commentary on Mencken's sense of familial propriety that one gets no sense of the drama that had just unfolded, nor the struggle that had preceded it, from the breezy opening lines of *Newspaper Days*: "My father died on Friday, January 13, 1899, and was buried on the ensuing Sunday. On the Monday evening immediately following, having shaved with care and put on my best suit of clothes, I presented myself in the city-room of the old Baltimore *Morning Herald*, and applied to Max Ways, the city editor, for a job on his staff. I was eighteen years, four months, and four days old, wore my hair longish and parted in the middle, had on a high stiff collar and an Ascot cravat, and weighed something on the minus side of 120 pounds. I was thus hardly a sight to exhilarate a city editor."

Hobson added another intriguing piece to the puzzle when he suggested that a pronounced class-consciousness was a mainspring of Mencken's personality. As we have seen, Mencken could poke fun at his own roots as a "larva of the comfortable and complacent bourgeoisie." But for all the good humor about his extended family that permeates *Happy Days*, Mencken had a deep-set family pride (especially in the academic accomplishments of his noble

German forebears); and he was painfully aware of his own lack of formal education at the hands of "the brethren who expounded *literae humaniores*," as he once put it. Moreover, and for all the china that got broken in his writing, Mencken was determined to make his mark as a man of solid accomplishment in the world—and thus he took satisfaction in later life from becoming a member of the boards of directors of both the *Sunpapers* and the Knopf publishing house.

Hobson drove the class analysis a bit too hard when he located Mencken's antipathy toward FDR in HLM's alleged belief that Roosevelt was a class traitor; Mencken's libertarianism, and Roosevelt's slipperiness, were sufficient reason for Mencken to loathe the New Deal, its politics, its moral pretensions, and its sundry coercions and propaganda campaigns. Still, the notion of Mencken as a man convinced that the proprieties of the middle (and, indeed, upper-middle) class were all that lay between him and chaos is an intriguing one, and may even help us understand some of the paradoxes that Hobson posits as distinguishing Menckenian characteristics: the anti-Victorian who in many respects led a decidedly Victorian life; the lampooner of the vulgarities of American democracy who defended the singularity (indeed superiority) of American speech; the author of that blistering critique of the South, "The Sahara of the Bozart," who did more than any other editor to foster the Southern literary renaissance during the 1920s.

But even here, important elements of Mencken's complexity seem to elude analysis. For if we are to understand the essential Mencken primarily in class terms, as a self-made bourgeois determined to preserve his hard-won respectability, then what are we to do with what Murray Kempton once called Mencken's "social outrage," which was captured in his 1924 column endorsing Progressive Party candidate Robert W. LaFollette over against John W. Davis and Calvin Coolidge?

There remains the Wisconsin Red, with his pockets stuffed with Soviet gold. I shall vote for him unhesitatingly and for a plain reason: he is the best man in the running, as a man. . . .

Suppose all Americans were like LaFollette? What a country it would be! No more depressing goosestepping. No more gorillas in hysterical herds. No more trimming and trembling. Does it matter what his ideas are? Personally, I am against four-fifths of them, but what are the odds? They are, at worst, better than the ignominious platitudes of Coolidge. . . .

The older I grow the less I esteem mere ideas. . . . There are only men who have character and men who lack it. LaFollette has it. . . . He is devoid of caution, policy, timidity, baseness—all the immemorial qualities of the politician. He is tremendous when he is right, and he is even more tremendous when he is wrong.

Similarly, the analytic prism of class does little to illuminate what Joseph Epstein one described as Mencken's exuberant iconoclasm and its appeal to the young across the barriers of class, race, and ethnicity. Thus, in his 1979 Mencken Day lecture at Baltimore's Pratt Library, Epstein reminded his audience of HLM's impact on the young Richard Wright, as recounted in his autobiography, *Black Boy*:

That night in my rented room, while letting the hot water run over my can of pork and beans in the sink, I opened *A Book of Prefaces* and began to read. I was jarred and shocked by the style, the clear, clean, sweeping sentences. Why did he write like that? And how did one write like that?

. . . Yes, this man was fighting, fighting with words. . . . Could words be weapons? Well, yes, for here they were. Then, maybe, perhaps, I could use them as a weapon. No. It frightened me. I read on and what amazed me was not what he said, but how on earth anybody had the courage to say it.

Mencken liked to describe his distinctive vocation as that of a "critic of ideas," and it is perhaps the greatest paradox of Mencken's literary life that his more formal philosophical, theological, and political speculations have worn poorly, though he believed them to be among his finest efforts. In a letter to James Branch Cabell explaining his intellectual scheme for the *American Mercury*, Mencken wrote that the new magazine would espouse "an educated Toryism," of the "true Disraelian brand." But how does Toryism, of any sort, square with Mencken's unmitigated belief in the inevitability of progress, especially scientific progress? Why did a man so preternaturally skeptical of all other claims to puissance (as he might have put it) maintain such a positivist cast of mind? And how did his positivism square with the gentler side of Mencken's religious agnosticism?

These may be questions of interest to only a few, however, and their lack of resolution need not interfere with anyone's enjoyment of Mencken's writing. After all, do we care all that much about Mark Twain's anti-Catholicism, Finley Peter Dunne's theory of the virtues, or Will Rogers's epistemology? Mencken's lasting reputation is built on his reporting, his philology, his skills as a memoirist, and his work as an editor—a role in which he had, arguably, his greatest influence on American letters.

Here, too, alas, Hobson's attempt to get inside Mencken's mind proved something of a disappointment. He skipped very lightly indeed over the surface of Mencken's literary criticism (where, according to Kempton, we find the "best Mencken," the first American critic to win the respect of Joseph Conrad); and there is nothing in Hobson to match the detail of Carl Bode's analysis of Mencken's two great magazine projects, the *Smart Set* and the *American Mercury*, in Bode's 1969 biography, *Mencken*. Nor does Hobson sufficiently explore Mencken's incapacities as a political prognosticator.

On a more personal level, Mencken's biographers describe, but never finally resolve, the puzzle of what appears to have been Mencken's essential loneliness. Why did he work so obsessively? Why did he party so hard, or struggle so assiduously to keep his friendships green? Why did he fall so quickly and completely into the pattern of the happy bourgeois husband during the brief five years of his marriage to Sara Haardt? One need not delve into what Mencken himself once described as "Freudian sewage" to detect a lonely man whose boisterous good spirits, iconoclastic public personality, and inimitable style of writing were in some part strategies to keep the demons of loneliness at bay. Perhaps loneliness is, in some measure, every writer's burden: no matter how wide one's circle of friends and colleagues, one is all alone when one picks up the pen or strikes the first letter on the keyboard. (I think it was another felicitous stylist, E. B. White, who said that before he sat down to write, he always had one dry martini, "for courage.") But however ubiquitous the problem may be among the scriveners, Mencken seems to have suffered it to a painful degree.

The question of Mencken's religious views—indeed, the question of whether he was in fact an anti-Christian bigot—was raised anew when Garry Wills defended the progressive, populist Bryan against the elitist, Social Darwinist Mencken in Wills's revisionist reading of the celebrated Scopes "Monkey Trial" in his book, *Under God*.

It may help, in assessing these charges, to remember that Garry Wills has been perfectly happy to use, indeed celebrate, Mencken when it suits his political purposes. Wills's contemptuous blast at the suburban-bourgeois Spiro Agnew, in *Nixon Agonistes*, is built around citations from Mencken's 1933 obituary column, "The Coolidge Mystery." Moreover, in his discussion of the Scopes affair, Wills failed to inform the readers of *Under God* that Mencken actually defended the right of the State of Tennessee to pass a law prohibiting the teaching of Darwinism in state-funded classrooms. Indeed, one suspects that what really cobs Garry Wills is that the Scopes Trial, and the interpretation of it that Mencken helped fix in the American mind, marked the end of the alliance between evangelicalism and "progressive politics." (Bryan's campaigns, Wills writes approvingly, had been "the most leftist mounted by a major party's candidate in our history.") For Garry Wills, such current enemies of civilization as the Moral Majority and the Christian Right are thus to be blamed on Mencken.

Certainly more generous, and I believe more balanced, is Joseph Epstein's defense of Mencken against the charge of callous elitism:

> In an odd way it was the common man, so regularly bilked by his clergymen, journalists, professors, politicians, in whose defense Mencken wrote. . . . Homo boobiens was, well, boobien, precisely because he fell—time and again, and yet again—for shoddy mental goods that made his life less good than it might have been, even under the restrictions of the tragic view. . . .
>
> What is more, whenever Mencken registers what might be construed as an objectionable or cruel opinion, one can count on discovering . . . acts of particular kindness that contradict that opinion. He attacks religion, for example, then enters into friendships with nuns and ministers; he relentlessly mocks the pursuit of men by women, then, in middle life, himself marries a woman whose death within a few years is certain. No evidence of envy or unseemly ambition is to be found in the record of his life. Although he did his best to hide it, the Holy Terror, the Bad Boy of Baltimore, appears to have been a very good man.

Perhaps Mencken's most succinct, and yet most telling, discussion of religious conviction comes in a letter he wrote to Marion Bloom, whom he came close to marrying on several occasions in the 1920s. In the wake of her experiences as a nurse in World War

I, Marion had become a devotee of Christian Science, a choice of sect guaranteed to set Mencken's teeth on edge. In trying to pry her loose from the shackles of "Ma Eddy," Mencken wrote, in a letter in 1921:

> The God business is really quite simple. No sane man denies that the universe presents phenomena quite beyond human understanding, and so it is a fair assumption that they are directed by some understanding that is superhuman. But that is as far as sound thought can go. All religions pretend to go further. That is, they pretend to explain the unknowable. As I said long ago, they do it in terms of the not worth knowing. . . . Anyone who pretends to say what God wants or doesn't want, and what the whole show is about, is simply an ass. . . .
>
> In other words, the objection to religion is that it represents an effort by ignorance to account for a mystery that knowledge simply puts aside as intrinsically impenetrable.

Throughout his mature life, Mencken insisted that he was not an atheist (for such a judgment would require a knowledge that was beyond "sound thought") but rather an agnostic. Asked once what he would do if on his death he found himself facing the twelve apostles, he answered (and in this instance we may be sure that beneath the humor lay deep convictions about intellectual honesty), "I would simply say, 'Gentlemen, I was mistaken.'" Imagine Carl Sagan ever having said such a thing about the possibility of his encounter with a postmortem minyan, and you begin to understand the difference between the agnostic Mencken and the true village atheist.

None of this is to deny that Mencken regularly made mock of religious convictions and practices. But he did it with a deftness and, in most cases, a good humor in which was rarely found the arrogance of sheer contempt. Moreover, Mencken was not insensible to the allure of religion or to religious contributions to what he

regarded as the world's meager stock of decency. Thus Mencken on
Roman Catholicism in 1923 (and in what some will regard as virtually a prophetic mode):

> The Latin Church, which I constantly find myself admiring, despite
> its frequent astonishing imbecilities, has always kept clearly before it
> the fact that religion is not a syllogism, but a poem. . . . Rome, indeed,
> has not only preserved the original poetry in Christianity; it has made
> capital additions to that poetry—for example, the poetry of the saints,
> of Mary, and of the liturgy itself. A solemn high mass must be a thou-
> sand times as impressive, to a man with any genuine religious sense in
> him, as the most powerful sermons ever roared under the big-top by a
> Presbyterian auctioneer of God. In the face of such overwhelming beau-
> ty it is not necessary to belabor the faithful with logic; they are better
> convinced by letting them alone. . . .

> [But the Roman] clergy begin to grow argumentative, doctrinaire, ri-
> diculous. It is a pity. . . . If they keep on spoiling poetry and spouting
> ideas, the day will come when some extra-bombastic deacon will as-
> tound humanity and insult God by proposing to translate the liturgy
> into American, that the faithful may be convinced by it.

Any serious analysis of Mencken's religious views must also contend with his deep disdain for theological liberalism, his intuition
(subsequently vindicated) that the quest for "relevance" would make
a wreck of mainline Protestantism, and his defense of the dignity
of the antimodernist position articulated for years by J. Gresham
Machen, whom he memorialized as "Dr. Fundamentalis" in the *Evening Sun* of January 18, 1937:

> The Rev. J. Gresham Machen, D.D., who died out in North Dakota on
> New Year's Day, got, on the whole, a bad press while he lived, and even
> his obituaries did less than justice to him. . . .

What caused him to quit the Princeton Theological Seminary and found a seminary of his own was his complete inability, as a theologian, to square the disingenuous evasions of Modernism with the fundamentals of Christian doctrine. He saw clearly that the effects that could follow diluting and polluting Christianity in the Modernist manner would be its complete abandonment and ruin. Either it was true or it was not. If, as he believed, it was true, then there could be no compromise with persons who sought to whittle away its essential postulates, however respectable their motives.

Thus he fell out with the reformers who have been trying, in late years, to convert the Presbyterian Church into a kind of literary and social club, devoted vaguely to good works. . . .

It is my belief, as a friendly neutral in all such high and ghostly matters, that the body of doctrine known as Modernism is completely incompatible, not only with anything rationally describable as Christianity, but also with anything deserving to pass as religion in general. Religion, if it is to retain any genuine significance, can never be reduced to a series of sweet attitudes, possible to anyone not actually in jail for felony. It is, on the contrary, a corpus of powerful and profound convictions, many of them not open to logical analysis. . . .

What the Modernists have done . . . [is] to get rid of all the logical difficulties of religion and yet preserve a generally pious cast of mind. It is a vain enterprise. What they have left, once they have achieved their imprudent scavenging, is hardly more than a row of hollow platitudes, as empty [of] psychological force and effect as so many nursery rhymes. . . . Religion is something else again—in Henrik Ibsen's phrase, something more deep-down-diving and mud-upbringing. Dr. Machen tried to impress that obvious fact upon his fellow adherents of the Geneva Muhammad. He failed—but he was undoubtedly right.

According to his own explicit instructions, Mencken had but the barest of agnostic funeral rituals, with merely a few friends and relatives gathered to bid him farewell before he was cremated and his ashes deposited next to Sara's in Baltimore's Loudon Park cemetery. But his sister Gertrude, with whom he had lived for years and for whom he retained a considerable (if occasionally exasperated) affection, was a pious lady of Episcopalian persuasion, and in her brother's memory she gave a gold chalice and paten to her parish, the Little Church of the Ascension. Some will regard this as an utterly quixotic gesture. I think Mencken would have appreciated it as an act of authentic familial piety, and perhaps as something more.

For if Mencken was the intrinsically lonely man suggested by Fred Hobson's biography, then his incapacity for, but appreciation of, the poetry of faith was doubly tragic. And this Menckenian, who believes that the old man did meet the twelve apostles in the early hours of January 29, 1956, would like to think that they—understanding the tragedy full well, honoring his frank acknowledgment of an invincible ignorance, and knowing his history and his habits—invited him in for a beer.

The Unjustly Unremembered Paul Horgan

Although my four years at Baltimore's St. Paul Latin High School coincided with the cultural meltdowns associated with the Sixties and its "Age of Aquarius," I was happily spared the kind of English-class reading lists with which students (and parents) have typically been afflicted in subsequent decades. It's virtually impossible to escape any high school in twenty-first-century America without having been compelled to read Kurt Vonnegut's vastly overrated *Slaughterhouse-Five* or Mitch Albom's treacly *Tuesdays with Morrie*. Worse, it's entirely possible to spend four years in a Catholic high school without ever having heard of, much less read, the great twentieth-century authors whose fiction reflects the Catholic sacramental imagination: Graham Greene and Evelyn Waugh, Flannery O'Connor and Walker Percy, to name just the all-stars. There's some serious cheating going on here.

Things were rather different in 1967, 1968, and 1969, when my English teacher was Father W. Vincent Bechtel: a holy terror, as my classmates and I thought of him then, but a man whose memory I now revere. Why? Because he threw me into the deep end of the pool of Anglo-American literature and told me, in so many words, to start swimming.

Father Bechtel had occasional intellectual quirks. A summer program at the Johns Hopkins University English department got him transiently infatuated with Freudian literary analysis, which, as I recall, led to some odd readings of Herman Melville (who is, er, odd enough in his own right). But even that crotchet of Father Bechtel's was to my ultimate benefit, for the memory of it caused me to laugh out loud years later at Frederick Crews's send-up of the Freudians in his masterful parody of trendy literary criticism, *The Pooh Perplex*. In the main, though, Father Bechtel was a classicist. He knew, as a matter of self-evident truth, that there was an Anglo-American literary canon. He believed that educated people should have read it, or should at least have read seriously *in* it. And he planted in me the seed of the conviction that knowing and learning to appreciate the canon is part of becoming the trustee of a civilization. These days, kids may read two or three novels over the summer and another one or two during the school year. Under Father Bechtel's tutelage (as I remember it now) or reign of terror (as I thought of it then), we read five or six novels during the summer and at least another half-dozen during the school year, not to mention plays, poetry, and short stories.

Please don't get the impression that Father Bechtel was a stick-in-the-mud, though. He had us read Salinger's *Catcher in the Rye* and the canonical American moderns: Faulkner, Fitzgerald, Hemingway, Sherwood Anderson, Eugene O'Neill, Tennessee Williams. At the same time, though, we were baptized by immersion into Jane Austen, the Brontës, Conrad, Dickens, Hardy, Hawthorne, Henry James, the aforementioned Melville, Shakespeare, and Mark Twain. All of which leads to the thought, hardly original, that everyone really ought to do high school English twice: the second time, when we're old enough to appreciate it.

Paul Horgan, whom almost no one remembers in the first decades of the twenty-first century, was one of the modern American writers whom I met through Father Bechtel. It was an introduction for which I've been grateful for the past forty years, for, in his day, Horgan was the embodiment of that seemingly now-extinct species, the "man of letters." He won the Pulitzer and Bancroft Prizes in history for his epic study of four cultures in the American Southwest, *Great River: The Rio Grande in North American History*. Twenty-one years later, in 1976, he won the Pulitzer again, this time for *Lamy of Santa Fe*, a magisterial biography of the émigré French prelate and pioneer who was Willa Cather's model in *Death Comes for the Archbishop*. (In preparing his Lamy biography, Horgan was allowed unprecedented access to the Secret Archives of the Vatican, thanks to a personal intervention by Pope John XXIII; the tale is nicely told in *Tracings*, a 1993 collection of some of Horgan's more memorable occasional pieces.) Horgan wrote sparkling, insightful essays and autobiographical reminiscences of events and people, including such literary giants as W. Somerset Maugham, T. S. Eliot, and Edmund Wilson; the devastatingly acerbic but nonetheless charming Washington hostess, Alice Roosevelt Longworth; and his friend Igor Stravinsky, the Russian composer. All in all, he published fifteen novels, seven books of short stories, eighteen volumes of essays, a volume of clerihews, a book of watercolors and drawings, and the libretto for a folk opera.

Born in Buffalo in 1903, he moved with his Irish-German family in 1915 to New Mexico, where the climate was thought to be better for his father's health. He was a cadet at the New Mexico Military Institute from 1919 to 1921, and then from 1922 to 1923. There, he met his lifelong friend, the prominent Southwestern artist Peter Hurd; and there he would work as librarian until joining the U.S. Army in World War II. The New Mexico years stuck with Paul Horgan in various senses of the term. Thus, insofar as Horgan figures in the American literary imagination today, it is as a "regional" writer—a literary craftsman who drew his materials from the Southwest and whose writing reflects a certain regional cast of mind: the first part of which is, at least in part, true enough, for many of Horgan's short stories and several of his novels are set in West Texas, New Mexico, and Arizona, and both his histories and his fiction reflect a fascination with the interaction of Native American, Spanish, Mexican, and Anglo-American cultures in that unique, and uniquely beautiful, corner of the United States. Thus the first Horgan novel Father Bechtel had us read was set in Arizona at the end of the U.S.

cavalry's struggle to pacify the territory; *A Distant Trumpet* is a just and fair portrait of the virtues and vices of Apaches, cavalrymen, and settlers, and a moving study of the meaning of manliness and leadership (it's been one of my standard Confirmation/Bar Mitzvah gifts for years).

On the other hand, Paul Horgan's literary sensibility and the distinctive cast of mind that shapes his work cannot be captured in regional terms alone, for by his own testimony, he was a product of the culture to which his family of writers, artists, and musicians had first introduced him in the northeast before their move to Albuquerque. As he once wrote, "I . . . derived most of my education informally from the cultural expressions best exemplified in the intellectual and artistic life of the East and of Europe, and I have been concerned with people without regard . . . to the 'typical' character imposed on either [the] eastern or western environment by other writers and observers." The interaction of cultures that he experienced in his own life and that he explored in his histories and his novels gave Horgan an insight into the universality of certain human affairs, temptations, and virtues. And, of course, another word for "universal" is "catholic"—as in "Catholic."

P aul Horgan did not wear his faith on his literary sleeve, so to speak. But it is impossible to read the first (and best) novel in his *Richard* Trilogy, *Things As They Are*, without quickly recognizing the Catholic sensibility that permeates the book. At the most obvious level, Richard (the youthful protagonist whose experiences mirror Horgan's) and his parents are manifestly Catholic in their belief and practice. Structurally, the book resembles *Death Comes for the Archbishop*, another "collection" of medieval-type vignettes that still holds together as a coherent novel (call those vignettes "miracle stories," if you've a broad understanding of the miraculous). But the Catholicity of Horgan's creation in *Things As They Are*, an exquisitely crafted book, is more than a matter of certain characteristics with which he invests his principal characters, or the literary structure of the work. It's a matter of a sensibility, an angle of vision, a way of seeing things—of seeing things "as they are," because that is the only way to see the extraordinary things that lie just on the far side of the ordinary. Seeing "things as they are," in other words, is the way to detect the divine at work in the human and the mundane.

Horgan's literary style is about as far away from Flannery O'Connor's as can be imagined. Yet much of Horgan's fiction, and especially *Things As They Are*, is an expression of O'Connor's "habit of being": that spiritual intuition that allows us to see life, not simply as one damn thing after another, but as a dramatic arena of temptation and fortitude, creation and redemption, sinfulness and grace—a cosmic drama being played out here and now, a drama in which God is producer, scriptwriter, director, and, ultimately, protagonist. Like O'Connor, the "hillbilly Thomist," Paul Horgan grew up in a time of saccharine devotional piety. Yet both of these writers knew that there is nothing less sentimental than Catholicism, because Catholicism is realism. And like O'Connor, Horgan grasped why: because it is through the Incarnation, a real event at a real time in a real place, that God's unsentimental, cleansing, and all-powerful love is decisively revealed—the divine mercy that is, according to the parable of the prodigal son, the defining characteristic of God's interaction with the world. Catholic realism doesn't deny "things as they are." Catholic realism doesn't deny the temptations of what an older generation called "the world, the flesh, and the devil." Catholic realism confronts the world, the flesh, and the devil in the confidence that, as Christ has conquered, so, too, may the people who are Christ's Body in history, by the divine mercy and grace.

Those confrontations, as experienced in the life of a sensitive and intelligent boy, set the narrative rhythm of *Things As They Are*. Childhood, Paul Horgan understood, is anything but carefree; "guilt," as he put it, is the "first knowledge," as remembering is the beginning of the stirrings of conscience. Thus young Richard confronts the classic temptations—of power, of ego, of false pride, of self-delusion, of ambition, of sex, of an overwrought piety that seeks to force God's hand—not in rollicking adventures like Tom Sawyer's or Huck Finn's, but in his utterly unremarkable and ordinary encounters with his parents and relatives, his friends, his pets, his parish and his priests, the tradesmen who come to his home and the families in his neighborhood. There is nothing sentimental or cloying here. There is, on the contrary, an acute, unsparing, yet sympathetic spiritual excavation of the process of growing up—a process that, as Horgan demonstrates in the two novels that continue the *Richard Trilogy* (*Everything to Live For* and *The Thin Mountain Air*), continues long after childhood.

In a letter to a friend, Flannery O'Connor once reflected on her own literary experience and that of the Catholic convert and novelist, Carolyn Gordon Tate: "I have never had the sense that being a Catholic is a limit to the freedom of the writer, but just the reverse. Mrs. Tate told me that after she became a Catholic, she felt she could use her eyes and accept what she saw for the first time, [that] she didn't have to make a new universe for each book but could take the one she found." I have no idea whether Paul Horgan knew Carolyn Gordon Tate, but the ten episodes in *Things As They Are* demonstrate a cradle-Catholic's complete agreement with a convert-Catholic's experience: there is no need to "invent a universe" in fiction, for an invented universe typically becomes an author's sandbox or playpen. The real universe—what we see and hear and feel and taste and experience—is adventure enough. It was adventure enough for the God who created it, redeemed it, and continually sanctifies it; it should be adventure enough for us, because amid the seemingly quotidian there are cosmic contests underway.

P rior to his death in 1995 at age ninety-three (he had left the Southwest in 1959 to teach and write at Wesleyan University in Middletown, Connecticut), Paul Horgan was never known as a "Catholic writer," in the sense that J. F. Powers (*Morte D'Urban*) was known as a "Catholic writer" or Chaim Potok (*The Chosen, The Promise, My Name Is Asher Lev*) was thought of as a "Jewish writer." Yet an argument can be made that Paul Horgan was the most accomplished Catholic man of letters in mid-twentieth-century America. Not because his fiction and his historical studies dealt over and over again with "Catholic" characters and situations (which they didn't), but because his remarkably wide-ranging corpus of work is shaped, sometimes overtly and sometimes subtly, by an unmistakably Catholic sensibility: a sacramental sensibility convinced that the ordinary things of this world are the vehicles of grace and the materials of a divinely scripted drama. Paul Horgan was too gifted a writer to beat you over the head with that message. It was almost always there, though, as this gifted, learned, and deeply humane novelist, essayist, and historian kept reminding his readers that seeing things as they are, in full, is the index of human, and Christian, maturity.

Part III

Catholics in These United States

The American Catholic Story, Contested

C atholics in America have rarely taken their history seriously. My own educational circumstances, which were hardly
unique, may illustrate the point. In nineteen years of a generally
excellent Catholic education in Church-sponsored schools between
1956 and 1975, I was never once offered instruction, much less a
a formal course, in the history of Catholicism in the United States.
And while this educational gap was perhaps understandable in a
community dominated until recent generations by immigrants and
their children, the strange ignorance of U.S. Catholics about their
story is nonetheless a formidable obstacle to ecclesial maturity, for,
as Cicero noted, "Not to know what happened before one was born
is always to be a child."

There are occasional signs that this self-inflicted amnesia is end-
ing. American Catholic history may not be so booming a discipline
as biblical studies or medical ethics, but even the most cursory survey
of the *American Catholic Studies Newsletter* (published by the Cush-
wa Center for the Study of American Catholicism at the University
of Notre Dame, itself an institutional expression of the growth of
the field) reveals a wide range of research, from classic institutional
histories and biographies of key figures to the new social history
with its emphases on patterns of community, spirituality, family life,
and education. Many Catholic dioceses are, at long last, taking their
archival responsibilities seriously, and new lodes of information are
being unearthed and mined.

This new vitality of interest in the American Catholic story is
surely to the good. It is good for the Church (both in the United
States and in Rome), good for the study of American religion, and

good for a more comprehensive understanding of the complex interaction of religion and public life in the ongoing experiment of American democracy. But there are no unmixed blessings in the tides of intellectual interest and fashion, as the discovery of Clio's charism among American Catholics illustrates. For parallel to (and in some cases generating) the explosion of historical knowledge about American Catholicism has come an effort to put that knowledge—better, a distinctive interpretation of that knowledge—to various partisan purposes in the Church's post-Vatican II struggles over the meaning of orthodoxy, authority, and ministry. Separating the wheat from that particular form of chaff is thus important.

To say that American Catholics have rarely taken their history seriously is not to say that there have never been serious historians of American Catholicism. Although they are largely unknown outside the American Catholic community (and scarcely better known within it, for that matter), John Gilmary Shea, Peter Guilday, Thomas T. McAvoy, and, pre-eminently, John Tracy Ellis were old-fashioned historians of genuine accomplishment who, in the late nineteenth century and the first half of the twentieth created the classic story line of American Catholicism.

It was a story written under the long shadow of nativist (and, it must be said, largely Protestant) anti-Romanism and its recurring charge that Catholicism—as a body of doctrine, a matter of personal conviction, and an institution—was incompatible with American democratic republicanism. Monsignor Ellis frequently quoted the remark made to him by Professor Arthur Schlesinger, Sr., that Schlesinger considered "the prejudice against your Church as the deepest bias in the history of the American people." Without getting into a bigotry sweepstakes, there is ample historical and contemporary evidence to suggest that Schlesinger's indictment was not a reckless one.

Classic American Catholic historians, as eager to challenge the nativist canard as other preconciliar Catholic intellectuals, adopted the "Catholicism/Americanism" tension as the principal theme of their story line. They sought to show how the Catholic people, and particularly their episcopal leaders, worked tirelessly to demonstrate in practice what they affirmed in principle: that there was no inherent conflict in being both a convinced Catholic and a patriotic American. Thus historical classicists like Shea, Guilday, McAvoy, and Ellis tended to highlight those great accomplishments of the Church in the United States—the assimilation of some ten million immigrants between the early nineteenth and early twentieth centuries, and the massive institution-building that paralleled the assimilation—that graphically and empirically refuted the spirit (and the letter) of Know-Nothingism. The brick-and-mortar church of the urban neighborhoods thus became the main character in the American Catholic story.

Given their justifiable concerns over problems of religious intolerance, the classic historians of American Catholicism, after a few ritual nods toward the Church of the Spanish and French explorers, liked to begin the Story of American Catholicism in 1634, with the founding of the proprietary colony of Maryland as a refuge for Catholics from the penal laws of England. These historians paid particular attention to the Maryland Act of Religious Toleration of 1649, which provided that no Christian in the province would "bee any wais troubled, molested, or discountenanced for or in respect of his or her religion nor in the free exercise thereof," nor could any person be in "any way compelled to the beleife or exercise of any Religion against his or her consent."

The story was then fast-forwarded to the time of the American Revolution. The thirty-five thousand Catholics in the thirteen colonies were less than one percent of the national population. But they were nonetheless blessed by great leaders, most prominent among them the Carroll cousins, Charles Carroll of Carrollton (longest surviving signer of the Declaration of Independence) and John Carroll, first archbishop of Baltimore and the first Catholic bishop in the United States. The "Carroll Church" was, in fact, the paradigm of American Catholicism most celebrated by the classic historians, and John Carroll himself was invariably presented as a model of leadership that his successors in the American episcopate would do well to emulate.

Archbishop Carroll's patriotism and his optimism about the American experiment; his ecumenism and his commitment to the constitutional separation of church and state; his active role in civic life; his passion for Catholic education; his non-sycophantic loyalty to the Holy See—these qualities of the "Maryland Tradition" were regularly celebrated in the classic historiography of American Catholicism. For it was precisely these qualities that, according to the standard account, allowed American Catholicism to weather the nativist assault and to get on with the parallel tasks of church-building and nation-building. Great episcopal figures of the antebellum period—for example, the Irish liberal John England of Charleston, and the pugnacious John Hughes of New York—were "fitted" into the Carrollingian story line (if I may be pardoned the neologism) even as their distinctive styles and the accomplishments of their episcopates stretched the boundaries of the Carroll Church. That style of Catholicism proved its tensile strength during the national cataclysm of 1861–65. Its unity in and with Rome kept American Catholicism from fracturing during the Civil War, according to the standard account. But the Church's (primarily Irish) ethnic concerns, and its nervousness about its position in the old Confederacy and the border states, conspired to keep it from seizing the great evangelical opportunity presented by black freedmen during Reconstruction.

The classic story line accelerated, and the central drama within it intensified, in the late nineteenth century. Here, the narrative was dominated by the struggle between the "Americanist" party (Cardinal James Gibbons of Baltimore, Archbishop John Ireland of

St. Paul, Bishop John Keane of Catholic University, and their
Roman agent, Monsignor Denis O'Connell) on the one hand, and
the "conservatives" (led by Archbishop Michael Corrigan of New
York and his suffragan, the redoubtable Bernard McQuaid of Roch-
ester) on the other—and it was rather clearly understood that the
Americanists were the good guys in the controversy. Things were,
of course, more complicated than that. Bishop McQuaid, the cur-
mudgeonly "conservative," initially opposed the definition of papal infallibility at Vatican I. Archbishop Ireland, the quintessential
"liberal," ruthlessly drove Eastern-rite Catholic emigrants and their
married clergy out of the archdiocese of St. Paul and indeed out of
the Church (thus earning himself the ironic title, among some wags,
of "Father of Russian Orthodoxy in America").

But where the two parties clearly divided was on the question
of American democracy and its distinctive resolution of the age-
old problem of church and state. The Americanists supported, even
celebrated, the American arrangement, while the conservatives (like
most senior Roman officials of the day) found it tolerable at best.
Charges of heresy flew back and forth.

Eventually, in 1899, the "Americanism" controversy was brought
to a formal conclusion by Leo XIII's apostolic letter *Testem Benevo-
lentiae*. The letter condemned certain "Americanist" propositions
(about spirituality, ecclesiology, the Church and modernity, and
church-state relations); but the pope also admitted his uncertainty
that anyone of consequence in the American Church held to the
proscribed notions. In the ensuing hermeneutic battle, Gibbons and
his party argued that Americanism was a "phantom heresy" (a position adopted by the classic historians of American Catholicism),
while Corrigan and his friends thanked Rome for having saved them
from the clutches of irresponsible Gallican innovators and sweaty
jingoists.

The Carroll/Gibbons tradition, according to the classic story
line, went into a fallow period after the deaths of the giants, Ireland

in 1918 and Gibbons in 1921. The end game of the Americanist struggle abutted the far more stringent Roman reaction to Modernism in the first and second decades of the twentieth century, and the Maryland Tradition of Carroll and Gibbons was superseded by the vigorous *Romanitá* exemplified by Cardinal William O'Connell of Boston. But the great tradition was kept alive in the social liberalism of the "Right Reverend New Dealer," Monsignor John A. Ryan, and was revived among the bishops in the late 1940s and 1950s under the episcopal leadership of men like Detroit's Edward Mooney, Chicago's Albert Meyer, and St. Louis's Joseph Ritter. The Maryland Tradition reached a particularly sharp edge of intellectual development at the Jesuits' Woodstock College outside of Baltimore, which housed the pioneer ecumenist Gustave Weigel and the great theologian of freedom, John Courtney Murray. Vatican II endorsed this revival and indeed the tradition of the Carroll/Gibbons Church, in *Dignitatis Humanae*, its Declaration on Religious Freedom (of which Murray was, of course, an intellectual architect).

By the mid-1960s, then, the tension that had driven the classic story line in the history of American Catholicism seemed largely resolved. The election of John F. Kennedy to the presidency in 1960, and Vatican II's endorsement of religious freedom as a fundamental human right, vindicated the confidence of Catholics in America and the American experience of Catholicism. Or so it seemed, until the ecclesiastical and political controversies of the postconciliar and Vietnam periods began to chip away at the Story of American Catholicism as told by the classicists.

T he classic story line held in the generation of scholars immediately following Monsignor Ellis. James Hennessy, S.J., Gerald Fogarty, S.J., and Marvin O'Connell, for example, were three distinguished historians who, with differences of emphasis and nuance, worked within the standard account while correcting its simplifications and amplifying its range of interests and concerns.

Hennessy's 1981 volume, *American Catholics*, enriched the classic portrait of Catholic Americans by focusing on Catholicism as a community of distinctive human beings, and not simply as a religious institution. Fogarty's study, *The Vatican and the American Hierarchy from 1870 to 1965*, offered a detailed portrait of the (sometimes tawdry) ecclesiastical politics that shaped the Americanist controversy, but, again, from within the general framework of the standard account with its emphasis on the "normative" status of the Carroll/Gibbons view of the American Church. In *American Catholic Biblical Scholarship: A History from the Early Republic to Vatican II*, Fogarty offered, among other things, a useful antidote to the claims of some Catholic restorationists that the anti-Modernist excesses of the early twentieth century were the invention of fevered post-Vatican II liberal imaginations. Fogarty's portrait of the persecution (there is no other word for it) of the Catholic University biblical scholar Henry Poels was a sobering reminder of how zeal for the Lord can, in the wrong hands, become mere zealotry. Marvin O'Connell's study, *John Ireland and the American Catholic Church*, demonstrated that biography in the grand manner and within the classic story line was still possible, even as contemporary research refined the standard account and our understanding of the major figures within it.

But as the twentieth century drew to a close, Fathers Hennesey, Fogarty, and O'Connell seemed to be a diminishing minority among scholars of American Catholic history, for they accepted, with various qualifications, the Shea/Guilday/McAvoy/Ellis historiography in its general outline of the Catholic Story in America. And it is precisely that account that has been challenged by a revisionist school whose manifesto was Jay P. Dolan's 1983 work, *The American Catholic Experience*.

The revisionists have brought new insights to the study of American Catholic history, particularly in terms of social history. Like Fernand Braudel and the *Annalistes* school in France, and in a manner not dissimilar to that of E. P. Thompson, Eric

Hobsbawm, and other Marxist historians in Britain, the revisionists are far less inclined, as a matter of principle, to investigate the doings of bishops and clergy, and far more interested in probing the daily lives and religious practices of American Catholics. This has, as I say, enriched our understanding of the American Catholic mosaic considerably.

But the revisionists' real interest, intellectually and, so to speak, politically, is historiographic. And their strategy, as an intellectual party, seems to be built around two lines of attack: to uproot the Shea/Guilday/McAvoy/Ellis standard account, and to replace it with a telling of the tale more congenial to their own ecclesiastical concerns, which involve the catalogue of "progressive" causes flogged regularly in the *National Catholic Reporter*—disentangling the American church from "Rome," "women's rights" in the Church, the "democratization" of Catholicism, and so forth.

If the classic story line stressed the essential continuity of the normative Carroll Church from the American Revolution to Vatican II (while taking account of the break in that trajectory occasioned by the Americanist and Modernist crises and the interwar "Romanization" of the American hierarchy), the revisionist story line stresses discontinuity: between the colonial period and the Catholicism of the Revolutionary period; between the first "republican" years of Carroll's episcopate and his later "conservative" period; between the Carroll Church and the "immigrant Church" that followed; between, most important, the working-class "Catholic ghetto Church" of 1925–55 and the postconciliar suburban Church of the 1960s and 1970s.

There was, to be sure, something a bit too neat about the standard account and its sense of American Catholic continuity, particularly in the scholarly generations running from Shea through the early Ellis. Yet what the revisionists propose is not to refine that account but to abandon it. The story line they would substitute is one whose thematic hallmarks are discontinuity across the generations from John Carroll to Joseph Bernardin and John

O'Connor; the radical pluralism of Catholic experience; the mediocrity and xenophobia of the preconciliar ghetto Church; and a chronic, usually nasty, tension between the Church in America and the Holy See.

This revisionist strategy involves a root-and-branch retelling of the American Catholic story from its beginnings. In terms of the colonial period, the good news is that the new historians have probed far more deeply than their predecessors into the non-English Catholic roots of Catholicism in America, and have added to our store of knowledge about colonial French and Spanish Catholicism— the latter, of course, being of particular importance today, given the prominent (and increasing) Hispanic presence in the American Church. The bad news is that the revisionists pay little attention to the religious-liberty dimension of the Maryland founding, and undervalue its importance as a breakthrough in religious tolerance with implications for Catholic participation in the subsequent church/state debate in the independent United States.

Indeed, the revisionist rereading of the Maryland colonial experience is a striking example of the school's tendency to turn what ought to be an amplification of our understanding of the past into an assault on the truth of the classic story line. The revisionists are surely right to remind us that the Calverts, founders of Maryland, were not plaster saints, but rather investors and proprietors who expected their colony to turn a profit. But why should such commercial concerns be thought to have precluded a commitment to religious liberty? Why couldn't the early Calverts have been *both* proprietors and exponents of religious tolerance? Do we have here an instance of "progressive" American Catholicism's skepticism toward capitalism distorting its historical perspective?

The real target of the revisionist rereading of the American Catholic "founding," however, is the work and reputation of Archbishop John Carroll. In the six-volume *Bicentennial History of the Catholic Church in the United States,* James Hennessy sums up, in contemporary form and with due regard for the archbishop's flaws, the classic case for Carroll:

> His Church was that which antedated in Catholicism the neo-ultramontane movement. In secular politics, he was a Federalist, a conservative, an admirer of George Washington. The "furious democracy" of France's revolution appalled him. . . . But he did not confuse [the] American and French revolutions, and he believed that the Church in the United States should be open to new forms of being and functioning that responded to the new setting in which it found itself. His working out of this in practice was not always easy nor was it always successful. John Carroll's "learning and abilities" were put fully to the test. On balance he met that test. His like has scarcely been known again in the history of American Catholicism.

Jay P. Dolan, on the other hand, will have none of this. In *The American Catholic Experience,* Dolan's final judgment on John Carroll is little less than scathing, for Dolan regards Carroll as having committed a kind of treason. Carroll, who had the opportunity to lead the way, in fact betrayed the possibility of creating a distinctively "American Church" by his ultimate (and, in Dolan's view, pusillanimous) acquiescence to Roman authority:

> With the spirit of independence, so manifest in the 1780s, gone, Carroll became increasingly dependent on the papacy. All throughout his career as a leader in the American Catholic community, he sought to maintain a balance between being a loyal American and a faithful Roman Catholic. It was a delicate balancing act; in his younger years, as a priest, he leaned toward the American spirit of independence; in his later years, as bishop, he moved closer to the stance of a Roman Catholic for whom the papacy was the vital center of the Church. Though he still held firm to his belief that the authority of the papacy was limited to "things purely spiritual," he no longer supported the idea of an *independent American Catholic Church* (emphasis added).

This view is, of course, dependent on Dolan's revisionist account of Carroll's early ministry as Superior of the Catholic Mission in the United States and as first bishop of Baltimore. Then, Dolan argues, Carroll understood the importance of creating a "republican" form of Catholicism in which the Church would absorb the new national experiment in democracy into its own internal life. Lay ownership and control of ecclesiastical properties, the election of bishops, decentralized Church authority, a vernacular liturgy, eschewal of a distinct Catholic educational system—in short, Catholic Congregationalism: this was the cause that, Dolan believes, Carroll should have espoused and would have led, had he not been spooked, as it were, by the excesses of Jacobinism in France and his own innate ecclesiastical conservatism.

Those who detect some affinity between Professor Dolan's revisionist designs for the truly "republican" episcopate of John Carroll and the agenda of certain parties *a gauche* in twenty-first-century American Catholicism will not be far off the mark. For just as revisionist historiographers of the Cold War reread the history of the Truman administration through the lens of their Vietnam passions, the new American Catholic revisionists view the episcopate of John Carroll—*the* paradigm in the classic story line—through the prism of their own agenda for Catholicism after Vatican II.

Despite a flurry of "independent" thinking during the Americanist controversy, the "republican" Catholicism that Archbishop Carroll allegedly betrayed lay essentially dormant, according to the revisionist story line, until the postconciliar period. The 165 years between Carroll's "turning" and the close of Vatican II were dominated by the construction of the "immigrant Church"—by which the revisionists mean (sometimes using the term itself, sometimes suggesting it by inference) the "ghetto Church." Moreover, "ghetto" here takes on the dreariest possible coloration: xenophobic, anti-intellectual, racist, sexist, authoritarian, Jansenist. Thomas Spalding, author of *The Premier See: A History of the Archdiocese of Baltimore, 1789–1989,* sums up the revisionist indictment in these terms:

> In an editorial entitled "Keeping Up with the Times," the *Baltimore Catholic Review* told its readers in the summer of 1921 that the Church "sees beyond the present and prepares for other times when jazz and noise and vulgarity shall have sickened their votaries." Her attitude toward the big questions "is the same today as yesterday." As non-Catholic America entered a period of doubt and disillusionment following World War I, "Catholics set out as 'providential hosts' to defend the values and promises of American idealism which seemed threatened by various forms of irrationalism." In their keeping innocence would survive.
>
> With a self-assurance that brooked no questioning, American Catholics would convince themselves that they were in the forefront of every important social, cultural, and intellectual movement in the country . . . Catholics would be daily reassured in the Catholic classroom, Catholic press, and Catholic pulpit that their Church had the answer to every question worth asking. Never would they think to look beyond these sources for confirmation.
>
> "We were, thus, a chosen people—though chosen, it seemed, to be second rate," recalled Garry Wills, a beneficiary of these reassurances and for several years a resident of Baltimore. The in-built inferiority of the ghetto church was carefully hidden by an apologetics ultimately rooted in neo-Thomism that would allow even literate Catholics to assume a God-given superiority. Upon this apologetical undergirding the Catholic ghetto of the twentieth century would be confidently constructed.

The classic story line, particularly in the hands of its more sophisticated practitioners, did not ignore the "immigrant Church"; indeed, it gave considerable attention to the assimilation controversies and other Irish/German tensions in the late nineteenth century. However, the classicists regarded the American Catholic immigrant saga as essentially a story of success. While the Church in Europe was losing the working class during the Industrial Revolution, American Catholicism, against the historical odds and in the face of vicious nativist opposition, brokered the passage of ten million immigrants into mainstream American society while retaining the religious loyalties of the overwhelming majority of these new citizens. Moreover, according to the standard account, that "success" was reconfirmed in the post-World War II period, when Catholicism was transformed from the working-class, urban-based Church into a middle-class and upper-middle-class Church demographically centered in the suburbs.

The revisionists, on the other hand, cannot seem to bring themselves to regard what they style the "ghetto Church" as the platform for any sort of success, religious, intellectual, or political. They accept, without much cavil, one of John Tracy Ellis's more dubious claims, namely, that American Catholicism had no intellectual life to speak of in the mid-1950s. They ignore, perhaps because they hold in contempt, the political success of the urban Catholic Irish, Italians, Germans, and Poles. They have little to say, perhaps because the data ill fit their historiographic image, about the fact that American Catholicism during this "ghetto" period produced great pioneers of the liturgical and social-action movements like Virgil Michel. Nor do they account for the fact that the Thomism they dismissively deprecate (while failing to recognize the variant schools within the Thomist family) was taken seriously as an intellectual tradition by such respected secular scholars as Robert Maynard Hutchins and Mark Van Doren. Nor can they explain how converts like Dorothy Day and Thomas Merton were attracted to this Church whose public face is taken to have been that of a xenophobic, anti-intellectual, politically reactionary ghetto. According to Wills and Dolan, only in the 1960s, when American Catholicism, personified by Daniel and Philip Berrigan, broke definitively with the "ghetto Church" and its flag-waving patriotism, did it become possible to reclaim, again and at last, the "republican" heritage betrayed by John Carroll and (most of) his successors.

Here, yet again, the revisionists have leaped from a valid historical point to an invalid historiographical conclusion. Of course there were strains of xenophobia in the immigrant Church, and some of them perdured into the 1960s. No one who reads Cardinal Lawrence Shehan's memoirs, in which he poignantly recalls being booed by masses of Catholic parishioners in 1966 when he testified before the Baltimore City Council in favor of an open-housing ordinance, can fail to realize that there were ugly elements in urban ethnic Catholicism. But, as Thomas Spalding himself demonstrated in *The Premier See,* the "ghetto Church" that produced racist parishioners also produced the priests and laity who were at the forefront of Baltimore's integration movement in the 1950s and 1960s.

Moreover, the revisionist account scarcely does justice to the immense vitality of Catholic life in, say, the Baltimore of Archbishop Michael J. Curley (1921–1947) or the Chicago of Cardinal George Mundelein (1916–1939). Spalding, in *The Premier See,* seems simultaneously baffled, charmed, repelled, and deeply impressed by Archbishop Curley and the Church he led. Curley, Spalding insists, had "little use for the values of mainstream America" (what those values are is left to the reader's imagination), and deliberately eschewed the Carroll/Gibbons tradition for a Church guided by "the myth of majestic changelessness." On the other hand, Spalding notes that Curley, with his "boldness and vigor," was "without doubt the most open, honest, and outspoken member of the American hierarchy" during the interwar period. What accounts for this curiously bifocal judgment? I suspect it may be due to the fact that Spalding, who has long and historic family connections in Baltimore, is somewhat less a revisionist on this matter of the "ghetto Church" than Dolan or Wills, and yet felt required to tip his historiographic hat at least modestly in that direction. Thus do intellectual fashions shape, posthumously, the reputations of great men.

T he revisionist deprecation of John Carroll and the even more lurid revisionist portrait of the "ghetto Church" are not simply matters of intellectual fashion, however. They are interpretations deeply, even determinatively, influenced by post-Vatican II Church politics. To construct an historical foundation for the "progressive" Catholic agenda they champion, Jay Dolan and others in the liberal Catholic opinion establishment had to make several moves. First, they had to distinguish the "bad John Carroll" from the "good John Carroll." Second, they had to show that the "bad Carroll" skewed the growth of American Catholicism away from its "republican" roots and toward ultramontanism. (Gibbons and Ireland must be chuckling in their postmortem circumstances over the thought that they were closet ultramontanes, but revisionist historiography permits few calibrations to the right of Catholic Congregationalism.) Third, they had to demonstrate that the net result of Carroll's betrayal was the "Catholic ghetto," whose evils must be catalogued in grim detail. Finally, they had to present Vatican II exclusively as the Council of *aggiornamento* ("updating"), rather than as the Council of an *aggiornamento* rooted in *ressourcement* (a "return to the sources")—including, it should be added, a return (in the Declaration on Religious Freedom) to the sources of authentic American Catholic liberalism in Carroll and Gibbons.

None of this, in its parts or as a whole, makes for an especially plausible or persuasive portrait of the American Catholic experience—unless one adopts what literary critic Frederick Crews once described as the "perpetually scandalized relation to the past" of "post-Sixties conformism." And that, alas, is a tough but accurate description of those revisionist Catholic historians who work diligently to rewrite the American Catholic story line in order to prop up the sagging cause of "progressive" Catholicism. These new historians of American Catholicism have, let it be freely admitted, opened some important windows of understanding. And doubtless some of their post-Sixties conformism is less a matter of an ideological agenda than of unexamined assumptions. But what might be called the "Jay Dolan Project" in American Catholic history is of a different magnitude entirely. For it is an interpretation of history intellectually rooted in what Philip Gleason has aptly described as "more fundamental changes in *theological* outlook." The Jay Dolan Project, in other words, is much less a matter of new facts than of new interpretive filters, of "a tendency to endorse as theological liberalism what the old [historiography] endorsed as social and procedural liberalism."

The proper analogy, again, is to the revisionist school of American historiography in the 1960s. As William Appleman Williams deliberately sought to reshape and radicalize U.S. foreign policy through a revisionist (and essentially Marxist) reading of the history of America's encounter with the world, so Jay Dolan and those of his persuasion have, with energy and imagination, sought to buttress the "progressive" agenda in postconciliar American Catholicism and the cause of an "independent American Catholic Church" by a radical retelling of the story that provides a usable history for their contemporary purposes. No doubt new light will be shed on the American Catholic experience as the Dolan school continues its work. But if the Williams analogy is apt, the Catholic revisionists will be in for an unwelcome surprise. For the net result of the revisionist/classicist battle over the origins of the Cold War was a strengthening of Harry Truman's posthumous claim to historical greatness—precisely the "myth" that the revisionists were most eager to debunk. Might the same be the happy fate of John Carroll and the Carroll Church when the debate over American Catholic historical revisionism runs its course?

"History is an antidote to despair," or so thought a college teacher of mine. Perhaps he would pardon my amending his *mot* to read, "History is an antidote to frivolity."

American Catholicism sometimes suffers from an excess of frivolity in the meridian years of its third century. A Church that is the
largest voluntary association in the country; a Church whose universal pastor, John Paul II, definitively answered Stalin's cynical query
about the pope's divisions; a Church that is, demographically, at its
strongest historical point of leverage in American society—this is a
Church that would seem well positioned to seize what Richard John
Neuhaus and others have seen as a possible "Catholic Moment" in
American history, *pro Deo et patria*.

Instead, the Catholic Moment proposition has been subjected to
the death of a thousand cuts from both opinion establishments, the
liberal and the conservative, in the American Church. The progressivist left refuses to concede the possibility of a Catholic moment
built around the authoritative interpretation of Vatican II taught by
John Paul II and Benedict XVI. The ultra-traditionalist right insists
that the *real* Catholic Moment was in the heyday of Archbishop
Curley when the "myth of majestic changelessness" prevailed against
all the Church's enemies, foreign and domestic.

Simply paying more attention to the Story of Catholicism in
America will not solve the problem of Catholic frivolity. Indeed, if
the revisionists come to dominate the field, their scandalized relationship to the past ("I thank thee, O God, that I am not like my
ancestors: racist, sexist, warmongering, environmentally insensitive,
subservient to Rome," etc., etc.) virtually guarantees more frivolity,
now extended back across several generations.

On the other hand, a renewed and amplified classic story line
could revivify the Catholic Moment proposition in several ways. It
could help distinguish what is authentically "American Catholic"
from what is merely post-Sixties conformism. It could suggest
models (Carroll, Gibbons, Murray) for the interaction between the
United States and Rome that mediate between Catholic Congregationalism and the tendency to see Catholicism in the United States

as a mere branch office of Roman Catholic Church, Inc. It might put to rest one of the least plausible feminist claims about the pre-conciliar Church, i.e., that it was an institution in which women were "disempowered." It would, in sum, usefully complexify the Catholic debate, and thus create the possibility of moving that debate to a more adult level of discussion.

Whom you would change, taught Martin Luther King, Jr., you must first love. Whom you would love, you must first know, because love is an act of the intellect as well as of the emotions. The new historiography of American Catholicism teaches, sometimes subtly and sometimes overtly, a contempt for the Catholic past, and indeed for the American past—which seems a dubious base on which to build the American Catholicism of the future. But neither can an American Catholicism capable of seizing a possible "Catholic moment" be built on the receding sands of a forgotten past.

Any possible Catholic Moment in American history will combine, as did the Second Vatican Council, a strategy of *aggiornamento* with a strategy of *ressourcement*. And that, it seems, is what the Carroll Church tried to do, at least in the standard account of the Story of Catholicism in America. Amplifying and refining that classic story line is thus an important intellectual exercise for the Church of the twenty-first century. And it just might be, as well, both an antidote to despair and a source of reasonable good cheer about the future.

U.S. Catholics
as They Were and Are

T he ideological pretentiousness sometimes found in the farther
reaches of postmodernist social history can be easily dismissed
as so much Marxist exhaust. A more modest approach to reading
history from the bottom up can, however, illuminate the past by
focusing on the loves, loyalties, and quotidian practices of ordinary
folk. Done right, that kind of social history can even unravel seemingly settled schemes of How Things Were. A classic example is Ea-
mon Duffy's 1992 book, *The Stripping of the Altars*, which, by demonstrating from parish records the remarkable tenacity of Catholic
popular piety in Tudor England, fundamentally altered the historiography of the English Reformation.

James O'Toole's 2009 volume, *The Faithful: A History of Catholics in America*, won't achieve anything nearly so grand in the field of
U.S. Catholic history. Still, the book is an interesting supplement to
the grand-sweep, classic Catholic historiography pioneered by Peter
Guilday in the 1920s and continued in our time by John Tracy Ellis
and James Hennessy. In fact, if someone were to marry an O'Toole-
like exploration of the way in which American Catholics actually
lived their faith to the classic Guilday-Ellis story line (which focused
on great episcopal leaders, Catholic institution-building, and the
American Church's struggles with anti-Catholic bigotry and Roman
incomprehension), the result would be something that has never existed: an engaging, comprehensive telling of the American Catholic
story in all its many-splendored and much-tattered complexity.

O'Toole nearly ignores the prelate-centered, bricks-and-mor-
tar institutional tale in order to reimagine the story of American
Catholicism as the story of "the faithful." He divides his study into

six (sometimes overlapping) periods, each symbolized by a paradigmatic lay figure of that era. The first four of these explorations are full of fascinating and evocative detail. To those who know only the Church after the Second Vatican Council, a lot of that detail will seem not so much quaint as utterly foreign.

The Catholic Church of the colonial period and the early American Republic (O'Toole does not, alas, explore the older, Spanish-colonial Catholicism of the Southwest) was largely a "priestless Church" in which the faith was transmitted, generation after generation, through home worship, pious books, and family catechism study. It was a Church in which, given the dire lack of clergy and the difficulties of travel, "making a spiritual communion" was far more frequent than the reception of Holy Communion itself (which, for many Catholics, was a quarterly or even an annual experience).

O'Toole's research suggests that this was more of a Bible-reading Church than the conventional story line has it, but those Douay-Rheims Bibles were complemented by popular devotional manuals such as Bishop Richard Challoner's *Garden of the Soul*, likely one of the best-selling Catholic books in the history of English-language publishing. The priestless Church contended with the sometimes fierce anti-Catholic bigotry of Protestantism, especially Puritanism; yet, as O'Toole reminds us, even a sometime Catholic-mocker such as John Adams could, in the aftermath of the American Revolution, make the largest single personal donation to the building of a Catholic church in Boston, the experience of the revolution having seemingly changed Adams's mind about the compatibility of "grandmother Church" (as he once called Catholicism) and democracy.

In his discussion of the Church in the antebellum republic, O'Toole focuses considerable attention on the Charleston experiment in Catholic constitutionalism. From 1823 until 1842, the Diocese of Charleston was governed by Bishop John England with the assistance of a House of Clergy and House of Laity, both of which met annually in a diocesan convention. The Charleston experiment was not replicated elsewhere, and in fact ended in South Carolina on the demise of Bishop England, an Irish emigré who had also launched one of the first and most consequential Catholic newspapers in America, the *United States Catholic Miscellany*, which had a national audience. Bishop England's constitutional experiment provides O'Toole with the prism through which he reads the early nineteenth-century struggle over trusteeism in the American Church. Along the way, O'Toole fails, perhaps, to consider how the more ardent advocates of lay ownership of Church property (a trusteeism that also entailed various degrees of lay control over local clergy appointments) were not, in other parts of the country, quite the gentlemen who made Bishop England's experiment work.

The trusteeship battle, which was eventually and inevitably won by the bishops, is something of a distraction from O'Toole's story line, which is far more interesting in its focus on the expansion and intensification of Catholic religious practice (as the available clergy increased considerably), the new Catholic interest in the papacy (reversing what O'Toole describes as a kind of Catholic apathy toward the Holy See prior to the period just before the Civil War), and the rise of violent anti-Catholic bigotry in such self-conscious centers of American progress as Massachusetts and Pennsylvania.

The political culmination of this bigotry was the Know-Nothing movement, which gave birth to the American party and ran Millard Fillmore for president in 1856. Its most intriguing artifact, however, was a piece of ecclesiastical porn by one Maria Monk: the *Awful Disclosures of the Hotel Dieu Nunnery in Montreal*, which was published in 1836 and was the best-selling book in the pre-Civil War period, save for *Uncle Tom's Cabin*. ("Maria Monk" was, in fact, a team of evangelical ministers; the book featured lurid tales of priest-nun liaisons, murdered infants buried in convent basements, and other fictional debaucheries.)

In his third period, the time of the Immigrant Church, O'Toole hews closest to the classic American Catholic historiography of Guilday and Ellis. Here, from the end of the Civil War to the 1930s, the focus is on organizational expansion and a vast program of institution-building—most of it funded, O'Toole notes, through lots of small donations rather than through today's familiar campaigns and their "leadership gifts." Vocations to the priesthood and religious life surged, parishes missions and novenas became popular, and magnificent churches were built. For the first time in American Catholic history, the multipriest parish was the norm; many newly ordained priests could anticipate a quarter-century apprenticeship before being given the responsibilities of a pastorate.

Catholic piety in this period came perilously close, at points, to confirming various anti-Catholic stereotypes. "Unworthiness," was, as O'Toole writes, "a persistent theme," so that the reception of Holy Communion at Mass reached what was likely a historic low; in Boston in 1899, to take one example, "a priest in a large parish of Irish and German immigrants reported that about seven hundred people were at his 7:45 Mass one Sunday morning, and that exactly forty of them came to Communion." Paraliturgical practices—later imagined to be ancient and enduring—in fact came into their own in this period; the two most prominent were the Stations of the Cross and Eucharistic Adoration followed by Benediction of the Blessed Sacrament (rather clumsily described by O'Toole as "a ceremony in which the priest blessed the congregation using a piece of consecrated eucharistic bread"). Marian piety and devotion to ethnic patron saints (St. Wenceslaus for the Bohemians, St. Patrick for the Irish, and St. Stanislaus for the Poles) flourished, as Catholics began to live in a spiritual geography that encompassed a vast array of characters, to be invoked by name in popular litanies of prayer.

Above all, this was the period in which the Catholic Church became the greatest assimilator of immigrants in American history—the institution that, more than any other, turned foreigners into

Americans. The numbers are simply staggering: 800,000 Irish in the 1840s, and 400,000 Germans in the same period. But that was a mere warm-up for the 1880s, in which 650,000 new Americans came from Ireland, along with 1.5 million from Germany, 300,000 from Italy, and another 300,000 from various bits of the Habsburg realms, swelling the ranks of Catholics in the United States through one of the greatest population transfers in history.

The organizational growth of the Church followed suit. There were seventeen U.S. dioceses in 1840 but sixty by 1880. American Catholics, O'Toole reports, were served by fewer than five hundred priests in 1840; there were nine thousand priests a half century later. One striking example sums up the process: "In the time it took for a Catholic girl born in Detroit in the 1880s to grow to adulthood, the Church around her had increased more than fivefold."

It was during this third period that Catholic urban politics and the long-lasting Catholic alliance with the Democratic party took shape, as more than a few immigrants worked their way into the American mainstream through the local police precinct and ward machine. Burghers of earlier stock began to complain of "cities held captive by Irishmen and their sons," which included New York, Chicago, and Boston, but also Kansas City and Omaha; "even in Salt Lake City," O'Toole writes (in one of those moments that make social history worthwhile), "the chief police detective was a man named Donovan." All of this led, of course, to the occasionally picaresque. Frank Hague, the boss of Jersey City from 1917 until 1947, "was a conspicuously observant Catholic . . . a regular in his local parish church, at least when he was not at one of the houses that graft had bought him at the shore or in Palm Beach."

Perhaps a story, untold by O'Toole, is not inappropriate here. In 1918, the city of Baltimore commissioned the Kirk-Stieff silversmiths to create, at public expense, a colossal silver service to be presented to Cardinal James Gibbons, the native son who was marking his golden jubilee as a bishop. Each of the hundreds of pieces in the service bore the cardinal's monogram and coat of arms; the silver-smiths also created a pattern that had never been used before (and has never been used since). The service was, presumably, gratefully received by the cardinal; for decades, it was prominently displayed in the dining room of the archbishop's house at 408 North Charles Street in downtown Baltimore.

Then, one morning in the 1950s, the rector of the old Baltimore cathedral came downstairs to find that the entire Gibbons silver service had been stolen. After absorbing the shock (and, perhaps, pondering the prospects of spending the rest of his clerical life in the extreme wilderness of western Maryland), the rector called the police, who informed the mayor—then, as for some years previous, one Thomas J. D'Alesandro, Jr., son of an Italian immigrant family and a devout parishioner of St. Leo's. (D'Alesandro's daughter, Nancy, would later become Speaker of the U.S. House of Representatives). Tommy, as everyone called him, took extreme offense at the theft, and put the word out on the street: "If that ****ing silver isn't returned in forty-eight hours, somebody's back is gonna get broken." The next morning, Our Lady of Fatima rectory in East Baltimore got an anonymous phone call: "Look in your trash cans." There was the Gibbons silver, all of it, in shopping bags. Some might call that "efficient local government"; in any event, it nicely illustrates the ethnic politics of the Immigrant Church, in the days before the American Civil Liberties Union and the U.S. Supreme Court got into the church–state act.

O'Toole suggests that the Church of Catholic Action, symbolized by Dorothy Day, followed the Immigrant Church, even if the two overlapped at points. Yet the Catholic Worker movement that Dorothy Day helped launch was only one expression of an enormous flourishing of lay Catholic organizations in the early and mid-twentieth century. The Holy Name Society, the Knights of Columbus, the Knights of St. Peter Claver (for

African-Americans, in that segregated era), the Daughters of Isabella, the Catholic Daughters of America, the St. Vincent de Paul Society, the Catholic Youth Organization, the Legion of Decency, and the Christian Family Movement—these and a myriad of other associations were essentially lay enterprises, and the rhythm of their activities was, for decades, the warp and woof of a distinctly Catholic civil society. (With the exception of the Knights of Columbus and one or two other examples, this rich associational life was rapidly destroyed by the liberal bureaucratization of the Catholic Church that began in the mid-1960s—a seemingly salient part of the lay Catholic story left unaddressed by O'Toole.)

Dorothy Day's radicalism went hand in glove with a deeply traditional piety; Dorothy, wearing a black mantilla while attending one of Fr. Daniel Berrigan's free-form liturgies in the 1960s, is an unforgettable image from that otherwise forgettable period. And in that sense, Dorothy Day was, despite her politics, a spiritual child of her Catholic era: a time of frequent confession, "visits to the Blessed Sacrament," the Forty Hours devotion, the family rosary, *Treasure Chest* (a Catholic comic book with a circulation in the hundreds of thousands), pilgrimages to Rome, adulation of the then-unassailable Pius XII, and better than 70 percent Sunday Mass attendance.

It was also the time when lay Catholics were prominent leaders of the American labor movement, even as the Catholic big-city bosses helped the Democratic party jettison Henry Wallace for Harry Truman in 1944 and then became an essential part of the liberal coalition that adopted a strong civil rights plank at the 1948 Democratic convention (both points unexplored by O'Toole). Catholic anticommunism was at its peak, symbolized by two Irish-American U.S. senators, "Tailgunner Joe" McCarthy of Wisconsin and John F. Kennedy of Massachusetts. Illustrating this point, O'Toole offers an evocative vignette that seems to come, not simply from another era, but from another planet: "In September 1959, when Nikita Khrushchev, the Soviet premier, visited the United Nations, more than 20,000 Catholics in Boston stood around the Bunker Hill Monument, which commemorated a battle of the American Revolution, to pray the rosary, asking God to frustrate the Russian's wicked schemes."

John F. Kennedy's rise to national prominence and his disentanglement of his politics from any tether to Catholic conviction (a point rightly noted by O'Toole) was a complex business, from which many hints about the future might have been read. Kennedy's election as president in 1960 marked, in one sense, the apogee of the Immigrant Church: as Joseph P. Kennedy was determined to prove through his sons, Catholics in the United States had finally made it. Yet Kennedy's aloofness from the Catholic associational universe also demonstrated the failure of the Church of Catholic Action to translate its reading of Catholic social doctrine into a practical political program that an attractive and knowledgeable Catholic politician could sell to the rest of America. Kennedy, who was far more the Harvard rationalist (and cynic) than the political by-product of *Rerum Novarum* and *Quadragesimo Anno*, helped make Catholics safe for America by "wearing his Catholicism lightly," as one Kennedy aide quoted by O'Toole put it (and not only in matters of the Sixth Commandment). That bifurcation of the theological and the spiritual from the mundane and the political, coupled with the Catholic migration to the suburbs and the disintegration of the urban Catholic cultures that had been such powerful transmitters of the faith, set the stage for many of the difficulties that would soon follow, in both ecclesial and public life.

The Faithful begins to flag, and finally to limp badly, when O'Toole comes into the sphere of living memory: Vatican II and the Church in the twenty-first century. The complex tale of Vatican II itself (which, admittedly, is not O'Toole's primary concern) is sketched as background in the familiar and dull categories of Catholic cowboys and Indians, with good liberals battling bad conservatives for the future of the Church. O'Toole paints a frank and depressing portrait of the collapse of Catholic liturgical and devotional practice in the years immediately following Vatican II. But he does not connect any dots between either the Council itself, or bodies of thought associated with the "spirit of Vatican II," and that collapse.

On the liturgy, he rightly laments that a silly season of liturgical kitsch ensued, while giving the enthusiasts of change for change's sake their innings: "After so many years of staring at baroque altarpieces whose design could be 'distracting,' one commentator concluded, 'the shock of a plain table with its rigid lines may be a good antidote for us.'" Yet O'Toole does not ask the obvious next question—an antidote to *what?*—nor does he explore the reasons behind what he accurately describes as the implosion of the Catholic belief system that stood behind both the Immigrant Church and the Church of Catholic Action.

O'Toole's survey of the wreckage is fair and instructive. And yet, some conjecture as to why the collapse of the idea of sin—and the concomitant collapse of an experience of grace—swept through the Catholic world of 1960s America would have been helpful. The liberal Catholicism of the post-Vatican II period was a hollow shell from which religious passion had been largely emptied, and that could not have been pleasing to the older generation of radicals. Despite her political myopia about the likes of Fidel Castro, the Catholic radicalism of a Dorothy Day was far more Catholic in its sense of the drama of sin and grace than the vapid liberalism that dominated the post-Vatican II Church. In other words, William F. Buckley, Jr., and the gang at *Triumph* magazine (both missing from O'Toole's account) weren't the only lay Catholics who thought that the immediate post-Vatican II Church was in serious trouble.

For with the collapse of distinctive Catholic practices (fish on Friday, the rosary, weekly Mass attendance, monthly confession) came a collapse of Catholic identity. And as the identity forged in the Immigrant Church and the Church of Social Action was being lost, the vacuum was intensified by a collapse of catechetics, such that by the mid-1980s, O'Toole notes, only one-third of Catholics in the United States could correctly name the four gospels of the New Testament.

There were, O'Toole notes, some countercurrents at work here— one of which was the wholly unexpected Catholic charismatic re- newal, whose origins O'Toole traces to a 1967 Duquesne University meeting of veterans of the Cursillo experience (a retreat movement that had begun to flourish in the late 1950s and early 1960s). In retrospect, the Catholic charismatic renewal now seems the first sign of what would, under John Paul II, become a veritable tidal wave of renewal movements and new Church associations, including Com- munion and Liberation, Focolare, the Neocatechumenal Way, and Opus Dei.

It is unfortunate that, after noting the rise of the charismatics, O'Toole gives little or no attention to these lay-dominated move- ments that are now, among other things, the seedbed of many priestly and religious vocations. Parallel lay initiatives in Catholic higher education—the University of Dallas, Thomas Aquinas Col- lege, Christendom College, Thomas Aquinas College—are not men- tioned, much less examined, in *The Faithful*, despite O'Toole's brief excursus on the postconciliar travail of Catholic higher education. He notes the expansion of "lay ministries" but without exploring the question of whether this has not amounted to a clericalization of the laity that is far removed from Vatican II's intention to ignite new forms of lay apostolate, evangelization, and mission in "the world."

O'Toole notes one of the great crises in the history of the American Church—the turmoil set loose by the 1968 en- cyclical *Humanae Vitae*—but he does so in conventional terms: Pat and Patty Crowley, the Chicago-based Christian Family Movement couple on Pope Paul VI's birth-control commission, didn't get their way, and all hell broke loose as a result. This doesn't take us much beyond the conventional liberal story line written at the time by the *National Catholic Reporter*; nor does it address the points that can be made in defense of *Humanae Vitae* and its analysis of the deleterious effects of widespread contraceptive thinking and practice on society and culture; nor does it notice the clerical bullying and liberal blackmailing that motored at least some of the dissent to the encyclical, as described in *L'Osservatore Romano* in 2008 by Baltimore-born Cardinal James Francis Stafford, in a striking memoir of his personal experiences at one of the ground zeroes of dissent.

As for the political politics (as distinguished from ecclesiastical politics) of the post-Vatican II Church, *The Faithful* notes Senator Edward M. Kennedy's "evolving position" on abortion, though O'Toole fails to explore what it meant that the Catholic layman who, above all others, could have led a national resistance movement to the abortion license imposed on the country by *Roe v. Wade* chose to do precisely the opposite. On the other side of the aisle, the most influential Catholic legislator of the last quarter of the twentieth century, Henry Hyde, is notable by his absence from O'Toole's account of the culture wars. According to *The Faithful*, Catholics became, in the 1980s, the "quintessential 'swing voters.'" But there is no digging inside the numbers to find what was, in fact, the new truth about "the Catholic vote," namely, that it was just like everybody else in that frequency of religious practice, not denominational self-identification, became *the* key indicator of voting behavior in post-*Roe v. Wade* America.

O'Toole neatly and accurately sums up the postconciliar decades by noting that "the clarity of the American Catholic world before Vatican II was replaced with both a new vitality and a new volatility." Yet he misses at least some of the vitality, and his tale of the most volatile moment in recent history—the Long Lent of 2002—contains some problems.

He correctly notes that the crisis of clergy sexual abuse was also a crisis of episcopal irresponsibility and misgovernance, and he rightly argues that no monocausal explanation of the enormous spike in predatory clerical sexual misbehavior will work (a point made by those whom O'Toole criticizes for highlighting the effects of doctrinal and moral laxness on the epidemiology of the crisis). But the story of that year of turmoil seems truncated in the book, perhaps because it is so Boston-focused and because it reveals O'Toole's evident sympathies for Voice of the Faithful, which is more accurately described as a gathering of veterans from the Revolution That Never Was than as a harbinger of a new lay Catholic responsibility and activism.

That said, O'Toole is certainly right to note that perhaps the most striking thing about the Long Lent of 2002 is that it didn't do more damage: Most Catholics, indeed the overwhelming majority of Catholics, made "the decision . . . not to abandon the Church in the aftermath of the scandal." Yet O'Toole doesn't follow up on that insight by exploring why the opposite was true in Boston, which a decade later was still reeling from the aftershocks of 2002.

A nother point that might well have received at least some attention in *The Faithful* is the fact that Catholic practice seems to have declined most precipitously in some of the former strongholds of progressive Catholicism. Chicago, for example, was the seedbed of a lot of the associational Catholicism that O'Toole celebrates in his description of the Immigrant Church and the Church of Catholic Action. Similarly, much of the liturgical and social-action liberalism of the immediate preconciliar period took its lead from what one historian of the Archdiocese of Chicago dubbed "this confident Church." Yet one would be hard put to describe Chicago Catholicism as a confident leader in the first three decades after Vatican II.

Figuring out how this happened, and why, would seem to be an urgent task. But it won't get done as long as certain of the stereotypes that mar *The Faithful* and distort its portrait of the immediate past continue to persist. Surely it is long past time to cease and desist on the notion of "John Paul II bishops" who were "selected for their undeviating loyalty to Roman policy"—which is to say, in the conventional argot, their conservatism. Cardinal Joseph Bernardin? Archbishop Daniel Pilarczyk? Cardinal Roger Mahony? Cardinal Theodore McCarrick? John Paul II appointees all, and, however else these men might be described, "conservative" does not seem the *mot juste*. The same criticism applies to O'Toole's seeming acceptance of the stereotype of the "John Paul II priest" as a liturgical ninny who wants to reassert clerical authority in parishes while wearing a cassock and a biretta. Alas, this cartoon is of a piece with O'Toole's general misapprehension of John Paul II as more medium than message. That the late pope might have been enormously successful with the young precisely because he challenged them to live lives of moral heroism against the conventions of the age is not a possibility seriously considered in *The Faithful*. Moreover, in a book focused in such an interesting way on the lay side of the American Catholic story, why is there so little attention to the impact that John Paul II had on lay Catholics, not least through the renewal movements and new Catholic communities noted above?

James O'Toole concludes his survey of Catholics in America with some modest predictions. A Catholic born in the United States today, he notes, "will be born in an era when, for the first time in its history, the infrastructure of American Catholicism will be shrinking rather than expanding." That same youngster will grow up in a Church in which the multipriest parish will be as much a vague memory as it was a pious aspiration in, say, 1820. The Church in America will be ever more richly textured ethnically, with Hispanic, African, and Asian strains adding new vitality to the mix. And, as white ethnic Catholics become more entrenched in the middle and upper classes of American society, these new Catholics will, at least for a time (and, in the case of the Asians, perhaps not so long a time) "reconnect the Church to its roots among the poor and working class."

One could have wished, in this context, for a more ample discussion of the debate over whether Hispanic Catholics should be rapidly assimilated into the mainstream (especially through the mastery of English); this is surely one of the great questions of the present on which the experience of the past can shed some light.

*T*he Faithful, while fascinating in many respects, is also frustrating. There is a danger in aiming so low in retelling the story of American Catholicism through the methodological canons of social history—namely, that one misses the many intriguing lay Catholic figures who were men and women of genuine accomplishment. I have made no comprehensive survey of the *dramatis personae* here, but it strikes me that a book telling the story of "the faithful" in America without ever mentioning the following members of the cast of characters is somewhat diminished:

- Leonard Calvert, the early colonial governor who made religious freedom a reality in seventeenth-century Maryland;
- Margaret Brent, another Maryland pioneer, a proto-campaigner for the legal and political rights of women and a stout Catholic who raised a company of volunteer soldiers to deflect an armed attempt by Virginia Puritans to take Maryland away from the Catholic Calverts;
- John Barry, one of the founders of the U.S. Navy in the Revolutionary War;
- Roger B. Taney, author of *Dred Scott*, one of the two worst Supreme Court decisions in history, and William J. Brennan, Jr., who participated (on the wrong side) in the other, *Roe v. Wade*;
- General Philip Sheridan, the leading federal cavalry officer during the Civil War;
- the student-seminarian volunteers of the North American College in Rome who, to a man, offered to take up arms in

defense of Pius IX when the Italian army was closing in on Rome in 1870;

- labor leader George Meany and financier John J. Raskob;
- urban Democratic bosses such as Chicago's Richard J. Daley and Pittsburgh's David Lawrence;
- authors Flannery O'Connor and Walker Percy;
- intellectuals such as Orestes Brownson, Mark Van Doren (a great influence on the young Thomas Merton), Michael Novak, and Gordon Zahn (the man perhaps most responsible for the beatification of the Austrian anti-Nazi martyr Franz Jaegerstaetter);
- politicians such as Eugene McCarthy and Henry Hyde (both of whom, in their distinctive ways, embodied a distinctively Catholic ethos in American public life far more than Clan Kennedy managed in all its generations);
- Omer Westendorff, an enormous (if often baleful) influence on liturgical music;
- Tom Monaghan, whose Legatus movement of Catholic entrepreneurs and professionals is one of the most successful twenty-first-century embodiments of the old associational instinct in American Catholicism.

Bringing people such as these into the story is essential, it seems to me, in marrying a social-history approach to the classic Guilday-Ellis story line and giving lay Catholics their due.

The fact that Catholics have made it in America—and the fact that this making it remains something deeply problematic—is neatly illustrated by pondering a photograph of the platform at the U.S. Capitol on Inauguration Day in 2009. There one finds the Catholic vice president of the United States, the Catholic speaker of the House of Representatives, and numerous Catholic cabinet officers. Sprinkled throughout the inaugural crowd are numerous Catholic members of the Senate and House (who form, in fact, the largest single religious group in the Congress). Yet as one keen observer has noted, the Catholic Church's core agenda of social issues would more likely be advanced if each of these Catholics were to be replaced by a Mormon.

The Radical Orthodoxy school would take this as confirmation of their claim that Catholicism and American democratic republicanism were never compatible—and proof that the United States is an ill-founded republic doomed from the start to decay into a dictatorship of relativism. That those who take this stance were AWOL from the presidential campaigns of 2000, 2004, and 2008, as they also were during the Long Lent of 2002, does not necessarily mean that their claim can be dismissed. Still, it does seem premature to declare defeat. The richness of the story told by James O'Toole, including its evocation of the struggles of the past, suggests that, while postmodern debonair nihilism may be an even more formidable foe than the bigotry of Know-Nothingism, Catholicism is not without its own strengths and its own capacity for resistance.

Indeed, the social doctrine of the Church, particularly as articulated by John Paul II, can give a more compelling account of the free and virtuous society than anything on offer in a standard Ivy League school's government department. And the attraction that many evangelical intellectuals feel for that social doctrine suggests that the story of religiously informed moral argument in American public life is not over, but is in fact heading into a new, more robust phase, in which classic Christianity versus neo-paganism, rather than Catholic versus Protestant, is the crucial fault line.

That the Catholic Church in America is headed into a new time of testing in the twenty-first century ought not be in dispute. That the Church is in a weakened condition to confront this challenge, because of a weakened sense of Catholic identity among the faithful, is not in doubt either. But history, pondered seriously, can be a source of hope as of despair. And while I have a hunch that James O'Toole and I have rather different political views, his refreshing, if often frustrating, retelling of the American Catholic story—through the prism of Catholic life as lived by the people who are the Church—is an antidote to gloom in a season of grave challenge.

The End of the Bernardin Era

C ardinal Joseph L. Bernardin died on November 14, 1996, after a moving and profoundly Christian battle with pancreatic cancer that edified Americans across the political and religious spectrums. Fourteen years after his holy death, the cardinal is primarily remembered for his end-of-life ministry to fellow cancer sufferers, for his chairmanship of the committee that produced the American bishops' 1983 pastoral letter, "The Challenge of Peace," and for his advocacy of a "consistent ethic of life." Those achievements were not the whole of the Bernardin story, however.

In his prime, Joseph Bernardin was arguably the most powerful Catholic prelate in American history; he was certainly the most consequential since the heyday of Cardinal James Gibbons of Baltimore in the late nineteenth and early twentieth centuries. In his early forties, Bernardin was the central figure in defining the culture and modus operandi of the U.S. bishops' conference. Later, when he became archbishop of Cincinnati and cardinal archbishop of Chicago, Bernardin's concept and style of episcopal ministry set the pattern for hundreds of U.S. bishops. Bernardin was also the undisputed leader of a potent network of prelates that dominated the affairs of the American hierarchy for more than two decades; observers at the time dubbed it the "Bernardin Machine." The machine's horsepower inevitably diminished after the cardinal's death. But it was still thought by many to have enough gas left in the tank to elect Bishop Gerald Kicanas of Tucson (who had begun his episcopal career as one of Bernardin's auxiliaries) as president of the United States Conference of Catholic Bishops (USCCB) in November 2010.

It didn't. Bishop Kicanas was defeated for the conference presidency by Archbishop Timothy Dolan of New York in a vote that left those bishops who still adhered to the Bernardin model speechless in disbelief. And if their stunned silence following the announcement of the vote did not conclusively demonstrate the point, the reaction to Archbishop Dolan's election in self-identified Catholic progressive circles—which ranged from bitterly disappointed to just plain bitter—confirmed that an era had ended and a corner had been turned in the history of Catholicism in the United States.

The Bernardin Era is over and the Bernardin Machine is no more. Understanding what that era was about, and what that machine embodied, is important for understanding the options the machine's demise had opened for a different pattern of episcopal leadership in the Catholic Church in the United States and a different mode of engagement between the Church and American public life.

T he era and the machine reflected the background, the perspective on the U.S. Catholic experience, and the ecclesiastical and political convictions of the man for whom both epoch and network were named.

Joseph Louis Bernardin was born in 1928 in Columbia, South Carolina, a son of Italian immigrants. Columbia was, and is, in the American Bible Belt, so Bernardin grew up in the least Catholic part of the United States—unlike, say, the prelates of his generation who were products of a vibrant Catholic urban culture in the Northeast and Midwest. Some of them may have lacked Bernardin's gracious manners and polish, but they never doubted that Catholics belonged in the United States. By contrast, an alert young man growing up in South Carolina in the years after the Al Smith presidential debacle could not have been unaware of Catholics being profoundly "other," indeed suspect.

After briefly exploring a career in medicine, Bernardin discerned a call to the priesthood, studied philosophy at St. Mary's Seminary in Baltimore and theology at the Catholic University of America, and was ordained a priest for the Diocese of Charleston in 1952. His ascent up the ecclesiastical ladder was swift, with Father Bernardin becoming Monsignor Bernardin only seven years after his ordination. In fourteen years in Charleston, Bernardin served four different bishops in a variety of administrative posts prior to being chosen auxiliary bishop of Atlanta. In April 1966, Bernardin received his episcopal ordination from the hands of Atlanta's first metropolitan archbishop, Paul Hallinan, the beau ideal of the postconciliar bishop within the progressive wing of the American Church and one of the grandfathers of the Bernardin Era and the Bernardin Machine. The other grandfather, Cardinal John Dearden of Detroit, plucked Bernardin from Atlanta to become the first general secretary of the National Conference of Catholic Bishops (NCCB) in 1968.

Bernardin and Dearden were the two dominant figures in the formative years of what was then a dyad: the NCCB, known internally as "the body," and the United States Catholic Conference (USCC), the NCCB's public policy arm. Dearden famously took counsel with the Booz Allen Hamilton management-consultant firm in designing the dyad's structure and procedures. But it was Bernardin who, more than anyone else, defined the structure's bureaucratic ethos, which deferred to "the body's" authority while establishing a conference "process" that gave its bureaucracy significant power and influence in U.S. Catholic affairs; as the conference's voice increased, that of individual bishops tended to decrease.

Bernardin's influence in shaping the bishops' conference and its public policy efforts would be closely identified with the man who would become one of the conference's most influential staff members, the Rev. J. Bryan Hehir, a Boston priest with a Harvard doctorate in political science. Hehir and Bernardin shared an ecclesiology (sympathetic to the progressive wing of the postconciliar spectrum, but careful not to appear radical); a politics (similarly tilted *a gauche*, but always with an eye toward "the center"); and a determination to put the NCCB and the USCC "in play" in American public life and keep it there. That determination, and the bureaucratic steps taken to give it force, were embodied in

Bernardin's style of leadership, which was silken on the outside (for Joseph L. Bernardin was a thoroughly charming man whose "Welcome to the club" phone calls to newly-nominated bishops were remembered by recipients with a warm glow years later) and quite tough on the inside (for Bernardin knew what he wanted the conference to do, knew how to make the conference do it, and knew how to get anyone who might be an obstacle out of the way).

Once Bernardin had finished his term as conference general secretary, Cardinal Dearden wanted him to have room to "operate," as the Detroit prelate once put it. And that, in Dearden's terms, meant that Bernardin ought to become the head of a large Midwestern diocese, en route to a traditional cardinalatial see. Thus in November 1972 Bernardin was named archbishop of Cincinnati, where he remained as metropolitan for a decade. But Bernardin's work was not limited to the city that specializes in chili with chocolate (a culinary curiosity that may have caused some distress to the archbishop, who knew his way around an Italian kitchen). In 1974, after a three-year interregnum in which Philadelphia's Cardinal John Krol served as NCCB/USCC president, Bernardin became the conference president, commuted regularly between Cincinnati and Washington, and put the Bernardin Machine into high gear. He was succeeded as conference president by five men (John Quinn of San Francisco, John Roach of St. Paul-Minneapolis, James Malone of Youngstown, John May of St. Louis, and Daniel Pilarczyk of Cincinnati) who were all members of the Bernardin Machine, and whose positions in the U.S. Church had no little to do with Bernardin's service on the Vatican's Congregation for Bishops (which Andrew Greeley once dubbed the "patronage office") and Bernardin's relationship with Belgian archbishop Jean Jadot, the Vatican representative in Washington from 1974 to 1980. In those halcyon days, Bernardin, master of the scene, could, with quiet confidence and no fear of contradiction, tell fellow American clerics that, "No, Jim Malone won't be the next archbishop of Cincinnati, but he will be the next president of the conference."

T he Bernardin Machine's approach to governance within the
    Church was frequently described as "collegial," but those
clergy and laity who, in their dioceses or in their interaction with
the NCCB/USCC, felt the sting of authoritarian Catholic liberalism in the 1970s and 1980s would likely demur. For the machine
was quite rigorous in enforcing its ecclesiology and its politics, and
it was perfectly capable of withdrawing its favor when bishops once
thought loyal club members showed signs of intellectual or ecclesiastical independence. One prominent example was Cardinal James
Francis Stafford, who retired as a curial official in 2009. Stafford was
thought part of the Bernardin world when, as an auxiliary bishop
of Baltimore, he was named a member of the U.S. delegation to the
1980 Synod on the Family. But he eventually took a different path,
in part because of his unhappiness with how Bernardin, also a member of the Synod, quietly tried to maneuver that body's deliberations
into a critique of Paul VI's teaching on the morally appropriate way
to regulate births in *Humanae Vitae*.

Stafford was surprised at this, but he shouldn't have been. For
the Bernardin Era and the style of governance characteristic of
Bernardin Machine bishops were deeply influenced by the Roman-
brokered "Truce of 1968," an ill-fated attempt to settle the disciplinary situation in the Archdiocese of Washington, where dissent
from *Humanae Vitae* was widespread and public. Whatever the
Vatican's intentions vis-a-vis the difficult situation in Washington,
what was learned from the truce were two lessons that would shape
an entire era of U.S. Catholic history. The first lesson was that the
Holy See would retreat from rigorously enforcing doctrinal discipline if it could be persuaded of the danger of schism. The second
lesson was that American bishops were ill advised to get out on a
public limb in defense of Catholic teaching (as Cardinal Patrick
O'Boyle of Washington had done by disciplining priests who had
publicly rejected *Humanae Vitae*), for that could result in the Holy

See sawing off the limb and leaving the bishop in question in a bad way.

Keeping peace within dioceses in the wake of the post-*Humanae Vitae* chaos thus became one of the prime imperatives of bishops adhering to the Bernardin model, even if that meant tolerating a measure of what Father Charles Curran liked to call "faithful dissent." Bishops who condoned "faithful dissent" were unlikely to be vigorous in enforcing catechetical standards or liturgical discipline. Their approach to problems of clerical indiscipline and malfeasance also helped shape the ecclesiastical culture in which incidents of the clerical sexual abuse of the young began to spike, and bishops turned to psychology rather than moral and sacramental theology in dealing with abuse cases.

As for its interaction with American public life, the Bernardin Machine was constructed at a moment when few could imagine a former Hollywood B-movie actor as president of the United States and a Democratic majority seemed locked in place on Capitol Hill. Thus the USCC in its first decades came to be regarded in Washington as an adjunct of the Democratic majority in the Congress, even as the bishops took some tentative steps into the murky worlds of radical activism by creating the Campaign for Human Development, which began to support programs of community organizing modeled on or promoted by Saul Alinsky's Industrial Areas Foundation.

Yet despite their occasional playing with Alinskyite fire, the politics of the bishops' conference during the Bernardin Era were more reflective of a determination to position the Catholic Church as part of a liberal vital center than they were of the politics of the American hard Left. A fine example of Bernardin's cast of mind and method in moving the bishops to address contested issues this way may be found in his chairmanship of the special NCCB committee charged with drafting a national pastoral letter on war and peace after the unthinkable had happened, the B-movie actor was in residence at 1600 Pennsylvania Avenue, and fears of a Reagan-initiated nuclear war were considered quite rational among U.S. Catholic bishops, intellectuals, and activists.

Archbishop Bernardin's shaping of the war/peace committee was a classic expression of his ecclesial and political modus operandi. As for the bishop-members of the committee, get the pacifist (Thomas Gumbleton) and the former military chaplain (John J. O'Connor) aboard in order to define the "extremes," then appoint two other bishops who could be counted on to follow the lead of Bernardin and the committee's chief staffer, Father Hehir, in defining the liberal "consensus." That, arguably, was clever, but not terribly original, bureaucratic maneuvering. What was more telling was Bernardin's instruction to the committee members at the beginning of their work: namely, that the one policy option they would *not* consider was unilateral nuclear disarmament. For that option, adopted, would brand the bishops as cranks who would no longer be "in play" in the public policy debate.

Yet, one wanted to ask at the time (and one wants to ask now), why not? If the bishops' committee on war and peace was an ecclesial body that would begin with moral theology and work its way to public policy from there, surely every policy option ought to have been on the table. Despite his insistence that the bishops were approaching this complex set of problems as "pastors and teachers" (a mantra of the bishops' conference), Bernardin's preemptive exclusion of the unilateralist option made clear that this was an exercise in which political criteria of viability would play a considerable role.

In the event, and despite all efforts to stay "in play," "The Challenge of Peace" quickly became a dead letter. Its recommendations on arms control were overrun by the debate inaugurated by the Reagan administration's Strategic Defense Initiative, as its assumption of the relative permanence of the Cold War became moot after the collapse of the Soviet empire in 1989–91. "The Challenge of Peace" sought to make a contribution to easing the undoubted dangers of the Cold War. By paying minimal attention to the potential of human rights activism in changing the internal political dynamics of the Soviet bloc, however, the bishops' letter missed what turned out to be the key, not simply to managing the superpower competition, but to freedom's victory over tyranny. (In his own reading of the undercurrents of history in the 1980s, Bernardin took a conventional liberal view. After a fellow guest at a dinner party in 1991 had spoken of John Paul II's pivotal role in the collapse of European communism, Bernardin, asked for his opinion, said that he thought Mikhail Gorbachev had been the key figure.)

Even during the years of its greatest influence, when Bernardin appeared on the cover of *Time* and his allies seemed fully in control of the bishops' conference, the Bernardin Machine was not omnipotent. Bernardin and those of his cast of mind seem not to have considered the possibility that, post-Paul VI, the College of Cardinals in 1978 would anticipate the American electorate in 1980 and do the unthinkable: elect a fifty-eight-year-old Pole with a sharp mind, a charismatic personality, and a firm will as bishop of Rome. It took some time for the effects of this dramatic change in the Vatican to be felt in the United States. Thus John Paul II, who seems to have had some doubts about the matter (perhaps because of that 1980 synod on the family), nonetheless acceded to the wishes of the Bernardin-dominated U.S. hierarchy by appointing Archbishop Bernardin as archbishop of Chicago in 1982 and nominating him to the College of Cardinals in 1983.

But if John Paul was willing to have Joseph Bernardin in Chicago and in the College of Cardinals, he was not willing to have one of Bernardin's proteges (and his former deputy at the bishops' conference), Thomas C. Kelly, O.P., as archbishop of New York after Cardinal Terence Cooke died in 1983. Kelly seems to have expected the appointment; he reportedly remarked to fellow bishops at Cooke's funeral that St. Patrick's Cathedral would "take some getting used to." But in a surprise at least as great as the 2010 Dolan/Kicanas election, the post instead went to John J. O'Connor after John Paul II rejected the Bernardinian *terna*, or list of possible nominees, submitted by the Congregation for Bishops. (John Paul asked the secretary of the congregation, the Brazilian Dominican Lucas Moreira Neves, whether he was happy with the *terna*, on which Kelly's name seems to have appeared in first place, reportedly followed by the names of John Roach and James Malone; Moreira Neves said he was not, and pulled out the O'Connor file.) O'Connor's staunch and unyielding pro-life activism as archbishop of New York was crucial in keeping that issue alive at a moment when the pro-life energies of the American episcopate may have begun flagging. In doing so, O'Connor, who had very little use for bishops' conference politics, set in place one of the markers that would eventually help displace the Bernardin approach to the Catholic Church's interaction with the U.S. public policy debate. After being named a cardinal in 1985, O'Connor's work as a member of the Vatican Congregation for Bishops was also important in putting brakes on the power of the Bernardin Machine to reproduce itself episcopally.

A further sign that the ecclesiology and leadership style of the Bernardin Machine would not go uncontested during John Paul II's pontificate came in 1985, when the pope summoned an Extraordinary Assembly of the Synod of Bishops to mark the twentieth anniversary of the conclusion of the Second Vatican Council and to consider the problems the Church had experienced in implementing the Council's teaching. The pre-Synod period was dominated by debate over a book-length interview with Cardinal Joseph Ratzinger, *The Ratzinger Report*, which was sharply critical of the kind of implementation of the Council that Bernardin and his allies favored (and led). In retrospect, though, the turning point

that the 1985 Synod represented for the Bernardin Machine and
the Bernardin Era only came into focus in a press conference marking the Synod's conclusion.

The Synod Fathers had recommended to the pope that a new
catechism be written. Asked by a reporter at the postsynod press
conference what he thought of that, Bishop James Malone, then
the NCCB president and very much Cardinal Bernardin's ally, said
that the reporter needn't worry, as neither one of them would live
long enough to see any such catechism published. Seven years later,
John Paul II issued the *Catechism of the Catholic Church*, which
gave lay people throughout the Church an instrument with which
to contest "faithful dissent," and which began a slow but steady
catechetical revolution in which the adventure of orthodoxy would
be stressed.

World Youth Day 1993 in Denver was another moment when
a prescient observer might have sensed the ebbing of the Bernardin
Machine's power, and perhaps the waning of the Bernardin Era.
John Paul was eager to hold a World Youth Day in the United
States; the bishops' conference and its Washington staff, which still
reflected the default positions Bernardin had implanted during his
years as general secretary and conference president, were dubious,
to put it gently. But the pope insisted, so the conference proposed
holding World Youth Day in either Buffalo (to take advantage of
that city's proximity to Canada) or Chicago (Bernardin's base). John
Paul, however, was intrigued by the idea of bringing World Youth
Day to Denver, a self-consciously secular city where Archbishop J.
Francis Stafford was working vigorously, and not without opposition, to bring the local archdiocese out of the Bernardin Era. The
pope won the argument; World Youth Day 1993 in Denver was
a tremendous success, and a marker was put down—the Gospel
without apology could be proclaimed with effect in a cultural environment that regarded the most challenging of Gospel demands
as bizarre. (Eleven years later, John Paul II was still chortling over

his coup. Looking at photos of Rocky Mountain National Park outside Denver, the aged and crippled pontiff smiled, stabbed the photo album with his index finger, and said "Denver! World Youth Day 1993. The American bishops said it couldn't be done. I proved them wrong!").

I n the last decade and a half of his life, Bernardin continued to advance a distinctive understanding of Catholicism's engagement with American politics. Even as work on "The Challenge of Peace" was being completed, the cardinal began promoting the concept of a "consistent ethic of life," which linked issues such as abortion, capital punishment, and arms control in what was quickly styled the "seamless garment." As articulated by Bernardin, the "consistent ethic" rooted itself in the foundational Catholic social-ethical principle of the dignity of the human person, and then suggested a moral symmetry between the defense of unborn life in the womb, the rejection of the death penalty, and resistance to the rearmament programs of the Reagan administration. Cardinal Bernardin was a committed pro-lifer; charges that he developed the "consistent ethic" approach in order to give cover to liberal (and pro-choice) Catholic legislators who were "good on capital punishment and nuclear weapons" were false. Intentions aside, however, the "consistent ethic" did help buttress the Bernardin Machine's "in play" approach to the Catholic Church and public policy, which inevitably blunted criticism of such determinedly pro-abortion Catholic politicians as Edward M. Kennedy and Robert F. Drinan.

Shortly before his death in 1996, Bernardin initiated the "Catholic Common Ground Initiative," an ongoing forum for fostering conversation across the spectrum of what had become, in the Clinton years, an increasingly polarized U.S. Church—a polarization that now seems, in retrospect, to reflect the further demise of the Bernardin Machine and the beginnings of an alternative correlation of forces within the American hierarchy. Because the Initiative

intended to include as full participants known dissenters from settled Catholic teaching, it was publicly criticized by former Washington archbishop Cardinal William Baum and Cardinal James
Hickey, then the incumbent in the nation's capital, for promoting a
false irenicism that tacitly accepted the notion of "faithful dissent."
Bernardin died before the Initiative could achieve any significant
critical mass; perhaps any such outcome was unlikely, given the
changing theological contours of the U.S. Catholic scene in general
and the American episcopate in specific. In any case, it was unlikely
that "common ground" could be found with those dissenters who
were in a state of psychological, if not canonical schism, imagining
themselves (as they did) the true Church of Vatican II. The Initiative nonetheless testified to Bernardin's enduring conviction that the
liberal/progressive consensus that informed the Bernardin Era and
guided the Bernardin Machine remained at the fifty-yard line of the
U.S. Catholic playing field.

T hree years after Cardinal Bernardin launched the Catholic
Common Ground Initiative, his successor as archbishop
of Chicago, Cardinal Francis George, O.M.I., redefined that playing field conceptually, declaring the liberal Catholic project dead
in an October 1999 lecture to mark the 75th anniversary of *Com-
monweal*. Cardinal George's remarks, which stressed a certain liberal
Catholic surrender to the ambient culture, brought into synthesis
several trends that had been underway in U.S. Catholicism throughout the John Paul II years, trends that ultimately undermined the
Bernardin Machine and that would ultimately draw the curtain on
the Bernardin Era.

One of these trends, which became a hallmark of Cardinal
George's own presidency of the bishops' conference from 2007–
2010, was an increased concern among bishops, clergy, and engaged laity about Catholic identity, which touched issues as various
as catechetics, liturgy, health care, and the relationship of Catholic

institutions of higher learning to the local church and its bishop. A second trend was the emergence of pro-life activism as *the* cultural marker of serious Catholicism in America. That trend, it should be noted, was itself accelerated by the U.S. bishops' 1998 statement, "Living the Gospel of Life," which effectively replaced the consistent ethic/seamless garment metaphors with a new image: the "foundations of the house of freedom," in which the defense of innocent human life from conception until natural death was understood to be fundamental, both theologically and in terms of sound democratic theory, in a way that other public policy questions engaging American Catholic attention were not. The third trend, most striking on campuses, was a willingness to reconsider, and in some instances enthusiastically embrace, the fullness of the Catholic ethic of human love, often by reference to John Paul II's Theology of the Body.

When John Paul II sent Archbishop Pio Laghi to Washington as apostolic delegate in 1980, the pope ticked off on one hand his concerns about the Church in the United States. He was worried about the effectiveness of the Church's evangelical mission, including the ways in which the sacraments were celebrated and religious education was conducted; he had serious reservations about the state of consecrated religious life in monasteries and convents; he thought priestly formation in seminaries needed to be tightened up; and he wanted a new approach to the appointment of bishops. The last amounted to a tacit instruction to dismantle the Bernardin Machine. It was an unlikely assignment for Laghi, who shared much of Joseph Bernardin's ecclesiastical sensibility; and while Laghi's arrival on Massachusetts Avenue did begin to blunt the capacity of the Bernardin Machine to reproduce itself by shaping the episcopal appointment process, it was the pontificate of John Paul II as a whole that proved the ultimate dismantler of the powerful ecclesiastical machine that Bernardin had built and operated with considerable skill.

John Paul II embodied a heroic model of the priesthood, and a heroic exercise of the office of bishop, that had a profound effect, over two and a half decades, on the Catholic priesthood and episcopate in the United States. The men who elected Timothy Dolan as USCCB president in November 2010 were men deeply influenced by the John Paul II model, as they were men intellectually formed by the Polish pope's dynamic magisterium on questions ranging from the Catholic sexual ethic to Catholic social doctrine. They understood, in a way that those who embodied the Bernardin Era did not quite seem to grasp, that it was important for the Catholic Church to be able to give a comprehensive, coherent, and compelling account of its faith, hope, and love in the *Cathechism of the Catholic Church*, just as they understood that the reaffirmation of classic Catholic moral theology in *Veritatis Splendor* was an important weapon in the war against what John Paul II's successor called the "dictatorship of relativism." And they were prepared to challenge the culture—and American politics—to rediscover the public policy implications of America's founding commitment to self-evident moral truths; they were not interested, in other words, in finding an agreeable fifty-yard line. They had learned from John Paul II and the Revolution of 1989 in east central Europe that seemingly invincible forces could be defeated, and they were determined to defeat, not find an accommodation with, the cultural forces that, in their judgment, were at war with the Gospel even as they were eroding the fabric of American life.

There was paradox here. Joseph Bernardin, growing up in that part of America where Catholics were most suspect, defined a style of engagement with American public life that put great stress on remaining "in play." The bishops who ultimately brought an end to the Bernardin Machine and the Bernardin Era grew up comfortably Catholic and comfortably American—and then came to understand that their Catholicism could require them to be forthrightly countercultural in dealing with American culture and politics. The paradox underscored that a sea-change had taken place, the effects of which were likely to be felt for generations.

T he ecclesiastical sensibility that characterized the Bernardin
    Era can still be discerned in several parts of the complex
reality that is the Catholic Church in the United States. That sensibility is perhaps most palpably felt in Boston, where Father Hehir wielded considerable influence over archdiocesan affairs in the
aftermath of the Long Lent of 2002 and has done so according to
the Bernardin model. The Bernardin ethos is also felt within the
bishops' conference bureaucracy, as it is within diocesan bureaucra-
cies. But if the Bernardin era is indeed over, one should expect to
see some continuing shifts of default position, not least within the
bishops' conference.

The conference might, for example, re-examine its habit of having a comment on virtually every contested issue in American public
life. The late Father Richard John Neuhaus used to say that, when
the Church is not obliged to speak, the Church is obliged not to
speak: that is, when the issue at hand does not touch a fundamental
moral truth that the Church is obliged to articulate vigorously in
the public policy debate, the Church's pastors ought to leave the
prudential application of principle to the laity who, according to
Vatican II, are the principal evangelizers of culture, politics, and
economy. The bishops' conference's habit of trying to articulate a
Catholic response to a very broad range of public policy issues un-
dercuts this responsibility of the laity; it also tends to flatten out the
bishops' witness, so that all issues become equal, which they manifestly are not.

In addition, the conference might re-examine its reliance on domestic policy default positions that were set as long ago as 1919,
when the National Catholic War Council (which begat the National
Catholic Welfare Conference, which begat the NCCB/USCC dyad,
which begat today's USCCB) issued the Bishops' Program of Social Reconstruction. Echoes of that program, filtered through the
liberal-consensus politics of the Bernardin Era, could be heard in
the Obama-era health care debate, with the bishops continually

stressing the moral imperative of universal health care. That moral imperative exists; but it is not at all clear that meeting it requires a first, indeed primary, recourse to governmental means. Or at least that is what the core Catholic social-ethical principal of subsidiarity, with its skepticism about concentrations of governmental power, would suggest. Putting that comprehensive vision—universality *and* subsidiarity—into play in the ongoing health care debate would be a genuine service to the country, and a distinctively Catholic service. Catholics bring a cluster of concerns to the table of the health care debate: they bring concerns about the unborn, the elderly, and the severely handicapped; they bring concerns for the poor and their empowerment; they bring concerns for maintaining a healthy pluralism in our national life through the principle of subsidiarity and the use of private sector mechanisms for solving social problems. It would be a real sign of movement beyond the public policy orientation of the Bernardin Era if that concern for linking universality to subsidiarity (which a few bishops began to articulate in 2009) were to achieve a higher prominence in the bishops' address to these issues, even as the USCCB continues to press hard on the pro-life agenda and the protection of the conscience rights of Catholic medical professionals.

Then there is the question of Catholic identity. Throughout his presidency of the USCCB in 2007–2010, Cardinal Francis George steered the conference toward a more intense focus on issues of Catholic identity as they touched on the work of Catholic colleges and universities, Catholic health care institutions, Catholic professional associations, and Catholic publications. Cardinal George's sense of urgency on these questions was primarily *ad intra*: it was important, he believed, for the bishops to take more seriously their roles as stewards of the integrity of Catholic identity. But that internal concern also bore on a public matter the cardinal discussed in an important lecture in February 2010 at Brigham Young University: the tendency in some quarters to privatize religious freedom, reducing that first of human rights to a matter of personal conviction and worship. As aggressive secularists and their allies in government continue their efforts to drive religious communities and religiously grounded moral argument to the margins of the public policy debate, the post-Bernardin bishops' conference will be required to be ever more vigilant in defending the rights of individual Catholics and the Church as a body to work within the democratic process according to religiously-informed moral convictions.

Finally, the post-Bernardin Era USCCB might re-examine one of the few enduring effects of "The Challenge of Peace," namely, its contribution to confused Catholic thinking about the intellectual architecture and purposes of the just war tradition. The country as a whole remains seriously disabled in its capacity to apply the canons of classic just war reasoning to the new world disorder; thus a fresh Catholic discussion of how Christians apply moral principles to world affairs would be an important public service.

The Bernardin Era was one of institutional maintenance and bureaucratic expansion in which a liberal consensus dominated both the internal life of the Church and the Church's address to public policy. It is not self-evidently clear what the post-Bernardin Era, just beginning in the second decade of the twenty-first century, will turn out to be. But if the Church's ordained leaders look to John Paul II as their model, they will increasingly embody an evangelical Catholicism that is unafraid to be countercultural in its engagement with public life, even as it stresses the imperative of radical conversion to discipleship and friendship with Jesus Christ as the *raison d'être* of the Church's existence. If they do so, these new-era bishops will help define a Catholicism in America in which the liberal/conservative taxonomy of the past two generations of Catholic life will crumble into irrelevance.

Part IV

The Sporting Life

Baseball: Then and Now and Whenever

Innocent of the game's history, sociology, or metaphysics, I learned my baseball in the late 1950s the old-fashioned way: sitting beside my grandfather Weigel in the lower deck of Baltimore's cavernous old Memorial Stadium, in the days when the Orioles seemed to have taken out a ninety-nine-year lease on sixth place in the American League.

You didn't have to buy tickets six months in advance, or cadge them from a friendly corporate public affairs officer, in that simpler age. Nor were you likely to have your beer (or, in my case in 1959, your popcorn or your Coke) knocked over by some broker as he shifted his cell phone from one hand to the other. Creature comforts were not much prized, either. Not only did "the stadium," as everybody called it, have no "luxury boxes"; in the lower reserved section, and throughout the upper deck and bleachers, it didn't have seats, period—just wooden benches, against whose splinters we protected ourselves by buying an *Evening Sun* as a seat-cushion on the way into the park. (Some fans preferred the *News-Post* as body armor, but being proper Baltimore bourgeois, we patronized the *Sunpapers* under all circumstances.)

In short, on those humid summer nights when Baltimore felt like a suburb of Calcutta you didn't come to the stadium to be seen, or to be "entertained," or to sip white zinfandel in an air-conditioned cocoon, or to make a real estate deal: you came for *baseball*. And under those happy conditions my grandfather taught me (and, later, my brother) the game.

He was not a voluble man, my grandfather Weigel, and he remained wholly untutored in what Mencken would have called the "wizard pedagogy" of John Dewey and Teachers College, Columbia University. But such was the efficacy of his instruction that, by the time we were eight or nine, my brother and I knew, not only the players and the rules, but at least the rudiments of pastime's inner architecture, in its subtleties, surprises, and strategems.

To take the most obvious, and most basic, example: we knew that the poor boobies who complained that "nothing ever happens in baseball" simply didn't know what they were talking about. For my grandfather had taught us, not only how to watch, but how to *see* what was going on. So we learned that there was more to pitching than balls and strikes: there were endless variations of speeds and locations; there were some things you did with some batters and other pitch sequences you avoided like the plague; umpiring was, at best, an inexact science, and the quirks of individual arbiters had to be considered.

Then there was defense. For whatever their other (and manifold) failings, the Baltimore Orioles that Paul Richards (the "Wizard of Waxahatchie") began to build in the 1950s could use the leather. Thus I learned to appreciate the skills and baseball intelligence of a string of astounding shortstops that ran in apostolic succession from Willy Miranda to Chico Carresquel to Ron Hansen to Luis Aparicio; these were also the days when Brooks Robinson began to redefine the playing of third base. And from all of this—the minute adjustments in the positioning of fielders; the footwork and timing around second during a double play; the stretch at first (never done better than by "Diamond Jim" Gentile); the coordination between outfielders and infielders to cut down arrant baserunners—I learned that, where the sadly uninstructed saw only inaction, there was, in fact, a hell of a lot going on.

My baseball education was furthered by other classic pedagogical materials: the radio, the sports pages of the morning and evening *Sun,* boys' baseball novels, baseball cards (ten for a quarter, with bubble gum, but without cash resale value). But it is to the personal instruction of my grandfather that I owe the most. And, as I found myself replicating his efforts with my own children, I came to appreciate the impact of his tutelage on my life more and more. For we learn baseball the way we learn religion: through stories, family traditions, and rituals. The refinements of doctrine, essential as they are, come later. First, we are converted.

This experience of an oral tradition—the narrative dimension of the game, which transcends and in fact creates the context for the true fan's other mania, namely, statistics—explains a lot of the grip that baseball has had on the national psyche for almost 150 years. The recreation of personalities, situations, plays, entire games, or for that matter entire seasons; the endless arguing about *what if;* the ongoing comparison of feats ancient and modern; the yarning, the embellishing, and the wild exaggerating: in all of this storymaking and storytelling, we are engaging in a national conversation that crosses the lines of class, race, age, and ideology like no other in our culture. I can happily talk baseball with people I find otherwise obnoxious, and with whom I agree on virtually nothing else; by the time they were teenagers my daughters could hold their own in friendly arguments at the ballpark with perfect strangers three times their age. The video revolution has ruined vast areas of American culture. But as long as there is baseball, millions of Americans will know how to tell a story.

Baseball-as-oral-tradition also helps explain why there have been very, very few great baseball movies. William Bendix as the Bambino in *The Babe Ruth Story* is a sad memory to be erased; William Bendix as a Marine who dies happy in *Guadalcanal Diary* because he's just heard on the radio that the Dodgers have won evokes something of the place that the game, and our personal loyalties within the game, hold in our lives.

G iven the breathtaking scope of his ambition, which
was to propose nothing less than a comprehensive
interpretation of post-Civil War America through the lens of a documentary history of baseball, I suspect that filmmaker Ken Burns
intended to break this pattern of cinematic failure and to make the
best baseball film ever. For everything about *Baseball*, the nine-part
(or "-inning," as he calls it) Burns documentary that appeared for
over eighteen hours on PBS in 1994, seemed intended to evoke the
label "epic": its length, its pacing, its structuring of the story, the
solemnity of the narration. And no one who loves the game will
gainsay Burns's genuine accomplishments.

As in his previous work on the Civil War, Burns displayed, in
Baseball, an uncanny ability to combine narrative and music with
the slow scanning of a still photograph to make an individual or an
event from the days before moving pictures come vibrantly alive:
John J. McGraw, longtime manager of the New York Giants and one
of the great figures of baseball's golden age, is a case in point here.
Burns also used old newsreel footage to great dramatic effect: in his
fourth episode (chastely titled "A National Heirloom" on TV, but
more aptly styled "That Big Son of a Bitch" in the film's companion
book), I watched the Babe Ruth whom many had thought washed
up in 1923 hit a home run in his first at-bat during the inaugural
game at Yankee Stadium, the "House That Ruth Built," and the
proverbial chills ran down my spine. More subtly, Burns indulged
a puckish sense of humor at times, as when Mozart's overture to *Le
Nozze di Figaro* provided the aural setting for a devastating narration
of the wreckage wrought by "George III" Steinbrenner on the proud
Yankee franchise in the first years of his ownership.

But a tension, barely visible at the beginning yet increasingly
evident over the course of nine episodes, ran through *Baseball*—
because, one suspects, it runs through Ken Burns. And that is the
tension between a baseball fan determined to produce an epic history of the pastime, and a child of the Sixties intent on driving home

a certain interpretation of the American national experience of race (and, to a lesser extent, class). So as Burns's nine-inning narrative unfolded, I found the baseball in *Baseball* increasingly and jarringly interrupted by the politics (which, not surprisingly, were entirely congruent with what one has come to expect from PBS).

The net result, alas, was not the epic that Burns wanted to create. *Baseball* has many magnificent moments. But the itch to admonish and to chastise (and in that nagging manner that makes upmarket liberalism so . . . well, so *annoying)* proved irresistible. And it most particularly damaged Burns's telling of the pivotal tale in the drama, the story of Jackie Robinson. Thus, after eighteen hours, I found myself thinking of *Baseball,* not as an American epic, but as something more akin to a seventh-grade social studies book from a progressive publisher, with lavish illustrations and a very politically correct text.

B efore getting further into the unpleasantness, though, let us pause and be grateful for the things that Ken Burns and his colleagues got right.

Baseball wisely ignored the oceans of ink spilt about the pastime's "pastoral" character and quite rightly positioned major league baseball as a quintessentially urban phenomenon. Many of its players may have come from the farms and the mines, especially in the early days. But when we say "baseball," we mean a city game whose most memorable moments have taken place, not in a massive concrete doughnut built alongside a freeway in the middle of nowhere, but in real ballparks whose architectural idiosyncrasies were determined by the quirks of the street-grid in the city neighborhoods in which they were built. (Indeed, part of the good news about the pastime since 1992 and the opening of Camden Yards in Baltimore is a trend toward replicating this classic architectural signature.)

The urban quality of baseball has to do with the game itself, however, not simply with its surroundings. From the beginning, professional baseball has exhibited the characteristic, distinctive to cities, of combining elegance and roughhouse in about equal proportions. The game mixes the athletic grace of a second-baseman "turning two" with the spike-sharpened aggression of a runner bent on breaking up the double play; within a single inning, the supreme control of a masterful pitcher can be complemented by the mad abandon of a centerfielder climbing a seven-foot wall to snag a potential home run.

All of which, to my mind, says "city," not "field of dreams." Moreover, the professional game has always been surrounded (and threatened) by three oppidan behaviors—drinking, brawling, and gambling: the last of which ruined the career and the reputation of one of the contemporary game's additions to the all-time pantheon, Pete Rose.

Without falling into a dour Calvinism, Ken Burns's film also rightly stressed that baseball is in large part about failure. A successful hitter fails seven times out of ten; a successful team loses 40% of its games. All of which teaches players, (real) fans, and managers (if not owners) a certain serenity. To be sure, it is the kind of serenity that comes only on the far side of great passion; but it is serenity, nonetheless. Earl Weaver, the Orioles' manager during fifteen of the team's glory years between 1966 and 1983, used to tell nervous sportswriters, worried about encroaching on the crusty genius's turf, "Relax. This ain't football. We do this every day." Someone—was it Ray Miller, Weaver's pitching coach?—once said that you can't play baseball with clenched teeth. The game is hard enough without tying yourself into a knot of anxiety, and baseball is a damned hard game to play well. And the hardness of the game—its technical difficulty, and the unforgiving way in which it winnows wheat from chaff—is the truth at the heart of the failures that define the rhythm of games and seasons and give baseball its distinctive moral texture. Thus no serious student of the pastime will quarrel with Burns's revisitation of such historic gaffes as "Merkel's Boner," "Snodgrass's Muff," Mickey

Owen's dropped third strike ("the condemned jumped out of the chair and electrocuted the warden," as one wag had it in 1941), and Bill Buckner's heartbreaking imitation of a croquet wicket in the sixth game of the 1986 World Series.

But the ubiquity of failure in baseball casts into greater relief the triumphs of the game's heroes, whose character and accomplishments Burns frequently captured with the deftness of a skilled miniature portraitist. Among the best of his sketches of the pastime's greats—themselves an entire gallery of Americana— are those of Cap Anson, a magnificent player and manager and an unreconstructed racist who drew the "color line" in 1888; Christy Mathewson, the "Christian gentleman" from Bucknell who was a nonfiction Frank Merriwell; Honus Wagner, the Pittsburgh Pirates' "Flying Dutchman," a gentle giant whom some still swear was the greatest player ever; Ty Cobb, "possessed by the furies," the antithesis of Mathewson and Wagner; the aforementioned McGraw; Grover Cleveland Alexander, the gifted but alcoholic pitcher who won the sixth game of the 1926 World Series with a massive hangover; Babe Ruth and Lou Gehrig; Carl Hubbell, master of the screwball, who struck out Ruth, Gehrig, Jimmy Foxx, Al Simmons, and Joe Cronin, seriatim, in the 1934 All-Star Game; the elegant Yankee Clipper, Joe DiMaggio; Willie, Mickey, and the Duke (Mays, Mantle, and Snyder); Hank Greenberg, pride of the Tigers, who came within an ace of topping Ruth's single-season home run record; Ted Williams, perhaps the greatest pure hitter ever; Stan "the Man" Musial; Carl Yastrzemski, who single-handedly drove the Red Sox to the 1967 American League pennant with what some believe was the greatest month a player ever had; Brooks and Frank Robinson, the heart and soul of the Oriole dynasty of the late Sixties and early Seventies; Sandy Koufax and Bob Gibson, flame-throwers both; Roberto Clemente, a magnificent Latino athlete driven by demons of resentment, and Henry

Aaron, the steady, undemonstrative African-American slugger who broke Ruth's career home-run record.

Baseball also explored the passions, foibles, and genius of some of the off-the-field figures who bent the game to their wills: Albert G. Spalding, the Gilded Age magnate who fancied himself the equal of Vanderbilt, Carnegie, and Rockefeller and manipulated the game into building him the country's greatest sporting goods empire; Ban Johnson, the autocratic founder of the American League; Kenesaw Mountain Landis, the commissioner who restored the pastime's integrity after the "Black Sox" fixed the 1919 World Series, but of whom Heywood Broun once wrote, "His career typifies the heights to which dramatic talent may carry a man in America if only he has the foresight not to go on the stage"; and Branch Rickey, whose distinctive combination of Methodist piety and a shrewd marketing eye led him to break Anson's color line by bringing Jackie Robinson to the Dodgers.

But it is the players, what was said of them, and what they said that are of enduring interest, and Burns's film serves up a good-sized helping of the pastime's more memorable *bons mots.* Thus we are made to recall the scouting report on Walter ("Big Train") Johnson: "He knows where he's throwing because if he didn't there would be dead bodies strewn all over Idaho." And Dizzy Dean's answer as to why he dropped out of the second grade: "I didn't do so well in the first grade, either." And the observations in epistemology vouchsafed by the Old Perfesser, Casey Stengel, and his star pupil (and prize player), Yogi Berra: "I made up my mind, but I made it up both ways"; "Baseball is 90 percent mental, the other half is physical."

*B*aseball also did a public service by introducing several generations of Americans to the Negro Leagues, to slugging catcher Josh Gibson, speedster James "Cool Papa" Bell, and pitcher-manager-entrepreneur Andrew "Rube" Foster, and to noble teams like the Homestead Grays, the Kansas City Monarchs, the Pittsburgh Crawfords, and the Baltimore Elite Giants. Burns also drew a handsome portrait of Satchel Paige, perhaps the only Negro League great whose name even the casual fan would recognize. But the finest work in *Baseball's* rendering of the Negro League experience was done by John Jordan ("Buck") O'Neil, a former Monarchs' first baseman and manager, whose position in *Baseball* was similar to Shelby Foote's in Burns's film on the Civil War: the man whose stories and comments you always want more of. O'Neil had, I think, precisely the right analysis of the Negro Leagues: they never should have happened, but, damn, they were great. The former judgment is, of course, the one more frequently encountered these days, and in fact it distorted the historical analysis in Burns's film—which, by presenting black baseball essentially over against the dominant white world, treats is as essentially a form of deprivation. But Buck O'Neil refused to have the meaning of his career forced onto any Procrustean bed of political correctness. "We loved it," was his summary comment on the not-always-easy life of segregated leagues and off-season barnstorming. "Why would you feel sorry for me? . . . We did our duty. We did the groundwork for the Jackie Robinsons, the Willie Mayses, and the guys that are playing now. So why feel sorry for me?" Why, indeed?

Finally, *Baseball* reminded America of the game's remarkable capacity for self-regeneration. The corruptions of Gilded Age baseball led to the reformation of 1876, in the establishment of the National League. When the Black Sox scandal threatened the game's future by trifling with its most precious asset—fan loyalty—Babe Ruth emerged as the people's choice. The decay of the sport during World War II was followed by a fifteen-year run that many consider the greatest period in the game's history. The doldrums of the late Sixties and early Seventies ended at 12:33 a.m. on October 22, 1975, when Carlton Fisk's home run off the left-field foul pole at Fenway Park ended the greatest World Series game ever played and launched a nationwide revival of interest in the pastime. And as Burns's *Tenth Inning* sequel to *Baseball* demonstrated when aired on PBS in 2010, the debacle of the 1994 labor dispute and the subsequent steroid era nevertheless gave way to more great baseball in the early decades of the twenty-first century, culminating in the epic 2011 postseason and a World Series for the ages.

Baseball also missed some important things. Burns was little interested in pitching, and two of the most game-changing developments of recent decades—the development of the slider and the split-fingered fastball, on the technical side, and the strategic emergence of the "closer," or late-inning relief specialist, as an essential weapon in any winning team's arsenal—simply go unremarked. Similarly, and with the obvious exceptions of Willie Mays's catch off of Vic Wertz in the 1954 World Series, and Brooks Robinson's grand larceny at third during the 1970 Series, great defense plays little role in Burns's baseball imagination. The uninitiate will also learn little about the strategy of baseball from *Baseball*: a curious oversight (given the number of brilliant managers who could have been interviewed) that risks confirming the complaint of the ignorant about "nothing happening" in those long moments between home runs.

Baseball also told us virtually nothing about the minor leagues, a once vast and flourishing network of professional teams now experiencing something of a renaissance after decades of troubles. Burns's tight focus on New York and Boston gets him into trouble here: thus we are not told that, for years, the Triple-A level Pacific Coast League (in which players of real ability spent entire careers and made serious money) prepared itself to become a third major league, only to have its thunder stolen when Robert Moses tried to break New York baseball to his bureaucratic, city-planning will, thus leading Walter O'Malley and Horace Stoneham to move the Dodgers and the Giants to the West Coast.

Students of the game will wonder why, in eighteen hours of film, time couldn't have been found to note the careers of Buck Ewing, Ed Delehanty, Billy Sunday, Nap Lajoie, George Sisler, Bill Dickey, Charlie Gehringer, Harry Heilmann, and Lou Boudreau, among the old-timers. I also found it strange that a film as self-consciously comprehensive as *Baseball* ignores, among the contemporaries, Johnny Bench, arguably the greatest catcher ever; Mike Schmidt, no match for Brooks Robinson with the glove, but overall, perhaps the best third baseman in history; George Brett, the finest bat of his time; Harmon Killebrew, who ranks high on the career home-run list (and who never laid down a sacrifice bunt in over 10,000 at-bats); and Dan Quisenberry, Rollie Fingers, and Goose Gossage, three exceptional relievers. I would also like to have seen a little more about umpires, who, with the exception of a cameo appearance by the legendary Bill Klem (author of the classic expression of nominalism, "It ain't a strike until I say it is, son") are notable for their absence from *Baseball*.

But these are, as they say, judgments calls: the kinds of things to be argued about, good-naturedly, during the off-season. The central flaw in *Baseball* lay deeper and was far more serious.

Irritating exercises in political correctness recurred throughout Ken Burns's film. Stephen Jay Gould, Doris Kearns Goodwin, Studs Terkel, George Plimpton, and Mario Cuomo were all given ample opportunities to offer portside commentary on the game and its meaning for the country, as was George F. Will from starboard. Thus the standard PBS ratio of liberal to conservative commentators was maintained, and Burns's viewers were denied what would have been intriguing comments from such conservative baseball aficionados as Donald Kagan, Leon Kass, Charles Krauthammer, and Hadley Arkes (author of one of the all-time great historical mnemonics: "I can always remember when St. Augustine was born. It was 1,600 years before Willy Mays robbed Vic Wertz

in the Polo Grounds"). Worse, viewers of *Baseball* are subjected to
a series of dull homilies from the first Governor Cuomo (all
variations on his 1984 address to the Democratic National Convention) on the inability of Americans to form "community"—even
as the film within which he is commenting constantly refutes his
claim. Cuomo, of course, never got out of the low minors; it would
have been interesting to hear from Kentucky Congressman and Senator Jim Bunning, a conservative Republican who won 216 major
league games as a pitcher for the Tigers, Phillies, Pirates, and Dodgers, or Senator Connie Mack, a Republican from Florida whose
eponymous grandfather was one of the game's greatest figures. But
that would have cut against the grain of the film's subtext, which
is that a proper understanding of baseball's history leads, without
much further analytic ado, to a politically correct understanding of
twentieth-century American history.

Given that hermeneutic preoccupation, it is no surprise that
Burns's portrait of baseball's ugly labor history depicted the owners as unremitting scoundrels and the players as hard-beset wage
slaves, at least until the dawn of free agency and the coming of the
mega-contract. I happen to think that there is considerable truth
in the first half of that analysis: baseball's owners have, historically,
shown incredible ineptness and stupidity in managing the pastime.
But Burns fails to explore how the explosion of wealth in baseball
has corrupted players as well as owners, for the former (with rare exceptions like Cal Ripken, Jr.) show as little interest in the integrity of
the twenty-first-century game as do the latter. Why, for example, did
the players not make reform of the game itself part of their demands
in the last several rounds of labor negotiations? Why have they never
demanded a say in re-establishing a commissioner with real authority to act "for the good of the game"? Why, in brief, are they, too, so
single-mindedly focused on the money? These are not questions that
fit easily into Burns's *gauchiste* understanding of labor/management
relations in baseball and America. But answering them seems as

urgent as condemning arrogant and irresponsible club owners who don't seem to understand that they don't "own baseball."

Then there are the throw-away lines in the script about "anti-communist hysteria during the Cold War"; the excessive attention lavished on Bill Lee, a flaky Red Sox pitcher who constantly appears in a "CCCP" (i. e., "USSR") baseball cap (would Burns have allowed him to wear a cap featuring a swastika?); the bland description of the urban riots of the Sixties—"American cities were set ablaze"—as if these were acts of God rather than acts of criminals; the morally offensive analogy between slavery and the old "reserve clause" (which, before free agency, bound a player to a team for his career); and the ritual bow to the Sixties as "a decade dedicated to change." But it is in dealing with the central figure of his history that Ken Burns fell flattest.

Seven decades after he became the first black American to play major league baseball in the twentieth century, Jackie Robinson's legend remains untouched by the passion for deconstructing heroes that has corrupted the United States since the Sixties. And that is precisely how it should be: for the Robinson legend "rarely deviates from reality," as one historian of baseball's desegregation put it.

Branch Rickey did in fact pick Jackie Robinson to break the color line because he wanted a warrior with the courage not to lash back against the crude racial abuse he was certain to encounter. Robinson did in fact respond with some of the greatest baseball in history, while keeping his bargain with Rickey, his mouth shut, and his fists to himself. And things did in fact turn around: first, on the Dodgers, and later throughout the pastime, as a one-time institutional bastion of segregation became a crucial instrument in the social revolution that was the civil rights movement in its classic period. Moreover (and this is a point on which Burns is silent), after his baseball career ended and the ideological contours of race politics changed with the emergence of Black Power and black separatism, Jackie Robinson remained committed to the ideal he and Rickey shared: the ideal most memorably articulated by Martin Luther King, Jr., the ideal of an America in which men were judged by the content of their character, not the color of their skins. When, in the early 1970s, Roger Kahn's masterful memoir of the Dodgers in their glory days, *The Boys of Summer,* brought Robinson back into the public eye, he told the author that he had been getting letters again, "mostly from people who believe in the right things. Integration."

Those who have been understandably exhausted by the claims of continuing victimhood advanced in the name of racial quota systems and an ever-expanding welfare state (not to mention the lunacies of "Afrocentric" school curricula and the anti-Semitism of Louis Farrakhan) are precisely those who should applaud George Will's assertion that, while Dr. King was the most important black American in our history, Jackie Robinson was second: a "very close second." For Robinson did, as the civil rights anthem promised, *overcome*, and the plain truth of the matter is that he overcame a lot: a late start in the majors (he was twenty-eight when he first joined the Dodgers); initially hostile teammates; vicious verbal abuse from fans, and the same—plus spikings and beanings—from opponents; above all, the enormous pressure of being first, and having to do it exactly right.

But Jackie Robinson not only overcame: he prevailed, because his exceptional athletic skills were combined with a ferocious com-petitiveness that made him, to many serious observers, the dominant player of his era (which was, be it remembered, the era of Mantle, Mays, and Williams). Leo Durocher, who managed Robinson on the Dodgers and against him for the Giants, once said of him, "Ya want a guy that comes to play. This guy didn't just come to play. He come to beat ya. He come to shove the goddam bat right up your ass." And because of that dramatic combination of will and ability, Jackie Robinson, the first African-American professional baseball player in the modern era, began, somehow, to transcend the conventional psychology of race even while remaining unmistakably, proudly, majestically *black*. As Roger Kahn put it, "Like a few, very few athletes, Babe Ruth, Jim Brown, Robinson did not merely play at center stage. He *was* center stage; and wherever he walked, center stage moved with him."

That Burns's *Baseball* came nowhere near to capturing the enduring qualities of Jackie Robinson so well as Kahn's *The Boys of Summer* is, in part, a further demonstration of the written word's superiority to celluloid. But only in part. For the deficiencies of Burns's political correctness were most glaringly apparent, and most distorting of his work, in his treatment of race and baseball, race and America, and Jackie Robinson.

As for race and baseball, Burns gave extensive play throughout the series to the commentary of Gerald Early, an African-American Studies professor at Washington University, who believes, according to publicity materials distributed by PBS, that "the drama of race [is] the true story of baseball." But Burns's own recreation of the stature of the Negro Leagues and his depiction of their linkage to the worlds of black entertainment, the black church, black higher education, and black criminality give the lie to the suggestion that black baseball should be thought of primarily over against the dominant white world: and thus in negative terms, as a form of deprivation. Professor Early describes the Negro Leagues as "a limited kind of life." For all that they regarded the color line as an evil, Buck O'Neil (and, I suspect, many other Negro League veterans) would have resented that deprecation of their culture and their accomplishments. And they would be entirely right to do so.

As for race and America, Burns was most unforgivably offensive when his script informed us that "by 1934, the world economy was in ruins and fascism was on the rise. In Germany, the National Socialists had come to power and had begun to institute exclusionary laws against Jews based in part on Jim Crow laws in the United

States." The implication would seem to be that Reinhard Hey-
drich, Heinrich Himmler, and Adolf Eichmann, sitting around the
conference table at Wannsee a few years later, were merely emulat-
ing the racial views of Cap Anson, Ty Cobb, and Kenesaw Mountain Landis: a grotesque diminution of the ideological horror and
singular evil of the Holocaust and an enormous slur on the moral
character of the United States. (It is also an inversion of history, for
it was German eugenic theory that tended to inform American racial laws in the 1920s and 1930s.)

A filmmaker who seems not to appreciate fully the rich human
texture of a lost world he has set out to re-create, and who appar-
ently thinks that Satchel Paige labored for the Kansas City Monarchs under the moral equivalent of the Nuremberg Laws, is not a
filmmaker, much less a historian, who is likely to do full justice to
the Jackie Robinson story: what it meant for baseball, what it meant
about America then, and what it could mean for an America in
which racism, white and black, remains a social evil. But that is not
the worst of it. For to suggest that Jackie Robinson, a commissioned
lieutenant in the United States Army during the war in which that
army defeated Hitler, was in reality the victim of a Hitler-like ideology, is to suggest that Jackie Robinson, an authentic America hero,
was something of a fool.

O n July 19, 1994, a game between the Seattle Mariners
and the Baltimore Orioles had to be cancelled because
tiles from the ceiling of Seattle's Kingdome had crashed down into
the box seats some hours before game time. It seemed, then, an apt
metaphor for what bid fair to become baseball's greatest season of
discontent: the pastime's ugliest venue, a monument to invincible
ignorance about how the game should be played, turned on the
game and made the playing of it impossible. As it happened, of
course, metaphor became prophecy when, on September 14, 1994,
the World Series was cancelled—a perfidy beyond the joint capacity

of Hitler and Tojo but not beyond the ken of the owners and players of the moment.

The 1994 strike and the steroid plague that followed (chronicled without fudging in Burns's follow-on film, *Tenth Inning*), demonstrated that, for all its continuing attraction, baseball is in need of serious reform. Nobody much cares if the National Basketball Association of the twenty-first century looks like the NBA of George Mikan and Dolph Schayes, for history is of little consequence in basketball. But if the baseball played by Frank Thomas and Ken Griffey, Jr. (not to mention Barry Bonds, Sammy Sosa, Roger Clemens, and Mark McGwire) appears alien to the pastime as played by Ruth and DiMaggio, Willie Mays and Bob Gibson, then something essential will have been lost.

"Artificial grass" that turns infields into pool tables and domes whose ceilings hide fly balls; commercial breaks that stretch out the time between and within innings; the mindless and greed-driven expansion of the major leagues; the designated hitter rule—all these recent innovations imperil the integrity of the pastime, as does the inability of the owners and the players union to come up with a business model that does not condemn half the major league teams to failure before the first pitch of the season is thrown. Then there is the glitzy mix of sex-rock-'n'-jocks that many owners and their marketing consultants seem determined to inflict on ballparks in slavish imitation of the NBA. For two decades, Baltimore's Camden Yards has been widely and rightly regarded (and emulated) as the paradigm for new ballpark construction. But it is becoming ever more difficult to hold a conversation—the essential complement to the watching of a game—there, because "classic rock" or country-and-western is constantly blasted out into the ballpark between innings. This and all the other nonsense paraphernalia of the "entertainment experience"—cutesy mascots cavorting around the stands, exploding scoreboards, ballgirls (whose purpose, the baseball classicist George Will once noted, is to entertain people who shouldn't be allowed in the ballpark in the first place)—ought to go.

Umpiring, long a source of exasperation, is also in desperate need of reform. The classic phrase, "a strike, letter-high," is never heard these days, because no umpire in either league calls balls and strikes today according to the established strike zone. This, and the umps' failure to enforce existing rules about delaying the proceedings (and, it should be admitted, thereby acceding to the demands of the TV advertisers), have conspired to turn the average ballgame into a three-and-a-half-hour affair. Enough. There may not be that much that can be done about the advertisers' imperatives (which would require a new asceticism on the part of bottom-line-driven owners), but surely umpires should be required to strictly enforce, not remake, the rules—and be dismissed if they don't.

Baseball should eschew further major league expansion. There are arguably too many major league teams as it is. But if contraction is impossible in this litigious age, there is no need to expand further. Television's control over postseason play must also be broken. If there were still a House Un-American Activities Committee, it would be fully justified in investigating how the networks, by insisting on late-evening East Coast starting times for postseason games, have deprived a generation of American children of their birthright: watching the World Series—just as their insistence on late afternoon games to fit their schedule imperils the integrity of the game by forcing it to be played in deep shadows. But that is a matter that can be easily resolved by moving afternoon playoff games back to the hallowed starting time of 1 p.m. And in seven-game postseason series, at least three games (and all Pacific and Mountain time zone games) should be scheduled for that hour; under no circumstances should a postseason game be scheduled to begin after 8 p.m. EDT.

Finally, and perhaps most importantly, the authority of the office of commissioner, which has been gutted by the owners with the acquiescence of the players, must be restored, and the commissioner empowered to act independently, once again, "in the best interests of the game." Rearrange the selection process so that the union, and, perhaps, sportswriters, representing the fans, have a voice in the commissioner's selection. But then get out of the way, and let a benign autocracy conduct the reformation that is needed.

"You can't kill it," Buck O'Neil averred toward the end of *Baseball:* an act of faith in the pastime's future that I would like to share. But one thing major league baseball teaches you is never to say "never" about major league baseball. Those owners and players who think that the pastime is infinitely plastic in its capacity to accommodate their avarice, and who imagine that fans will remain loyal unto death under any circumstances of abuse, are betraying their stewardship—and risking the wrath.

John Unitas vs. the Klingons

The National Football League is the most successful professional sports operation in history, a money-making machine that never seems to sleep. But is the twenty-first-century game as sound as the balance sheet, or has the corporate-bureaucratic ethos that keeps the NFL purring in profitability trickled down to the playing field, with unhappy results?

Consider an offhand comment by then-Washington Redskins offensive coordinator Al Saunders in August 2006. The Redskins had just lost their third straight preseason contest amidst another torpid performance by Mark Brunell, the team's multimillion-dollar-per-year quarterback. Yet Saunders, who was pulling down a healthy $2 million-per-annum himself, wasn't worried: "The good news is that in our system, we're not asking Mark to win the game for us. . . . We're asking him to manage the game . . . not to try to do too much and [to] let the offense work for him."

During the NFL's Golden Age, one could no more have imagined a coach telling the great John Unitas to just manage the game than one could have imagined Pope Julius II asking Michelangelo to "manage" the painting of the Sistine Chapel ceiling. ("Just follow my plan and let the paint work for you.") But in recent decades, the bureaucratization of pro football on the field has resulted in a game in which "system" trumps personal initiative, and even more importantly, personal responsibility, time and again. Tom Callahan's *Johnny U: The Life and Times of John Unitas*, one of the finest sports biographies ever written and a fine evocation of American sports in the late Fifties and Sixties, explains why this should be a matter for regret, and not simply for NFL fans.

According to no less an authority than *Sports Illustrated*, John Constantine Unitas, who died in 2002 at age sixty-nine after suffering a heart attack on a treadmill, was the greatest quarterback in NFL history. To mark his death, *SI* created a statistical matrix, the "U-ratings," to prove its point mathematically. But those of us who watched him, and idolized him, for the seventeen years during which, as quarterback of the Colts, he was the uncrowned king of Baltimore and the man who, arguably, did more than anyone else to make the NFL the glittery success it is, didn't need statistics to tell us that. As Baltimore-bred Frank Deford wrote shortly after Unitas's funeral, we knew that this was the guy on whom you'd bet, not just the game or the season, but a whole lot more: "The best quarterback ever? The best player?" Deford asked. "Let me put it this way: If there were one game scheduled, Earth versus the Klingons, with the fate of the universe on the line, any person with his wits about him would have Johnny U calling the signals in the huddle, up under the center, back in the pocket."

Calling the signals and playing to win—not managing a "system." "Systems" are for Klingons. Talent, imagination, physical courage, leadership, and coolness under fire are for men. And John Unitas was a man, of a distinctively American sort.

You don't have to be born in western Pennsylvania to be a great quarterback, but it helps: or so names like George Blanda, Jim Kelly, Johnny Lujack, Dan Marino, Joe Montana, Joe Namath, and Babe Parilli suggest. Kelly, with Marino one of the two best quarterbacks never to win an NFL championship (and the last to call his own game, rather than having plays sent in to him from coaches on the sideline or up in a skybox) attributes western Pennsylvania's disproportionate share of the quarterbacking greats to the local work ethic; as he told Tom Callahan, "I know the Marino and Montana families very well, and I know Dan and Joe were brought up on the same thing I was brought up on—and all of western Pennsylvania is built on—a work ethic that says, 'What you get out of something depends on what you put into it.'" Philosopher

Michael Novak, who grew up in those parts, thinks it's also a matter of the region's east-central-European heritage: "You're down 19–7 with only seven minutes to play? Big deal. It's been that way for a thousand years."

That was John Unitas's world: the ethnic (in his case, Lithuanian) and family-centered world of Depression-era steel mills and mines and coal-delivery trucks where, if they were lucky, the family got a few dollars for each ton of coal Unitas's father shoveled into someone's basement. The elder Unitas died at thirty-eight, technically of kidney failure and pneumonia, more likely of sheer exhaustion. His son showed his form early: five years after his father's death, after John and his sister had been bitten by a rabid dog and required twenty-one injections all over their bodies, his sister Shirley, sensing her brother's stoicism, refused to cry. As they were about to get off the streetcar on the way home, John turned to Shirley, still biting her lip against the pain, and whispered, "It's only a needle, Toots." As Callahan nicely puts it, he was Johnny Unitas at ten.

It took a while for the world to figure out what being Johnny Unitas meant, however. After an impressive high school career, he didn't make it to what every Catholic football player in the immediate post-Knute Rockne era imagined to be the Promised Land, Notre Dame; an assistant coach feared that the university would be "sued for manslaughter" if the Fighting Irish played a five-eleven, one-hundred-thirty pound quarterback. So Unitas settled for a scholarship to the University of Louisville where, throughout his collegiate career, he pretty much was the football team. Yet he showed enough form—and enough of that laserlike arm—to attract some professional attention. The Pittsburgh Steelers drafted him in the ninth round in 1955—and then cut Unitas at the end of the preseason. (Around the same time, the Steelers passed on drafting Lenny Moore and Jim Brown, thus hitting the trifecta of worst-ever NFL drafting decisions.) Unitas, who had married in college, went to work on a Pittsburgh construction gang to support his young family, and played $6-per-game sandlot football on a local semipro team called the Bloomfield Rams.

The Baltimore Colts of the early 1950s were a monument to ineptitude, but by mid-decade some shrewd drafting—crucial in the days before free agency made for virtually unlimited player movement around the league—was laying the foundations of a winner. The Colts thought they had the answer at quarterback in Oregon All-American George Shaw. But when Shaw tore up his knee in 1956, his replacement was a skinny kid from Pittsburgh whom Don Kellett, the Colts' general manager, had signed off the waiver wire for the price of an eighty-cent phone call—and who, given the chance he'd never been given in his home town, had made an impression during training camp and preseason. Rushed into the game as Shaw's backup, John Unitas threw his first NFL pass—which was promptly intercepted by the Chicago Bears' J. C. Caroline and returned for a touchdown. It was an inauspicious beginning (and the Baltimore papers began howling), but despite the loss to the Bears, some of the Colts liked what they had seen in the skinny kid during the brief months they'd known him.

Colts like Gino Marchetti, the defensive end who had enlisted in the army after a high school scrape ("I figured I could either face the Germans or I could face my father"), who had fought in the Battle of the Bulge at eighteen, and who had played his collegiate football on an undefeated University of San Francisco team that refused to go to the big southern Bowl games because doing so would have meant leaving their two black stars back in the Bay Area. Colts like defensive tackle Art Donovan, son of the referee of the two Joe Louis-Max Schmeling heavyweight fights, who prepared for NFL combat by taping old issues of *Time* and *Newsweek* to his shins. Colts like Raymond Berry, the myopic split end with one leg shorter than the other who invented what we mean today by "wide receiver"; Alan "the Horse" Ameche, the Heisman Trophy winner from Wisconsin who looked more like a tenor in a Verdi opera than a fullback; and

Jim Mutscheller, the daily Mass-going tight end from Notre Dame who had fought as a marine in Korea and who, as Callahan writes, "had a look in his eye that could bore a hole in a vault." They would all become friends on a team that, with its ethnic and racial diversity (and tension), was a kind of NFL analogy to the Brooklyn Dodgers of *The Boys of Summer,* as the Colts showcased such prototypical black football greats as the aforementioned Lenny Moore, offensive tackle Jim Parker, and defensive tackle Eugene "Big Daddy" Lipscomb. Berry would become Unitas's other half, the two working for hours after practice, refining their timing, devising plays that Unitas would store on the hard drive of his beautiful football brain, ready to be retrieved at the right moment.

Which would be a moment of Unitas's own choosing, for after he became the Colts' starting quarterback midway through the 1956 season, Unitas was both the team's on-field leader and what in today's bureaucratized NFL would be called the offensive coordinator (not to mention the quarterback coach). He'd talk the game plan over with head coach Weeb Ewbank and others on Ewbank's staff; but when new offensive assistant coach Don McCafferty asked him, in 1959, "John, do you want any help on Sunday?" Unitas had his answer ready: "Mac, if you're *positive* they're going to blitz, let me know. Otherwise, sit back, relax, and enjoy the game."

Unitas could get away with that because, the year before, he had led the Colts to the 1958 NFL championship in what is now habitually referred to as "The Greatest Game Ever Played," the first (and, to date, only) championship game in NFL history settled in sudden-death overtime—and, thanks to television, the game that indelibly impressed the NFL on the national psyche and thereby changed the way Americans spend Sunday afternoons in the fall and winter.

The crucial play in the Colts' epic fourth-quarter drive, which tied the game with seven seconds left (thus setting up the dramatic overtime), had been conceived more than two years before, in one of those endless postpractice sessions between quarterback Unitas and receiver Berry. The two had been working on the timing of square-ins, in which the receiver runs an L-shaped pattern, when Unitas asked Berry what he would do if a certain linebacker were lined up directly in front of him. Berry replied that he'd give him an outside fake, try to make the linebacker come after him, and then "jump underneath him like this" to break into the clear. Unitas nodded, and didn't say a word about the maneuver until December 28, 1958, when there was a minute left in regulation time and the sun was setting over Yankee Stadium on a cold winter's afternoon. When the Colts came to the line of scrimmage, second down and ten on their own twenty-five, Berry saw New York Giants linebacker Harlan Svare standing straight in front of him—and glanced over at Unitas. "I'll never forget the look John gave me," Berry told Tom Callahan decades later, "the look we gave each other. I made the fake I had described to Unitas two years earlier, and Svare came right after me. I jumped underneath him and John zipped it on a perfect line" leading to a twenty-five-yard gain, a first down at midfield, and, ultimately, the tying field goal that made possible the Colts' overtime victory. No offensive coordinator, equipped with instant replay, a three-inch-thick playbook, and a computer, called that play. It was called by a supreme football intelligence at work on the field, retrieving the necessary information and applying it with a contagious confidence.

That confidence, which was matched by an equally striking humility, was one reason why John Unitas's teammates followed him unreservedly. Another reason was Unitas's conviction that he was, despite being the main man, a teammate. "How can I help you?" he'd ask in what halfback Alex Hawkins once called "his cathedral": the huddle. "Is there anything I can do?" Once, in the Unitas cathedral, future Hall of Famer Jim Parker told Unitas, "That f***in' [So-and-So] just called me a nigger.' Unitas said, 'We can't have that.

Let him through this time.' John hit him right in the forehead with a bullet pass. He fell like a f***in' tree," Parker recalled (with evident relish). But perhaps above all, his teammates respected Unitas's willingness to take responsibility, not only when he was throwing those lasers to Berry and Lenny Moore, but when he missed (which, in the nature of the case, he did 45 percent of the time), or when his receivers failed him. Gino Marchetti again:

> "What really impressed me about Unitas was that, when he threw an interception, he didn't wave his arms all around or anything like that. You know, like quarterbacks do to signal to the crowd that it wasn't really their fault. He'd quietly go up to the intended receiver and say, 'You weren't where you were supposed to be on that play. If you don't start studying and know your plays, I'll never throw to you again.' Then, when the newspaper guys came into the locker room, John would say, 'My fault. Overthrew him.' His throwing hand is blown up to twice its size and [one of the local beat reporters] puts it to him, 'John, I guess you didn't have a very good day because of your hand.' And he says, 'My hand didn't bother me at all. I just had a terrible day.' If John wanted to, he could have held up that hand and said, 'Take a picture of this, why don't you?' What do you think would have been the lead story? But that wasn't him. He took the bad with the good. No rah-rah stuff. No bullshit. Dead honest with himself. Dead honest with you, if he trusted you. The better I got to know Unitas's character [in 1956–57], the more excited I became about our chances."

Which were, as it turned out, rather good chances at that. The Colts took the NFL title in 1958 and 1959 and won Super Bowl V in 1971; several other times during the Sixties, they fielded what was arguably the league's best team, only to have bad luck or scheduling vagaries deny them the chance to play for the championship. In 1969, they lost Super Bowl III to Joe Namath and the upstart New York Jets (coached by Weeb Ewbank, coach of the Colts' 1958 overtime victory), in part because Don Shula (who would go on to become the winningest coach in NFL history) didn't get Unitas into the game soon enough. Yet, in an irony about which Unitas never complained, it is Vince Lombardi's Green Bay Packers, not John Unitas's Baltimore Colts, whom most people associate with the NFL's Golden Age. (Unitas, for his part, made a point of making friends with another undersized and understated quarterback, the Packers' Bart Starr.)

The Baltimore Colts were sold in 1972 to Robert Irsay, an air-conditioning mogul and shamelessly mendacious self-promoter who would later steal the team from Baltimore (in the middle of the night, no less) and move it to Indianapolis—an act of perfidy that, for Baltimoreans, has consigned Irsay to that circle of the Inferno where New Yorkers long ago put Walter O'Malley (who moved the Dodgers to Los Angeles) and Horace Stoneham (who moved the baseball Giants to San Francisco). Unitas's last season in Baltimore was the first of the Irsay era; Irsay essentially ran Unitas out of town, before he stole the Colts. After trying to make a go of it in San Diego, Unitas retired—but not before giving invaluable tutelage to a young quarterback, Dan Fouts, who, on his own induction onto the Pro Football Hall of Fame, publicly thanked Johnny U.

Like many others in the football pantheon, Unitas tried his hand as a color commentator on TV; it didn't work, but he did leave to posterity one immortal line, about a quarterback whose fluttering passes were in sharp contrast to Unitas's: "Billy Kilmer throws an option pass. You have the option of catching either end of the ball." A happy second marriage and three new children brightened Unitas's last two and a half decades, during which he suffered business reverses and lost the use of the right hand that had once thrown an NFL-record numbers of touchdown passes; the delayed effects of old injuries forced the best quarterback ever to learn to write left-handed, in his sixties.

Unitas never cottoned to the idea of the "Indianapolis Colts" and asked that his records not be included in the Indy Colts' press guide. But to this day, there is a special tribute to Unitas at every Baltimore Ravens' home game. Raymond Berry, with whom Unitas is ever identified in the memories of their fans, offered a eulogy at the 2002 funeral Mass in Baltimore's packed-beyond-capacity Cathedral of Mary Our Queen, in which he said that Unitas had "made the impossible possible." But he did more than that. For as Berry said to his departed teammate, "You did more than perform on the field. Individual achievements and glory didn't have a place on your priority list. All of us knew that you were focused on . . . winning the game. You didn't care who did what. Just do our jobs when called on, and we all win together. The Colts were a team, and your example and leadership set the tone."

It was a different time and a different ethos, of course, in those days when John Unitas walked the gridiron like a slope-shouldered, bandy-legged hero, something out of *High Noon* by way of the Pittsburgh sandlots. Everybody, Unitas included, had an off-season job, selling paint or insurance or cars or whatever, because NFL salaries wouldn't support a family. Not only were there no agents, there was no hired help, either: Unitas laid the linoleum in the row-house kitchen of Alan Ameche, who scored the winning overtime touchdown in 1958. They were beer drinkers, not steroid ingesters, Unitas and Marchetti and Donovan and all the rest, and while most of them lived comfortably after their playing careers, and some of them became very wealthy from business, none of them became millionaires from football—as top draft choices do today before they've strapped on an NFL helmet.

The story of John Unitas is almost inconceivable today, in an NFL dominated by the likes of tweeting wide receiver Chad Ochosinco (formerly "Chad Johnson," before renaming himself after his uniform number). Peyton Manning, who showed his respect for the Master by asking for number 18, one digit below Unitas's fabled "19," is perhaps closest to the archetype. But does that mean that Unitas's story is, ultimately, a futile one, good only for its capacity to evoke nostalgia?

I think not. John Unitas never thought of himself as anything other than an honest craftsman, a professional who was proud to play football and play it well. But in plying his trade, he embodied a set of several distinctively American qualities: self-reliance; the work ethic; individual excellence married to a passion for the team; confidence tempered by humility; physical and mental toughness; loyalty; a democratic, as distinguished from aristocratic, sense of dignity and honor. Those qualities of character, so essential to a democracy (and especially to a democracy under assault), will commend Unitas's life and accomplishments to future generations of Americans, no matter what happens to the NFL (much less to the Chad Ochosincos of the world). Americans beyond the legions of NFL fans owe Tom Callahan a debt of gratitude for reminding us who John Unitas was, why he mattered—and why he matters still.

Part V

Remembrance

Pope John Paul II
(1920–2005)

He once described his high-school years as a time in which he was "completely absorbed" by a passion for the theater. So it was fitting that Karol Józef Wojtyła lived a very dramatic life. As a young man, he risked summary execution by leading clandestine acts of cultural resistance to the Nazi occupation of Poland. As a fledgling priest, he adopted a Stalin-era nom de guerre—*Wujek* [Uncle]—while creating zones of intellectual and spiritual freedom for college students; those students, become senior citizens themselves, called him *Wujek* to the end. As archbishop of Kraków, he successfully fought the attempt by Poland's communist overseers to erase the nation's cultural memory. As Pope John Paul II, he came back to Poland in June 1979; and over nine days in which the history of the twentieth century pivoted, he ignited a revolution of conscience that helped make possible the collapse of European communism a decade later.

The world will remember the drama of this life even as it measures John Paul II's many other accomplishments: his transformation of the papacy from a managerial office to one of evangelical witness; his voluminous teaching, touching virtually every aspect of contemporary life; his dogged pursuit of Christian unity; his success in blocking the Clinton administration's efforts to have abortion-on-demand declared a basic human right in international law; his remarkable magnetism for young people; his groundbreaking initiatives with Judaism; his robust defense of religious freedom as the first of human rights.

And, in the remembering, certain unforgettable images will come to mind: the young pope bouncing infants in the air and the old pope bowed in remembrance over the memorial flame at Yad Vashem, Jerusalem's Holocaust memorial; the pope wearing a Kenyan tribal chieftain's feathered crown; the pope waving his papal cross in defiance of Sandinista demonstrators in Managua; the pope skiing; the pope lost in prayer in countless venues; the pope kneeling at the grave of murdered Solidarity chaplain Jerzy Popiełuszko; the pope slumped in pain in the Popemobile, seconds after taking two shots from a 9mm semi-automatic—and the pope counseling and encouraging the would-be assassin in his Roman prison cell.

Some will always dismiss him as hopelessly "conservative" in matters of doctrine and morals, although it is not clear how religious and moral truth can be parsed in liberal/conservative terms. The shadows cast upon his papacy by clerical scandal and the misgovernance of some bishops will focus others' attention when considering his legacy. John Paul II was the most visible human being in history, having been seen live by more men and women than any other man who ever lived; the remarkable thing is that millions of those people, who saw him only at a great distance, thought at his death that they had lost a friend. Those who knew him more intimately experienced a profound sense of personal loss at the death of a man who was so wonderfully, thoroughly, engagingly human—a man of intelligence and wit and courage whose humanity breathed integrity and sanctity.

So there are many ways of remembering him. Pope John Paul II should also be remembered, however, as a man with a penetrating insight into the currents that flow beneath the surface of history, currents that in fact create history, often in surprising ways.

In a 1968 letter to the French Jesuit theologian Henri de Lubac, then-Cardinal Karol Wojtyła suggested that "a degradation, indeed a pulverization, of the fundamental uniqueness of each human person" was at the root of the twentieth century's grim record: two World Wars, Auschwitz and the Gulag, a Cold War threatening global disaster, oceans of blood and mountains of corpses. How had a century begun with such high hopes for the human future produced mankind's greatest catastrophes? Because, Karol Wojtyła proposed, Western humanism had gone off the rails, collapsing into forms of self-absorption, and then self-doubt, so severe that men and women had begun to wonder whether there was any truth at all to be found in the world, or in themselves.

This profound crisis of culture, this crisis in the very *idea* of the human, had manifested itself in the serial crises that had marched across the surface of contemporary history, leaving carnage in their wake. But unlike some truly "conservative" critics of late modernity, Wojtyła's counterproposal was not rollback: rather, it was a truer, nobler humanism, built on the foundation of the biblical conviction that God had made the human creature in his image and likeness, with intelligence and free will, a creature capable of knowing the good and freely choosing it. That, John Paul II insisted in a vast number of variations on one great theme, was the true measure of man—the human capacity, in cooperation with God's grace, for heroic virtue.

Here was an idea with consequences, and the pope applied it to effect across a broad spectrum of issues.

One variant form of debased humanism was the notion that "history" is driven by the politics of willfulness (the Jacobin heresy) or by economics (the Marxist heresy). During his epic pilgrimage to Poland in June 1979, at a moment when "history" seemed frozen and Europe permanently divided into hostile camps, John Paul II demonstrated that "history" worked differently, because human beings aren't just the by-products of politics or economics. He gave back to his people their authentic history and culture—their identity; and in doing so, he gave them tools of resistance that communist truncheons could not break. Fourteen months after teaching that great lesson in dignity, the pope watched and guided the emergence of Solidarity. And then the entire world began to see the communist tide recede, like the slow retreat of a plague.

After the Cold War, when more than a few analysts and politicians were in a state of barely restrained euphoria, imagining a golden age of inevitable progress for the cause of political and economic freedom, John Paul II saw more deeply and clearly. He quickly decoded new threats to what he had called, in that 1968 letter to Father de Lubac, the "inviolable mystery of the human person," and so he spent much of the 1990s explaining that freedom untethered from moral truth risks self-destruction.

For if there is only your truth and my truth and neither one of us recognizes a transcendent moral standard (call it "*the* truth") by which to settle our differences, then either you will impose your power on me or I will impose my power on you; Nietszche, great, mad prophet of the twentieth century, got at least *that* right. Freedom uncoupled from truth, John Paul taught, leads to chaos and thence to new forms of tyranny. For, in the face of chaos (or fear), raw power will inexorably replace persuasion, compromise, and agreement as the coin of the political realm. The false humanism of freedom misconstrued as "I did it *my* way" inevitably leads to freedom's decay, and then to freedom's self-cannibalization. This was not the soured warning of an antimodern scold; this was the sage counsel of a man who had given his life to freedom's cause from 1939 on.

Thus the key to the freedom project in the twenty-first century, John Paul urged, lay in the realm of culture: in vibrant public moral cultures capable of disciplining and directing the tremendous energies—economic, political, aesthetic, and, yes, sexual—set loose in free societies. A vibrant public moral culture is essential for democracy and the market, for only such a culture can inculcate and affirm the virtues necessary to make freedom work. Democracy and the free economy, he taught in his 1991 encyclical *Centesimus Annus*, are goods; but they are not machines that can cheerfully run by themselves. Building the free society certainly involves getting the institutions right. Beyond that, however, freedom's future depends on men and women of virtue, capable of knowing, and choosing, the genuinely good.

That is why John Paul relentlessly preached genuine tolerance: not the tolerance of indifference, as if differences over the good didn't matter, but the real tolerance of differences engaged, explored, and debated within the bond of a profound respect for the humanity of the other. Many were puzzled that this pope, so vigorous in defending the truths of Catholic faith, could become, over a quarter-century, the world's premier icon of religious freedom and interreligious civility. But here, too, John Paul II was teaching a crucial lesson about the future of freedom: a broad, even universal, empathy comes through, not around, particular convictions. There is no Rawlsian veil of ignorance behind which the world can withdraw, to emerge subsequently with decency in its pocket.

There is only history. But that history, the pope believed, is the story of God's quest for man, and man then taking the same path as God. "History" is His-story. Believing that, Karol Józef Wojtyła, Pope John Paul II, changed history. The power of his belief empowered millions of others to do the same.

Henry J. Hyde
(1924–2007)

In September 1984, as I was beginning a sabbatical year at the Woodrow Wilson International Center for Scholars, I had lunch one day in the Members' Dining Room of the U.S. House of Representatives with a Seattle congressman, Joel Pritchard, then in the midst of a bout of chemotherapy. A portly gentleman came up to our table to ask Joel how he was feeling; Congressman Pritchard then introduced me to Congressman Henry Hyde. Hyde politely asked what I was doing in town, and I explained that I was exploring Catholic thought on war and peace at the Wilson Center. Hyde smiled and went off to his own lunch.

Fifteen minutes later, he came back and asked me, "Have you ever written anything on church and state?" I replied that I had, and would be happy to send him some things—which I did. To make a long story short, Hyde had been asked by the Thomas White Center at the Notre Dame Law School to give a lecture in response to the "I'm personally opposed, but . . ." abortion politics of Mario Cuomo and Geraldine Ferraro. (Note to the young: Cuomo was a three-term governor of New York whom the Great Mentioner was forever electing president of the United States; Ferraro was the vice-presidential candidate on a ticket that carried one state and the District of Columbia). So I pitched in with drafting the speech, which was intended both as a rebuttal to Cuomoism and as a positive statement of how Catholic understandings of the dignity of the human person should engage the public square—a phrase Richard John Neuhaus was just then introducing into the national vocabulary.

From such an utterly serendipitous beginning came one of the great friendships of my life and a twenty-year collaboration that would teach me a lot about how American politics really works.

Henry Hyde, who died on November 29, 2007, was, without exaggeration, a singularity. As Clement Attlee once said of Winston Churchill, Henry's personality resembled a layer cake.

There was the Hyde who reveled in the contact sport that was (and is) Illinois politics, and who regaled friends with Mr. Dooley-like stories of campaign shenanigans and naughtiness (on both sides of the partisan divide); and there was the Hyde who was a close student of history, one of the most avid readers in the House of Representatives.

There was the Hyde who was the undisputed legislative leader of the American pro-life movement, the man who almost single-handedly kept the federal treasury out of the abortion business; and there was the Hyde who defied some conservative orthodoxies by arguing that it was nonsensical to claim that the Second Amendment created a constitutional right for eighteen-year-olds to own AK-47s and other assault weapons.

There was the Hyde whom Cokie Roberts (no conservative) once described to me as "the smartest man in Congress"; and there was the Hyde who was one of the best joke-tellers of all time.

There was Hyde, the ambitious politician; and there was the Hyde who passed up what would turn out, later, to be a chance to become Speaker of the House, because he had given his word to minority leader Bob Michel to vote for Michel's candidate for whip.

There was the Hyde who was a master of rhetorical cut-and-thrust, the greatest extemporaneous debater in recent Congressional history; and there was the Hyde whom the likes of Nancy Pelosi liked, respected, and perhaps even came to love.

One indelible memory that captures Henry Hyde in full involved Thanksgiving 1986. Henry's prostate was acting up so he spent the holiday in Georgetown University Hospital. When I went to visit him on Thanksgiving Day, I found him sitting up in bed, tubes running in and out of him, smoking a six-inch-long cigar, watching on TV as his beloved Bears played the Lions—and reading a massive scholarly tome on William Wilberforce, the British parliamentary scourge of the slave trade. (I asked Henry whether he'd had a lot of visitors. He replied that a guy who was interested in running for his seat had come in and expressed grave concern. Said Henry, in a growling whisper, "I told him, 'The last words you'll ever hear me say are gonna be, 'Get your foot off the oxygen hose.'")

He loved the U.S. House of Representatives, and while he made important foreign policy contributions as one of those conservatives who married a profound concern for international human rights to a principled anticommunism, I think Henry most enjoyed chairing the Judiciary Committee after the Republicans took control of the House in January 1995. His remarks during the Committee's first meeting under his chairmanship are worth remembering:

In our American system, justice is not an abstraction. Like all the virtues, justice is a moral habit; we become a just society by acting justly. The duty to "promote justice," which we lay upon ourselves when we pledge to defend the Constitution, is a duty we exercise through the instrument of the law. [For] the "rule of law" distinguishes civilized societies from barbarism.

That simple phrase—"the rule of law"—should lift our hearts. To be sure, it has little of the evocative power of Lincoln's call to rebuild a national community with "malice toward none" and "charity for all"; to celebrate the "rule of law" may stir our souls less than MacArthur's moving call to "Duty, Honor, Country." But if that phrase lacks the eloquence of Lincoln and MacArthur, it nonetheless calls us to a noble way of life.

Legislators—makers of laws in a democratic republic—are involved in a vital task. Ours is not just a job; public service in the Congress is not just a career. What we do here, we ought to do as a matter of vocation: as a matter of giving flesh and blood to our convictions about justice— our moral duty to give everyone his due. I have been in public life long enough to know that not every moment in politics is filled with nobil-ity. But I have also been in public life long enough to know that those who surrender to cynicism and deny any nobility to the making of the laws end up doing grave damage to the rule of law—and to justice. If we don't believe that what we are doing here can rise above the brokering of raw interests—if we do not believe that politics and the making of the law can contribute to the ennobling of American democracy—then we have no moral claim to a seat in the Congress of the United States.

It was a touching confession of political faith, and Henry's con-clusion was met with applause and cheers. Even such sworn partisan foes as the ranking minority member, John Conyers, and the ul-tra-pro-choice Patricia Schroeder were moved, and leaned across to shake the new chairman's hand. (Chuck Schumer, if memory serves, continued to eat a jelly doughnut while chatting on the dais with his friend, California's Howard Berman.)

In less than four years' time, of course, chairing Judiciary got Henry embroiled in the impeachment inquiry against President Clinton. Hyde was a model of fairness throughout, as even a Clin-ton defender like Barney Frank acknowledged. His own falls from grace, decades in the past, were dredged up by reporters, aided and abetted (I am convinced) by unscrupulous Clintonistas, all of whom somehow imagined that the impeachment inquiry was about extra-curricular sex. Henry was hurt, badly, and even talked of resigning. I remember telling him that no two people I had ever met had been more married than he and Jeanne (who had died in 1992), and that he owed it both to her forgiveness and his duty to press ahead. Which he did, in the conviction that President Clinton had put the Congress and the country in an impossible position: for how could the nation have as its highest law-enforcement official a man guilty of a crime—perjury—for which more than a hundred other men and women were serving time in federal prisons?

When the House managers solemnly carried the Articles of Impeachment across the Capitol to the Senate, Henry Hyde saw in Trent Lott's eyes (as he told me late that night) that "we're not going to make it; Trent won't fight." Rather than let the trial of the president descend into farce, Henry tried heroically, through the force of argument and rhetoric, to keep the country focused on the nobility of the rule of law—as he did in opening the Senate trial for the House managers:

> Every senator in this chamber has taken an oath to do impartial justice under the Constitution.
>
> The president of the United States took an oath to tell the truth, the whole truth, and nothing but the truth in his testimony before the grand jury, just as he had, on two occasions, sworn a solemn oath to "faithfully execute the laws of the United States."
>
> The case before you, Senators, is about the taking of oaths: the president's oaths, and your own oaths.
>
> That is why your judgment must rise above politics, above partisanship, above polling data. This case is a test of whether what the Founding Fathers described as "sacred honor" still has meaning in these United States: two hundred twenty-two years after those words—*sacred honor*—were inscribed in our national charter of freedom. . . .
>
> In recent months, it has often been asked—it has *too* often been asked— so what? What is the harm done by this lying, by this perjury?
>
> The answer would have been clear to those who once pledged their sacred honor to the cause of liberty. The answer would have been clear

to those who crafted the world's most enduring constitution. And the answer should be clear to us, the heirs of Washington, Jefferson, and Adams, Madison, Hamilton, and Jay.

No *greater* harm can be done than breaking the covenant of trust between the president and the people; among the three branches of our government; and between the country and the world.

For to break that covenant of trust is to dissolve the mortar that binds the foundation stones of our freedom into a secure and solid edifice. And to break the covenant of trust by violating one's oath is to do grave damage to the rule of law among us.

The Senate acquitted the president; but students of American history will read Henry Hyde's remarks during the impeachment inquiry and trial for decades after President Clinton's memoir (with its bitter criticisms of Hyde) is pulped.

Late in the Reagan years, House Speaker Jim Wright (of all people) asked Henry to speak at a luncheon Wright was hosting for newly elected members of Congress, shortly after their election. Henry graciously congratulated the neophyte solons, cracked a few jokes, and then got very serious. "You are basking in the glow of victory," he told these as-yet-unsworn-in men and women, "and that is entirely understandable. But permit me to suggest, on the basis of long experience, that if you don't know what you're prepared to lose your seat for, you're going to do a lot of damage up here. You have to know what you're willing to lose everything for if you're going to be the kind of member of Congress this country needs." That was Henry Hyde. And even his most bitter enemies knew that he spoke the truth.

Once, addressing the National Right to Life Convention, Henry reminded the ground troops of the pro-life movement that they were not "playing to the gallery, but to the angels, and to Him who made the angels." When I learned of his death, I imagined the angels giving him a rousing, Chicago-style welcome. So, I expect, did today's holy innocents, the unborn, whose cause he led for decades with wisdom, wit, and effect. If it is too much to ask that we'll ever see his like again, it is always a good thing to be thankful that, as a nation under God and under the rule of law, we had his services for so long.

Aaron Jean-Marie Cardinal Lustiger (1926–2007)

As the shadows of a Christophobic secularism that carries with it the ancient disease of anti-Semitism lengthen across twenty-first-century Europe, visitors to the Cathedral of Notre-Dame in Paris will do well to ponder a relatively new commemorative marker in that great and venerable Gothic space, whose beauties were known by Thomas Aquinas during his teaching days in the City of Light. The marker carries this inscription:

> I was born Jewish. I received the name of my paternal grandfather, Aaron. Having become Christian by faith and by baptism, I have remained Jewish as did the Apostles. I have as my patron saints Aaron the High Priest, Saint John the Apostle, Holy Mary full of grace. Named 139th archbishop of Paris by His Holiness, Pope John Paul II, I was enthroned in this cathedral on 27 February 1981, and here I exercised my entire ministry. Passers by, pray for me. +Aaron Jean-Marie Cardinal Lustiger, Archbishop of Paris.

Two young men whose names would become familiar throughout the world attended the same political science lectures at the Sorbonne in the early 1950s. One was the son of Polish-Jewish parents; the other came from Cambodia. One had lost his mother in Hitler's Holocaust; the other would ignite a holocaust. One had converted to Catholicism; the other had converted to Marxism. One would live to become the embodiment of humane, intellectually coherent religious faith, and thereby give hope to his people. The other would marry irrationality to viciousness, and his name would become a curse among his people.

One was named Aaron Jean-Marie Lustiger. The other was named Pol Pot. A novelist of sufficient imagination could turn that scene—Lustiger and Pol Pot, in the same Parisian classroom—into a gripping tale about divergent roads taken, and the consequences that followed in the late twentieth century, from an acceptance or refusal of Pascal's Wager. As I came to know and esteem him over a decade, it was self-evidently clear that Jean-Marie Lustiger really did believe in God; he didn't simply live "as if God existed," and things changed around him, for the better, because of that. But how different the worlds that Pol Pot touched and desecrated would have been if that young Cambodian had accepted Pascal's challenge, even without making Lustiger's act of faith.

We first met in Washington in 1986 or so, when Cardinal Lustiger was visiting America with a group of young aides. After a formal session at the Woodrow Wilson International Center for Scholars, the cardinal and I fell into more informal conversation, and I asked him whether this was his first trip to the U.S. Oh no, he answered, he had once hitchhiked across the country. I asked him when. "1968," he replied. I suggested that he might have chosen a more tranquil year.

Cardinal Lustiger was very helpful to me as I was preparing *Witness to Hope: The Biography of Pope John Paul II*, and we stayed in touch over the years. Early in 2006, one of his assistants, Jean Duchesne, told me that the cardinal, quite ill with cancer, wanted to see me before he died, in order to share some memories of, and reflections on, the last years of John Paul II. We spent ninety minutes together in the cardinal's modest Paris apartment in December 2006 and had a conversation that I shall always remember for Lustiger's Christian lucidity and tranquillity in thinking out loud about death, in the very face of death. I asked for the cardinal's blessing as I left;

I shall always cherish the memory of his hands on my head and his thin arms drawing me into a final embrace. Here was a man of God; here was a man. The first explained the second.

As archbishop of Paris and one of the most prominent members of the College of Cardinals for more than two decades, Jean-Marie Lustiger embodied precisely the Catholicism imagined by Pope John XXIII and the Second Vatican Council: a Church engaged with the modern world; a Church that had opened its windows to modernity in order to invite modernity to open its windows to the worlds of transcendent truth and love. Like Blessed John Paul II, Cardinal Lustiger was completely convinced, on the basis of both faith and reason, that being a Catholic and being an engaged, compassionate, intelligent human being, dedicated to healing the world's wounds and advancing the cause of human freedom, were two sides of the same coin.

Both these Christian giants believed that the biblical story—the story that begins with God's self-gift to the People of Israel and that continues in the Church—is in fact the story of humanity, rightly understood. The biblical story and the human story don't run on parallel tracks, as if we have on one track "creation, fall, redemption, etc." and on another track "ancient civilization, the middle ages, the age of science, etc." Rather, it's all one track: the biblical story *is* the human story, read in its true depth. For Cardinal Lustiger, the "choice of God" (the title of one of his best-selling books) was also the choice for a genuine humanism, the choice for a life without fear of final oblivion—the fear that was one root of the lethally different choice his Cambodian classmate had made.

Because he came from a human world outside the worlds-within-worlds of French Catholicism, Jean-Marie Lustiger could see things perhaps more clearly than others of his fellow French Catholics. He could see, for example, that both the conventional Left and Right options among French Catholics were, in fact, no options, for both imagined the Church wedded to worldly power: in one case, the power of the revolution (however it might be conceived); in the other, the power of the old order. As Lustiger understood it, though, the Church was not in the business of aligning itself with worldly power of any sort. The Church was in the business of evangelization, of service, of mission, of witness to the truths about the dignity of the human person on which the rights of man most securely rest. The Church's public business was forming a culture of authentic freedom: a culture that could form the kind of citizens who can live freedom nobly, rather than meanly or selfishly.

C ardinal Lustiger was a wonderful human being—intelligent, caring, wry in a funny way—because he had been transformed by the power of God, through the Holy Spirit. His great desire was that others might share in the gift he had been given, the gift of faith. That gift led him to read situations in their true depth, often against the grain of conventional wisdom. And here was another quality he shared with John Paul II: the capacity to read the dynamics of history in depth. Like the man who took a great risk in appointing him archbishop of Paris, Lustiger (who took no less a risk in accepting John Paul's appointment) understood that the most dynamic force in history over time is neither politics nor economics, but rather culture: what men and women honor, cherish, and worship; what men and women are willing to stake their lives, and their children's lives, on.

Everyone worships; the question is whether the object of our worship is a worthy one. Having lived and died in the conviction that worship of the God of Abraham, Isaac, Jacob, and Jesus is true worship, Aaron Jean-Marie Lustiger, a son of Israel become a son of the Church, became a blessing for the world.

Avery Cardinal Dulles, S.J. (1918–2008)

I t was my privilege to count Cardinal Avery Dulles, S.J., as a friend for more than a quarter-century. Truth to tell, though, I had "known" Avery long before I met him, for I began reading him when two of his books, *Apologetics and the Biblical Christ* and *Models of the Church,* were assigned in my sophomore college theology classes, back in (gasp!) the first Nixon Administration. When we finally met in person in Washington, in 1985 or thereabouts, Avery's reputation as Catholic America's unique theological reference point was well established. What was immediately evident about the man himself was his unaffected naturalness, his preternatural calm, and his good humor.

From the mid-1970s on, Avery was a sign of contradiction within an ever-more-left-leaning U.S. Catholic theological establishment. He was one of the Catholic signatories of the 1975 Hartford Appeal for Theological Affirmation, an ecumenical challenge to then-dominant revisionist and secularist tendencies in academic theology. Dubbed the "Hartford Heresies" by its critics in the establishment theological guild, the Appeal in fact marked one of the points at which Catholic theology in the United States began to reground itself in the Church's ancient and ongoing tradition, rather than imagining that theology (and everything else, for that matter) had started all over again with the Second Vatican Council.

Taking a leadership role in the theologian's guild wasn't a pleasant task for Avery, a private man who relished serious argument but who had no taste for polemics. Yet he acceded to the wishes of his colleagues and served as president of the Catholic Theological Society of America during one of its most difficult periods. A

CTSA-commissioned study of sexual morality couldn't bring itself to condemn bestiality; Church authorities were (rightly) aghast; the experience of defending orthodoxy while leading the society through the ecclesiastical donnybrook that followed doubtless reinforced Avery's longstanding dislike of the spotlight.

He never made a point of his lineage, but if the United States had an aristocracy, he would have been indisputably a member of it. His great-grandfather, his great-uncle, and his father all served as Secretary of State—as his uncle had been founding director of the CIA and his aunt had negotiated the Austrian State Treaty that got the Red Army out of Vienna a decade after the end of World War II. Yet for all that he didn't make a big deal out of being something like American aristocracy, Avery remained a man of deep, if usually understated, filial piety and came to his father's defense when historians stewed in the juices of the 1960s began to attack John Foster Dulles's reputation. In a 1994 lecture at Princeton, Avery met the fashionable liberal critique of Foster Dulles (as a political Manichaen who had wed hyper-Calvinism to American chauvinism) in the calm, scholarly spirit with which he handled theological controversy. His conclusion was both just and loving: "At a distance of a generation or two, I think we may judge that my father made the kind of contribution to which he felt called—that of a Christian layman concerned with developing a world order consonant with Christ and the Gospel. [Thus] he was able to make a coherent and, to me, convincing case that a nation cannot be enduringly strong and prosperous without adherence to strong spiritual and moral principles."

How did the staunchly Presbyterian Dulles stock— John Foster Dulles had, among other things, been the most prominent Protestant layman in the United States in his day—produce a Catholic convert, a Jesuit priest, and the first American theologian to be raised to the cardinalate?

The answer was encoded in the motto on Cardinal Avery Dulles's coat of arms, *Scio cui credidi* [I know in whom I have believed]: St. Paul's simple-yet-profound explanation to Timothy of why he was not concerned about his sufferings or his future. That faith came to Avery Dulles in stages. He left prep school an agnostic, but a chance encounter with a blossoming tree during his undergraduate years at Harvard inspired the conviction that the world was governed by "an all-good and omnipotent God," as he later put it. How might that conviction be embodied institutionally, though?

Slowly, Avery Dulles came to appreciate the subtlety, depth, and coherent structure of Catholic doctrine. Here was the truth, nobly expressed: the only possible response was to adhere to it, heart, mind, and soul. That is what Avery Dulles did for sixty-eight years, after entering into full communion with the Catholic Church in 1940. Adherence to the truth of Catholic faith was also the organizing principle of his extensive theological work—more than twenty books and over seven hundred articles. Avery Dulles was a theologian of the tradition, explicating ancient truths, stretching them a bit, exploring their implications, but never seeking cheap originality or sound-bite fame.

That modesty of purpose went hand-in-hand with an evangelical modesty of person and a tart sense of humor. As for the modesty of person, one does not often see cardinals of the Holy Roman Church repairing their battered shoes with duct tape, or walking across campus in a cheap blue windbreaker; Avery's sartorial style would have caused heartburn at Men's Wearhouse, much less Brooks Brothers. There was no affectation here, though. Avery Dulles took a vow of poverty when he entered the Society of Jesus and he kept it, as he kept his vows of chastity, obedience to superiors, and that special obedience to the bishop of Rome that is the distinguishing hallmark of classic Ignatian life. As for the tart humor, I well remember the night Richard John Neuhaus was received into full communion with the Church in the chapel of the archbishop's residence in New York, with Avery and me as his confirmation sponsors. Cardinal John O'Connor did the liturgical honors, and then invited us to cocktails and dinner. As the Scotch began to flow, Avery said to Richard, "Well, Richard, it was all very nice, but I missed the part from my day where you had to publicly abjure your previous heresies."

A very's nomination as a cardinal at age eighty-two came as a complete surprise to him, if not to others. The night it was announced, my wife and I were entertaining friends who were also close to Father Dulles. As dinner began, the phone rang: it was the newly-nominated cardinal, who brushed aside my congratulations and asked whether it was possible for him to be dispensed from the canonical requirement of a cardinal being a bishop. I assured him that the dispensation would be readily given by the Holy Father, as it had been for other elderly theologians whom John Paul II had honored with the red hat. There was a sigh of relief on the other end of the line and I asked him why he was so worried about being a bishop. "I'm too old to be running around New York doing confirmations," came the eminent reply.

Still, cardinals employ the miter and crosier when they preside liturgically. So on the night of February 23, 2001, Cardinal Avery Dulles, S.J., processed into the Church of the Holy Names of Jesus and Mary on the Via del Corso to take possession of his Roman "title," vested as none of us had ever seen him before. At which point one colleague leaned over and whispered, "Now we know what Abraham Lincoln would have looked like in full pontificals."

Perhaps a bit closer to the truth, however, was the image of Avery a few days before, sitting in the cortile of the Pontifical North

American College, receiving well-wishers while seated, an hour after receiving the cardinal's red biretta (which in his case fell into John Paul II's lap when Avery bent over to kiss the pope's ring). I watched from a distance, and the sensation was eerie: one could imagine John Henry Newman sitting for the familiar 1881 portrait by Sir John Everett Millais.

M y favorite Dulles memory, however, involves a black-and-white photo, not a lecture or a book. In it, Avery, his lanky torso clad only in a dark t-shirt, is standing at the bar in New York's Union League Club, having just performed a modest striptease of sorts for an ecumenical and interreligious group of theologians.

It was, in a sense, my fault: in a fit of whimsy, I had had t-shirts made from the cover of my book, *Catholicism and the Renewal of American Democracy*, for which Avery had kindly provided a glowing front-cover blurb. One of the shirts went to Father Dulles, with a note explaining that this would make him the best-dressed theologian at Fordham University. Some weeks later, at a meeting organized by Richard Neuhaus (then still a Lutheran), Avery caused consternation in the Union League Club bar by taking off his suit jacket (itself a grave offense in the very proper ULC) before starting to peel off his shirt. "He's had a stroke," people thought. "Somebody call 911!"

But there had been no stroke. Father Dulles just wanted to show off his new t-shirt. The photo of Avery and his crooked grin, surrounded by Catholic, Protestant, and Jewish theologians cracking up, is one I shall cherish *ad multos annos* as a foretaste of the comradery of heaven.

Richard John Neuhaus
(1936–2009)

T he conventional story line on Richard John Neuhaus holds
that his eventful life was defined by change, transition, even
rupture: Lutheran pastor's kid becomes teenage hellion becomes Lutheran pastor becomes Catholic priest; Democratic Congressional
candidate becomes adviser to Republican presidents; Sixties' radical becomes Eighties neoconservative. And truth to tell (as Richard
liked to say), there's at least something to this.

The early influences on his religious thought and sensibility included the Lutheran theologian Arthur Carl Piepkorn (who taught
him to think of Lutheranism as a reform movement within the
one Church of Christ) and Rabbi Abraham Joshua Heschel (from
whom he drew the idea that Christianity and Judaism were necessarily locked into a conversation from which both ought to benefit);
his later interlocutors in matters theological shifted to include the
German Lutheran Wolfhart Pannenberg (whom he introduced to
the English-speaking world), Joseph Ratzinger (later Pope Benedict
XVI), and Pope John Paul II.

He worked with Martin Luther King, Jr., and Ralph David Abernathy in the classic period of the American civil rights movement;
his chastisement of William F. Buckley, Jr., in a letter complain-
ing about *National Review*'s stance on civil rights legislation, led to
lunch and then to thirty years of friendship, conversation, and collaboration.

He was typically labeled a "conservative" Catholic in his latter years; yet for more than four decades, he was at the intellectual center of both the ecumenical and interreligious dialogues, in
partnership with a diverse crew that included, at various moments,

Cardinal Avery Dulles, the Rev. William Sloane Coffin, Jr., Charles W. Colson, Alexander Schmemann, Rabbi David Novak, and Rabbi Leon Klenicki.

He was an early supporter of Jimmy Carter who became a counselor to George W. Bush; with the sociologist Peter Berger, he pioneered a new way of thinking about "mediating structures" (or voluntary associations) in society, thereby providing the intellectual foundation for Bush's faith- and community-based initiative.

He was a vocal critic of America's war in Vietnam who helped cause a major rift in the postwar peace movement by criticizing the new communist government's persecution of religious believers.

His friends and familiars included prominent American public intellectuals of all faiths and no faith; on different days, he could be found arguing amiably and intensely with Henry Kissinger about morality and foreign policy, and then with Norman Podhoretz about the proper interpretation of Isaiah and St. Paul. In tandem with colleagues like Michael Novak and Robert Benne, he made a Christian moral case for the superiority of the free market over socialism; yet by his own choice, most of his pastoral work as both Lutheran pastor and Catholic priest was in poor and working-class parishes. He loved music, especially Bach, and he loved to sing; but he couldn't carry a tune to save his life. He was a brilliant preacher and a wonderful raconteur who also suffered through his dark nights.

Anyone whose journey through this world spanned that range of experiences and touched that wide a cast of characters obviously went through some changes over time. Yet, as I reflect back on thirty-one years of friendship and collaboration with Richard Neuhaus, I am far more impressed by the consistencies than by the discontinuities in his life and thought.

To begin with, he was a thoroughgoing Christian radical, meaning that he believed that the truth of Christian faith was not just truth-for-Christians, but the truth of the world, period.

As with his hero, John Paul II (and contrary to the conventional wisdom on "tolerance"), that conviction opened him up to serious conversation with others, rather than shutting down the argument. Yet his basic theological and philosophical convictions, and the intellectual sophistication he brought to their defense, had resonances far beyond the boundaries of the religious world. For those convictions also undergirded the two big ideas that he put into play in American public life.

The first of these ideas, laid out in his 1984 bestseller, *The Naked Public Square*, involved that hardy perennial in the garden of American controversy, church and state. Neuhaus's position was that the two pieces of the First Amendment's provisions on religious freedom were in fact one "religion clause," in which "no establishment" of religion served the "free exercise" of religion. There was to be no established national church, precisely in order to create the free space for the robust exchange of religious ideas and the free expression of religious practices. In making this case, Neuhaus changed the terms of the contemporary American church-state debate, arguing that the Supreme Court had been getting things wrong for more than half a century by pitting "no establishment" against "free exercise," with the latter increasingly being forced into the constitutional back seat. It was a bold proposal from a theologian and has increasingly been vindicated by much of the recent legal and historical scholarship on Supreme Court church-state jurisprudence.

Neuhaus's convictions about the meaning of religious freedom in America also reflected his consistent defense of popular piety and the religious sensibilities of those whom others might consider "simple" or "uninformed." If 90 percent of the American people professed belief in the God of the Bible, he argued, then there was something profoundly undemocratic about denying those people— a super-majority if ever there was one—the right to bring the sources of their deepest moral convictions into public debate, even if they sometimes did so in clumsy ways.

That populism was also at the root of Neuhaus's second big idea: that the pro-life movement was in moral continuity with the classic civil rights movement, because pro-life claims were rooted in the same moral truths for which he had marched with King and Abernathy across the Edmund Pettis Bridge outside Selma, Alabama. The pro-life position, Neuhaus insisted, was a matter of the first principles of justice, and those principles could not be sacrificed to what some imagined to be the imperatives of the sexual revolution. Thus as early as 1967, he warned his liberal and radical friends that their advocacy of "abortion rights" was a betrayal of their previous commitments. For to deny the unborn the right to life was to shrink the community of common protection and concern in America, whereas the whole point of the civil rights insurgency had been to enlarge that community by finally including African-Americans within it.

On a related set of questions, Neuhaus was also concerned with elitism and its corrosive effects on the poor people he served. He often spoke of his experience of reading an early essay on "quality of life," back in the embryonic days of what would eventually come to be known as bioethics. The author described "quality of life" in terms of income, education, recreational opportunities, and so forth; then, as Neuhaus told the story, "I got into my pulpit on Sunday, looked out at the congregation, and realized that not a single person there had what was being described as 'quality of life.'" Something was seriously wrong; and so the dignity of every human life, not its alleged "quality," became the conceptual basis on which he entered the bioethics struggles that now define such a significant part of the national agenda in the twenty-first century.

Both of these Big Ideas—no war between "free exercise" and "no establishment," and the pro-life movement as the natural moral successor to the civil rights movement—intersected in what Richard Neuhaus, public intellectual, thought of as his life's project: the creation of a "religiously informed public philosophy for the American experiment in ordered liberty," as he frequently put it. Understanding each of the pieces of that puzzle is important to understanding the man.

A "religiously informed public philosophy" was one that took account of the American people's abiding religiosity, but "translated" biblically informed moral convictions into a language that people of different faiths or no faith could engage in. The American "experiment," for Neuhaus, was an unfinished, and indeed never-to-be-finished, political project. American public life, as he understood it, was a constant testing of whether a nation "so conceived and so dedicated" could "long endure": thus Lincoln's question at Gettysburg was a question for every generation of Americans, not just the generation of the Civil War. And then there was "ordered liberty," in which the adjective captured Neuhaus's conviction (which paralleled that of the classic English liberal and historian of freedom, Lord Acton) that political liberty was not a matter of doing whatever we like, but of having the right to do what we ought.

R ichard John Neuhaus's lifelong habit of serious conversation—typically complemented by bourbon and cigars—was fed by his voracious reading. The breadth of his professional reading was on display every month in his personal section of *First Things*, the magazine he launched in the early 1990s; fittingly enough, the section was styled "Public Square," and its large readership marveled at the amount of material Neuhaus read, digested, and commented on every four weeks. Our twenty-two years of vacationing together at his cottage on the Ottawa River introduced me to the more personal side of my friend's unquenchable thirst for challenging ideas, preferably couched in good writing: one year, he would read Macauley's *History of England*; another year, it would be Gibbon's *Decline and Fall of the Roman Empire*; yet another, Aquinas's *Summa Theologiae*. And on at least three occasions during those two decades, he read through virtually all of Shakespeare. Yet the same man could spend the late evenings howling with laughter over DVDs of *Talladega Nights*, *Best in Show*, or *A Mighty Wind*. (Lest I cause scandal, I should add that he also appreciated serious movies, and that his leisure reading included mystery writers such as P. D. James and Ellis Peters. If memory serves, he also claimed to have read *Scoop*, Evelyn Waugh's send-up of journalism, at least ten times.)

The public world, where he spent much of his working life as writer and editor, thought of him as a controversialist, which he surely was (and a very skillful one at that). But what the public world rarely saw was the man who spent countless hours counseling young people, or receiving unannounced and uninvited visitors to his office who just "had to meet Father Neuhaus," or hearing confessions and saying Mass in his parish. He could be fierce, rhetorically; but those whom he led through the thickets of religious quandaries, vocational discernments, or psychological crises knew him to be remarkably patient and gentle.

And so, while he was arguably the most consequential American religious intellectual since Reinhold Niebuhr and John Courtney Murray, his memory will long be cherished by people who knew little of his public life, but did know him to be a man of conviction, conscience, and compassion—a true pastor. Which is no bad way for the man who dubbed his poor Bedford-Stuyvesant parish "St. John the Mundane" to be remembered.

Leszek Kołakowski
(1927–2009)

Leszek Kołakowski, who died at eighty-two on July 17, 2009, will be remembered by the world of letters as one of the leading philosophers of the late twentieth century, a man whose magisterial *Main Currents of Marxism* will be read centuries from now by anyone interested in getting at the intellectual roots of one of modernity's most consequential—and lethal—bodies of thought. His native Poland will remember Kołakowski as one of a small group of intellectuals who, in the aftermath of Hungary-1956 and Czechoslovakia-1968, turned their backs on theoretical Marxism as well as on the Communist Party, wrecking their own academic careers but laying some of the paving stones that would eventually lead to the Solidarity movement, the nonviolent collapse of European communism, and the triumph of freedom in much of central and eastern Europe.

Those memories will be true to the man and his accomplishment. But when I think of Leszek Kołakowski, the first thing that comes to mind is perhaps the worst dive I've ever been in: the hard-currency bar in the basement of a five-star (sic) Moscow hotel in October 1990.

I was in the Soviet capital with a group of American political thinkers and writers, meeting for a week with men and women who thought of themselves as the democratic opposition to Mikhail Gorbachev—whom none of them imagined to be much of a democrat. It was a week of bad food, intense conversation about the legal and cultural building blocks of democracy, irritating surveillance from the KGB, and the exhilaration of fomenting a democratic revolution in the belly of the beast, so to speak. When we first got to our hotel rooms, it was obvious even to amateurs that they were bugged. So my colleagues and I agreed that we would meet occasionally in the hotel's hard-currency bar, admission to which required either U.S. dollars or Deutschmarks, for debriefing and planning. We figured that the excruciatingly loud rock music—and not very good rock at that—would forestall eavesdropping on our conversations about that day's happenings, and the next day's plans, by any ferrets who happened to be lurking about.

It was an awful dump, with wall-to-wall German prostitutes standing along the perimeter, the air impossibly thick with smoke. The sight of Leszek Kołakowski in that dive, sitting on a shabby divan and dispensing wisdom while sipping cherry brandies and politely batting away the fräuleins who tried to plop themselves on his lap, is one I shall never forget.

Just as unforgettable, though, was the walk I took with Leszek one day, down at the bottom of Red Square. A kind of tent city had been set up there, full of poor people from the countryside who had come to Moscow to ask for a redress of their various grievances, many of which were displayed on crudely fashioned homemade posters. The exquisite sensitivity with which the great philosophical pathologist of Marxism engaged one after another of these sad souls—listening carefully, offering words of encouragement—bespoke a decency and a capacity for human solidarity that was nothing short of inspiring. Indeed, one of the few other men in whom I sensed similar attributes was another Pole: Karol Wojtyła, Pope John Paul II.

Were it the only thing he ever wrote, *Main Currents of Marxism*, Kołakowski's three-volume masterwork, would nonetheless have made him a worthy first recipient of the Library of Congress's Kluge Prize for lifetime achievement in the humanities and social sciences. *Main Currents*, however, was only one part of Kołakowski's extensive oeuvre, which combined the kind of rigorous logic for which pre-World War II Polish philosophy was noted with wit and literary grace. Kołakowski's small book, *Why Is There Something Rather Than Nothing? 23 Questions from Great Philosophers*, is a gem that ought to be required reading for every college freshman—for Kołakowski was a brilliant teacher as well as a gifted writer, a man who forced you to think even when you disagreed. Then there is *My Correct Views on Everything*, in which he explains his break with Marxism (while eviscerating the British Marxist, E. P. Thompson, who wrote a notorious "Letter to L. Kołakowski") and then goes on to explore Christianity and classical Liberalism in a brace of finely-honed essays. Kołakowski's philosophical works on religion ought to give the New Atheists pause; they, and others, might begin with *Religion: If There Is No God—On God, the Devil, Sin, and Other Worries of the So-Called Philosophy of Religion* (Leszek did have a way with titles).

But in trying to summarize the achievement of a brilliant and original thinker who endured both political exile and a lot of physical suffering, I still return to those days in Moscow in October 1990, albeit to a scene from which Leszek was absent. Another colleague and I decided to spend a few free hours exploring the Kremlin, and enlisted as guide and translator a bright young Russian who had been hanging around the hotel lobby, obviously looking to practice his English. He took us to one of the newly restored cathedrals inside the Kremlin walls, where we soon found ourselves standing before a brilliant fresco of the Last Supper. There was no doubt that it was the Last Supper; it couldn't have been anything else. Yet this obviously intelligent young Russian looked at us and said, "Please tell me: who are those men and what are they doing?"

That was what seventy years of Marxism had done to a generation: it had lobotomized them, culturally. Leszek Kołakowski's philosophical project was a long, rigorous, deeply humane protest against that kind of spiritual vandalism. Kołakowski knew that European civilization was built on the foundations of biblical religion, Greek philosophy, and Roman law—the conviction that life is not just one damn thing after another; a robust confidence in the human capacity to get to the truth of things; and a settled determination to order societies by means other than sheer coercion. Leszek Kołakowski's defense of the civilization of the West against the barbarism he was convinced was inherent in the Marxist enterprise was an impressive intellectual accomplishment. It was also the accomplishment of a noble soul.

Robert Charles Susil
(1974–2010)

Four days after my son-in-law, Rob Susil, re-entered Johns Hopkins Hospital, where he died of an aggressive sarcoma on February 5, 2010, the Catholic Church marked the Feast of the Presentation of the Lord and read the Gospel of Simeon's prophecy to Mary—that a "sword will pierce through your own soul" [Luke 2:35]. That image of a sword, often described as a sword of sorrow, is the first of the traditional "seven dolors" of Our Lady of Sorrows, commemorated throughout the Church on September 15, the day after the Feast of the Triumph of the Cross. Yet if Mary is the first of disciples and the model of Christian discipleship, then the sword of sorrow must pass through each disciple's life, too, configuring Christians more closely to the Son from whose pierced side flowed blood, water, and the Church.

All those who loved and esteemed Rob Susil were pierced by that sword in the weeks before his death. He and my daughter, Gwyneth, fought gallantly against his sarcoma since after it was diagnosed in March 2008, with the able assistance of the entire Hopkins medical family—of which Rob, as a specialist in radiation oncology completing his Hopkins residency, was a valuable and beloved member. There are, however, things that even the best medicine cannot do, at even the greatest medical centers in the world. So those who loved Rob and shared his deep Catholic faith prayed for a miracle, and were joined in that prayer by people all over the world. The miracle did not come; we know, however, that those prayers opened channels of grace and healing of which we are unaware, but for which we are grateful.

When Rob and Gwyneth first started seeing each other seriously, and after we were introduced, my wife said, "So, what do you think of Rob?" "Think?" I replied. "Smart, handsome, funny, 110% Catholic, loves Gwyneth, and likely to have an income. He's straight out of son-in-law Central Casting." He was so much more, though.

Rob was a brilliant young scientist, who held M.D. and Ph.D. degrees—and who didn't tell me that he had co-authored numerous scholarly articles until I saw the galley proofs of a forthcoming one when I was helping him and my daughter move into their first apartment. He had a great appetite for learning; weakened by chemotherapy and anemia, he was nevertheless maintaining his research program, and the day before his last hospitalization, I was planning to drive him to Philadelphia so he could work on an academic paper with a colleague. He was an extraordinarily committed husband and father: he and my daughter shared one of the great marriages I was ever privileged to witness, packing a superabundance of love, devotion, and mutual support into five and a half years, and his joy in being "Daddy" to William was itself a joy to behold. And he was a man of faith, whose faith sustained his good humor, his clearmindedness, and his determination during an illness about which he, a consummate young professional, knew all too much. That faith was matched by Gwyneth's; more than one friend, in the week before Rob died, described Gwyneth's strength and dignity as that of a biblical heroine. I am a suspect witness, of course, but I could not agree more.

When I put Gwyneth's hand into Rob's at the foot of the altar at St. Jane Frances de Chantal Church in Bethesda, Maryland, on August 14, 2004, the day of their wedding, I was able to get out three brief sentences before my throat tightened up and my eyes became misty: "You two are great. Be great for each other. Let Christ be great in you." Gwyneth and Rob were all of that, and more, as they finished medical school together, did residencies together, brought William into the world together, and felt the sword of sorrow pierce their souls together. All of that good lives on, I am certain—as I am certain that I shall pray for the divine assistance through my son-in-law's intercession in the future.

Acknowledgments

The essays in this book have been developed from articles, essays, columns, and reviews previously published in various journals.

First Things was the original home of "The Sixties, Again and Again and Again"; "Scoundrel Time"; "Truths Still Held?"; "Blair, Benedict, and Britain"; "St. Evelyn Waugh"; "Making Sense of H.L. Mencken"; "The American Catholic Story, Contested"; "U.S. Catholics as They Were and Are"; "The End of the Bernardin Era"; and my remembrance of Henry J. Hyde. The first three of these essays were adapted from my annual William E. Simon Lecture, sponsored by the Ethics and Public Policy Center in Washington, D.C., and made possible by the generosity of the William E. Simon Foundation, its board and its staff. Special thanks at the Simon Foundation go to William E. Simon, Jr., J. Peter Simon, James Piereson, and Jennifer Wotochek.

Commentary invited me to, well, comment on Ken Burns's *Baseball* and Tom Callahan's biography of John Unitas.

In its initial form, "Rescuing *Gaudium et Spes*" was a lecture given at the Pontifical Theological Faculty of St. Bonaventure, the *Seraphicum*, in Rome, at an international theological conference marking the thirtieth anniversary of John Paul II's election. It was subsequently published in *Nova et Vetera* (Volume 8, Number 1 [Winter 2010]) as the centerpiece of a symposium; the *Nova et Vetera* essay included extensive notes, which scholars and students may find helpful.

"Benedict XVI and the Future of the West" was originally a lecture delivered at St. Patrick's Church, Soho, London, to mark the church's re-opening after an extensive renovation; the lecture was subsequently published in *Standpoint*.

"The Unjustly Unremembered Paul Horgan" is an adaptation of the foreword I wrote for the Loyola Classics edition of Horgan's *Things As They Are*.

My remembrance of Pope John Paul II was, in its initial form, published in the *Wall Street Journal*, while the elegy for Cardinal Jean-Marie Lustiger was commissioned by the Archdiocese of Paris. The remembrances of Cardinal Avery Dulles, and of my son-in-law, Robert Susil, are based on *Catholic Difference* columns that were syndicated by the Archdiocese of Denver to the Catholic press throughout the United States. My remembrance of Richard John Neuhaus, in its original form, appeared in *Newsweek*, while my essay on Leszek Kołakowski was published by *National Review Online*, and was based on remarks I made at a memorial conference held at the Washington offices of the National Endowment for Democracy.

I am grateful to the editors who commissioned these works in their original form and to the publications themselves for permission to use that material, in developed form, in this book.

Practicing Catholic, like *Against the Grain*, was first imagined by John Jones of the Crossroad Publishing Company, who worked with my literary agent, Loretta Barrett, to bring the book to the public; I am, as always, grateful to both. John Zmirak was a helpful partner in bringing the project to a conclusion, as Gwendolin Herder was a supporter of the book from the beginning.

For reasons explained in the Preface, I am happy to dedicate this book to David Brewster and his wife, Joyce, in partial discharge of a great debt of gratitude and in thanksgiving for more than three decades of friendship.

G.W.
26 November 2011
The First Sunday of Advent